Soulsong

Soulsong

SEEKING HOLINESS, COMING HOME

greatest gift is HOME

Critical !

cf. Padovano (p 30)

THOMAS A. FORSTHOEFEL

ORBIS BOOKS

Maryknoll, New York 10545

Founded in 1970, Orbis Books endeavors to publish works that enlighten the mind, nourish the spirit, and challenge the conscience. The publishing arm of the Maryknoll Fathers and Brothers, Orbis seeks to explore the global dimensions of the Christian faith and mission, to invite dialogue with diverse cultures and religious traditions, and to serve the cause of reconciliation and peace. The books published reflect the views of their authors and do not represent the official position of the Maryknoll Society. To learn more about Maryknoll and Orbis Books, please visit our website at www.maryknoll.org.

Library of Congress Cataloging in Publication Data

Forsthoefel, Thomas A.
   Soulsong : seeking holiness, coming home / Thomas A. Forsthoefel.
     p. cm.
   Includes index.
   ISBN-13: 978-1-57075-683-2 (pbk.)
   ISBN-10: 1-57075-683-X (pbk.)
    1. Spiritual life. 2. Self-actualization (Psychology)—Religious aspects. 3. Theological anthropology. 4. Saints. 5. Holiness. I. Title.
BL624.F6635 2006
206'.1—dc22

                     2006013478

To my mother and father

and

to all

who listen

well

Critical!
Care

Life is a good teacher and a good friend.

—Pema Chodron

Contents

Preface

When I first proposed a book on holiness to Orbis Books, I saw it as a natural extension of my scholarly work on the nature of religious experience. Arriving at an idea for a new book in this way is not at all unusual. Writers working on one project often recognize a train of thought that seems to require a more complete treatment of it, so they propose a book to a publisher. Since my first book asked the question "What do we know through religious experience?," the next question seemed to emerge naturally, namely, "What do we know through the lives of the saints?" And so I proposed something of a cross-cultural examination of holiness, perhaps adapting the approach of Avery Dulles in his study of the church. In this case, I wanted to consider models of holiness but not limit reflections to a single religious tradition. Instead, I wanted to peer into other traditions to discover what we might learn from them. And so, in one sense, this book does indeed flow from my earlier work.

But life intrudes and presses its demands. Just as I began writing the book, I suffered a painful crisis that changed the book as it has changed me. While the book always intended to examine key themes in human unfolding, a new personal urgency emerged and suddenly much more was at stake for me. Although the questions inspiring the book were never merely intellectual, they became far more personal and existential, cutting to the quick of my life.

The book's evolution in a way mirrors my own. The book is the same, in key ways, as I originally proposed, but it is quite different, too. It is no longer the academic tome I imagined, but different, with an identity at once more simple and complex, now drawing from different genres to explore cross-culturally the meaning and value of holiness. Similarly, I am the same person as I was before my crisis, but I am profoundly different now, too, having tried to internalize the lessons of a life curriculum. So, just as the book has its continuities and development, I see in my life certain continuities—key streams in my being—and my own inner unfolding, that is, new ways of being on the path of becoming. For many of us, this process is not easy, at least sometimes. But microdevelopments in our unfolding humanness—call them instances of growth—are the promise of the path to wholeness, and wholeness is always related to holiness. This seems to be the course of things in life. We are who we are—a leopard doesn't change its spots, after all—but we do have the capacity to grow, and that perhaps is our most distinctive trait as humans.

As if to bring this truth home—that we do have key streams in our identity, even as we stumble through our uncharted inner terrain—I came to see that the book itself emerged from a deeper stream in me, one that became clear during a recent move. As I sifted through a forgotten box of essays, I came across a yellowed sheet of onion paper on which was typed, in the blurry ink of an ancient typewriter, a brief, unpublished essay. The essay, written over twenty-five years ago, was titled "In Praise of Saints and Saintliness." It was a brief reflection on holiness, written when I served as a lay volunteer in India. There, as a recent college graduate, I came to know of the impact in India of Father Francis Schlooz, a Salesian of Don Bosco, and Mother Teresa. That essay was never published, in part because I never really knew precisely for whom it was written. I realize now, of course, that I wrote it for myself. There, in incipient fashion, I began, in a serious and self-conscious manner, reflecting on holiness and authentic human flourishing, which are the heart of *Soulsong*. It is now evident to me that questions about holiness and what we know in the lives of the saints have been pivotal issues in my life, long before the acuity emerging from recent trauma. Over the years, I now recognize, I have given ample reflection on holiness and authentic human flourishing—in my scholarly training, religious formation, experiments in faith-based activism, and teaching. In this key stream of my life, I have been blessed in encountering, in one way or another, others who also are committed in faith and resolve to the full expression of their humanity. The authentic expression of our human being, in the wide compass of wisdom and love, is our holiness; it is our soulsong. Owing to our great planetary diversity, this expression itself is necessarily diverse, which is why, in this book, I include both Western and non-Western examples of saints and the religious wisdom that informs their lives.

"In Praise of Saints and Saintliness" could qualify as the subtitle of this book. That essay reflected a passionate intensity, a proverbial youthful idealism that perhaps saw holiness in categorical terms: the saints were the superheros of the religious life, somehow perfect, far beyond the usual capacities for wisdom and generosity. Indeed, I close that essay recalling Father Zossima's sobering words in *The Brothers Karamazov*: "The world has not seven righteous men." I conclude, however, "even if there are precious few, the world has everything to gain from them."

A key theme of this book is found in that last line of my essay: we have everything to learn from the lives of the holy ones. We learn how to "be here," how to be more fully human. The paradox we see in many religious traditions is that in the encounter of our own humanity, we discover our divinity, too. And yet, I have a different view than Father Zossima: the world is not limited to only a few saints. The saints are here, and they are many. Indeed, they are you and I. The saint is not the action figure of the spiritual life, ripped with spiritual abs, perfect. The holy one is anyone, anywhere, loving well and living wisely, expressing authentic humanness in the context of faith, action, and constructive habits of heart and mind. The holy ones are you and I as we gradually and patiently make inroads into a life of wisdom and compassion. The saints are not perfect; they are whole. They integrate the wisdom of their lives in a coherent and potent self-expression, perhaps first marked by rich self-acceptance. This authentic life-expression is what I call soulsong.

There is great wisdom out there as we review the weave of our lives in its rich pastiche of gift and glory, heartache and pain, saintliness and sin. We do ourselves a great service if we listen to that wisdom, even if comes from religious contexts different from our own. Hindu teachers sometimes use the metaphor of bees drawing pollen from a wide variety of flowers in order to produce something rich, flavorful, and unique. This is what I hope to do in this book. My intention here is to draw on a variety of sources, religious and poetic, in order to create something rich and flavorful on its own terms, but, more importantly, as an account by which readers see and savor the beauty of their lives, perhaps hear in some way their own soulsong.

In this book, I draw on the lives of the holy ones, some well known, others not well known, and consider the religious values and wisdom that inform their authentic life-expressions. These expressions then become mirrors of our own becoming. The holy ones become teachers, but not in the sense of requiring anyone to follow lockstep one's own path. Rather, the holy ones mirror qualities already present in ourselves, the expression of which allows us to be more who we already are. Indeed, in this sense everything and everyone finally become teachers, if we are open to learning. Every element of our lives—good, bad, ugly, indifferent—is curriculum for our wholeness, and wholeness is intimately related to holiness.

I wish here to give thanks to all the teachers in my life for calling me, in a variety of ways—some easy, some not so easy, some brutally difficult—to a path of deeper authenticity and truth. Every person named in this book has been an important teacher to me. I wish here to acknowledge them and to honor them. Many others, unnamed, also suffuse this book. Here, too, I honor them. And to all the teachers in my life, named or unnamed, I offer heartfelt gratitude.

I wish to acknowledge by name two persons, Robert Ellsberg, my editor, and Peggy Brace, the artist whose original artwork serves as the cover of this book. Robert sometimes reminded me of the Hindu god Ganesha, who carries a noose, not to string someone up, but to rope in the devotee if he or she strays too far off the path. My style in this book is discursive, almost conversational, and is, I hope, well suited for its audience. I appreciate Robert's patience and encouragement on many fronts, not to mention his efforts, like Ganesha, to rope me in when I wandered too far off the path. This Robert did with an instructive mix of encouragement, honesty, and sensitivity, all of which became for me yet another model of authenticity, one that extended beyond the limits of mere professionalism.

I want to thank Peggy for her own gifts in art and in matters of the heart. Peggy's calm and gentleness, and her own deep appreciation of religious wisdom, drew me to ask her to create something evocative of the themes of the book. I wanted something unique, perhaps spared the obvious and overused representations of religious symbolism. And this, I think, she has done, and exquisitely, too. The best art and poetry naturally express the experience of the artist but then trigger something potent in those who listen well or behold it with openness. I am tempted to offer my interpretation of the cover, but I will not do that, for it would subvert something essential to this project. The cover and the book are both served by the goals of *presentation*, with the aim of stimulating insight, reflection, inspiration, and creativity. I think Peggy's artwork does this, and this I hope *Soulsong* does, too.

Peace and blessings.

1

Toward Holiness

ON THE COGNITIVE VALUE OF THE SMILE

The Gift
Breath sweeps across the waters,
dancing
across the tumbling cascades
on the surface
of great silence.

THIS BOOK BEGINS from a smile, or, rather, a sequence of smiles. Not the blank, empty "smily face" ubiquitous on bumper stickers and bookbags in the 1980s but something richer and more soulful. Scholars of religion debate long (and loudly at times) the interpretation of sacred literary texts, such as scriptures, but also sacred visual texts, such as ritual performance or iconography. I would like to propose, as a motivating force for this project, another visual text, however fleeting, that deserves thoughtful reflection, too: the smile. We all are familiar with

1

smiles and the response they provoke in us—validation, affirmation, joy. The smile of a lover, the smile of a child, the smile of friend—all of these generate a sense of acceptance, affirmation, validation, a sense of well-being. The smile of a saint generates many of the same emotional responses but with some differences. The smile of a saint seems to carry different (I hesitate to say deeper) overtones, somehow "speaking" to a broader affirmation and validation, a more inclusive acceptance that somehow settles the soul in peace and calm. Let me illustrate this with several examples.

When I was working on my dissertation in India, I would on occasion visit temples with my wife, Therese, and my children, Andrew and Caitlin. In India, there is no shortage of heroic stories of saints and seers, some far-fetched and dubious, perhaps revealing more about the needs of the author and audience than about the subjects themselves. While fantastic stories of mystics and saints abound in Hinduism, one thing is clear in that tradition: the whole of reality is embraced in the divine, and this can be revealed in the luminous smile of a saint.

One of the central practices in Hinduism is *darshan*, "seeing and being seen" by the divine. This practice works on the assumption that the sacred permeates the visible world; the divine is dynamically present in temple images, in natural bodies, and in holy people. To "take *darshan*" means to benefit by the exchange of sight between god and devotee. As the eyes are the windows to the soul, this exchange involves a transfer of holy power, a blessing to the beloved.

One hot tropical day Therese, Andrew, Caitlin, and I visited the Shiva temple in Tiruvannamalai, an old temple town with a long history of saints and seers; some stories about them were fabricated no doubt for tourists afflicted by what Chogyam Trungpa called "spiritual materialism." I recall being corralled by a "guide" to visit—for a fee, naturally—a three-hundred-year-old yogi, still living in a cave. I kindly declined. It was clear that some holy men (*sadhus*) were on the dole, more interested in a free meal or a few rupees than any genuine spiritual realization.

In the temple, however, Therese and I both noticed a dignified, old *sadhu* circumambulating a shrine as part of his prayer (*puja*). There was something profoundly sincere about him, and a gentle peace, an unaffected detachment, seemed to flow from him. The way he carried himself was marked by that elusive, difficult-to-define quality that is recognizable when seen: genuineness. Later, we left the temple and pushed into the crowded streets, gripping the hands of Andrew and Caitlin lest we get separated. In the crush of the crowd, Therese and I happened at the same time to look behind us, and the same gentle old *sadhu* stood calmly, raised his staff in blessing and smiled. Something very peculiar happened, still not easily articulated. Something was given or transmitted amid the bustle of that day, and it happened to both of us, simultaneously. We looked at each other and said, "Did you see that?" at once astonished and puzzled by the power of a simple smile and brightness in the eyes. We immediately looked behind us once more, and he was gone, as if he had vanished. There was something mysterious about that smile and the exchange of sight that occurred in that brief gaze. Something happened in that encounter, a profound validation, but one more inclusive or comprehensive than "Have a nice day!" His eyes, that smile, communicated something dynamic yet difficult to articulate. And though it seems extravagant to say this, I will: I do not think it is far-fetched to say that certain smiles *do* communicate something about the nature of reality in its most complete context. Some smiles come from the soul and speak to the soul. Let me offer several more examples.

After finishing my dissertation, a heady philosophical study of Hindu texts on religious experience, a series of smiles, begging for reflection, seemed to emerge in my introductory course in religious studies. The primary objective of the course—and this book—is to consider deeply what it means to be human. What does it mean to "be here"? *How* shall we be in our *being here*? What do we have to go on? What do we do in the face of pain? It may be the case, as Elie Wiesel registers in his memoir, *Night*, that there always exists a power in the question that cannot be captured by the answer. No categorical answer ever captures the mystery of life or that of our own unfolding. Perhaps there is no categorical answer. Perhaps we only asymptotically approach the answer. We can only plumb the depths, and they are unfathomable. As we step onto the path of authentic becoming, the source of our holiness, we may feel distressed by the lack of maps, but we are not without guidance. There is wisdom in our religious traditions, and there is the gift of those who have lived lives well. This book draws on both resources as it considers what it means to be holy.

When we reflect on lives lived well, we see authenticities shaped by spiritual commitments and ethical choices. We see examples or models of what it means to be human; the luminous manner in which this life is lived reveals, at the same time, what it means to be holy. Exquisite humanness *is* holiness. In the examples of the holy ones, we glean hints of being and becoming and these resonate, strike a chord in us, awaken something deep. And so we learn from others—those who ask basic human questions and, following Rainer Maria Rilke, by living them, walk into the answers. The way they live the human question becomes the cogent word of their lives. For those of us on the path forming our own cogent word, we do well to listen to the lucid expression in the lives of the holy ones. In doing so, we avail ourselves of the opportunity to discover— or recover—something deep, maybe hidden, in our own. Listening to the lives of others allows the question of our lives to surface, and thereby we become rich with possibility.

To stimulate reflection on the "human question" in my introductory courses, I use several films, including the extraordinary documentary on Mother Teresa by Ann and Jeannette Petrie. This film really is a case study in compassionate service, a premier dynamic, in the Christian account of things, to usher in the reign of God. The film also is an example of one woman stepping out—setting aside the chorus of nay-sayers and stepping into her deepest authenticity, and because this authenticity was *hers*, it was holy. Mother Teresa is a saint above all because she was no one other than herself, and that is the essence of her holiness. Her life then became the lucid expression, the cogent word, of her being. In that film, a young man appears to be deeply moved by the Missionaries of Charity, and he makes the observation that the nuns say very little but teach a great deal without words. How so? By what they do and by their *smiles*.[1] Later in the course, I use another film, *Compassion in Exile*, a documentary on His Holiness the Dalai Lama. *Compassion in Exile* makes another rich case study in compassion, and those from a Christian perspective find great parallels between the Dalai Lama's meditation of exchange (mindfully receiving the anger and hatred of the Chinese and extending compassion back to them) and Jesus' call to radical forgiveness in the Sermon on the Mount. Indeed, the Dalai Lama considers the Chinese to be his greatest teachers, for responding to destructive actions and policies requires the greatest love. In this regard, we might recall the words of Jesus, "it is easy to love those who love you, for even the tax collectors do the same." Love always is hardest in the crush of loss and sorrow, but to love then, ripened by time and grace, is perhaps the greatest opportunity for self-transformation. Yet, when I ask my students what strikes them most about the film—which includes raw, if brief, footage of Chinese brutality against Tibetans—they typically mention above all the radiant smile (and infectious laugh) of the Dalai Lama. A smile and simple joy seem more communicative of the essence of the Dalai Lama than even his profound words of compassion for the Chinese who have occupied Tibet since 1950 with terrible brutality. His luminous smile is on the cover of *An Open Heart*, the Dalai Lama's rich presentation of Buddhist meditation. Looking at the cover, I am reminded of a comment of a friend who suggested that his official title—"His Holiness the Dalai Lama"—should be changed to "His Happiness the Dalai Lama." The observation is not trivial, for happiness is intimately related to health, and health is at the root of holiness. Happy people are attractive, and nothing communicates the simple joy of "being here," more than a soulful, loving smile.

Sometime later, I happened to attend a lecture by Robert Thurman, one of the leading authorities in Tibetan Buddhism.

In his reflections on the life of Siddhartha Gautama, the one who was to become the Buddha, Thurman offered an intriguing comment about Siddhartha's enlightenment. In Buddhist terms, he was now awakened; he now saw things as they are. But, as Thurman rightly observed, to see "reality as it is" could be devastating if the truth of reality were fundamentally negative or vicious. Such an idea is sometimes held by persons loathe to the notion of a supernatural infusion in reality, mixed as it is with spectacular glories and devastating limitations. To see reality as somehow ultimately and decisively negative is an entirely reasonable possibility based on the evidence of nature and human will—one could tally up the tornadoes, cataclysms, diseases, crime, wars and conclude that the universe is a lagoon of misery, bereft of a beneficent presence. Waking up to that, for some, may be sobering but also liberating. But, as far as I can see, a comprehensive negative evaluation of reality is not the last word on things according to most religious traditions, including Buddhism, which also describes the supreme goal, nirvana, as the supreme bliss (*parama sukha*).

When the Buddha pronounced his first noble truth, "Everything is suffering," he was hardly a prophet of gloom. He issued a realistic observation of change and our resistance to it, which typically issues in frustration and discontent. Still, frustration is not the last word on things in Buddhism. After his night of enlightenment, Thurman noted, Siddhartha *smiled*. He could have seen reality in its completeness and recoiled in horror. And if the horror was the decisive truth, then ignorance might, after all, be merciful, if not bliss! But, instead, the Awakened One *smiled*. And in that smile was completeness, the truth of the universe revealed in the upward turn of the lip.

The secret smile also appears as a central formative image in the Zen tradition as well. One day the disciples of the Buddha gathered round him, awaiting his discourse. He looked at a flower, and while his most of his disciples waited for a verbal teaching, one of them, Kashyapa *smiled*. The Buddha passed the flower to him and announced, "There is a Supreme Dharma, a Wonderful Truth: words cannot reach it, words cannot teach it." The transmission of the teaching occurred silently and was confirmed by a smile. Here, the smile both transmits and confirms truth. Indeed, the smile contains understanding, even as that understanding transcends concepts.

The mystery of the smile is also seen in the classic novel *Siddhartha*, by Herman Hesse, a text that many teachers use in their courses owing to its astute existentialist insights. At the conclusion of the book, the struggling Siddhartha finds peace— not through the mechanism of formal religion but through the truth of his unique path, which included arduous asceticism, the categorical rejection of spiritual striving, an embrace of sensual excess, and dismal failure too. When he falls—when he comes to terms with his brokenness—he softens. He is humble. Siddhartha's integration and healing occur gradually and are facilitated by listening to a flowing river in the presence of a compassionate friend. The river, always one but always changing, becomes a metaphor for the process of becoming. Applied to one's life, this process therefore must leave nothing out; it is all-inclusive and embraces everything: good and bad, saintliness and sinfulness, light and dark, all of it.

At the end of the novel, his boyhood friend Govinda, always the seeker, always the follower, is reunited with Siddhartha. He clearly sees that his old friend has found peace, and, deeply frustrated by his own lack of serenity, he asks, "Give me something to help me on my way, Siddhartha. My path is often hard and dark."[2] Siddhartha *smiled*. And that smile was revelation, disclosing to Govinda the sanctity of everything—the deeply human, the passion, the goodness, the rounds of birth and death, the unity of it all in a constantly evolving process, free of judgment, full of acceptance. In experiencing the wholeness of his life, Govinda touches his own holiness. Hesse writes,

> this smile of unity over the flowing forms, this smile of simultaneousness over the thousands of births and deaths—this smile of Siddhartha—was exactly the same as the calm, delicate, impenetrable, perhaps gracious,

perhaps mocking, wise, thousand-fold smile of Gotama, the Buddha, as he perceived it with awe a hundred times.[3]

Something was transmitted in this exchange for Govinda, who was unsure whether it lasted for a second or for a thousand years, but he was struck by the poignant mix of joy and sadness, a sense of being "wounded deeply by a divine arrow." Govinda then smiled too, bowing down, finally bursting forth in uncontrollable tears, for the smile of Siddhartha "reminded him of everything that he had ever loved in his life, of everything that had ever been of value and holy in his life."[4] In a sense, this is both the process and goal of this book, namely, to consider what has been of value and holy in my life and to share it with the aim of evoking the same in yours.

So, what exactly do smiles have to do with holiness? Everything. Something known and knowing occurs in a smile. The smile contains, perhaps, everything we need as humans to negotiate the convoluted paths of our lives. The smile addresses very local realities, but it also intimates and transmits something broader, something bolder, something utterly free. We live in a world shaken by tumult, disorder, and abject confusion. Even religious traditions, supposed anchors in the sea of storm, often become some of the worst causes of storms. To what do we turn for reassurance? Where is some consolation amid the heartache of personal and social chaos? Overwhelmed, we might think that abject destruction has the last word on reality. Our own suffering and that which we witness everywhere bear down upon us, and we feel our world—and perhaps our hearts—closing. And then we see a smile of someone special. It could be the smile of one's beloved, a smile that somehow holds everything in great tenderness. Or it may be a smile of a child, a smile that reminds us of beauty and innocence in the world. Or it may be the smile of ordinary persons who have lived life in extraordinary ways. These people seem to have won something for their efforts, a peace that, far from being disingenuous in the face of the world's troubles, often appears to penetrate much deeper than those struggles. Their smiles seem somehow to possess extra value, owing to the host of choices made in their lives, all of which become a cogent word, an exquisite soulsong back to God. Their smiles are congruent with a particular vision of reality, one in which love and kindness, and not aggression or despair, speak the last word, no matter the extent of sorrow and suffering.

The Saints

These people are the saints, a term inevitably coded with traditional conceptualizations and pieties. To disabuse these standard pieties, I think of the campus minister at my colleague's alma mater, who apparently would greet each student he met with an exuberant, "Hey, saint!" or "How are you, saint?" Saints are not etheric, disembodied entities. They are you and I as we grapple with the central question of existence: what does it mean to be human? What does it mean to be here? How shall I be in my being here? The term "holiness" comes packaged with baggage, too. And indeed, as a lexical item, its meaning changes under broader cultural and religious conditions that change too. What counts as holiness in an earlier era might be considered pathological in ours. For the purposes of this book, I take holiness to be directly related to health and wholeness. Indeed, the word's root, *hal*, includes wholeness, health, and well-being in its semantic range. Seeking holiness in a world of conflict is essential to our well-being *and* the well-being of others. This does not mean we are required to construct massive social service projects, though, for some, this may be a natural expression of their soulsong, the sacred gift of their lives. Our authentic humanness by itself extends value and care and well-being to others, often in discreet and hidden ways. Exquisite humanness *is* holiness. Holiness issues in communion of heart, and communion is the road home. Indeed, it is home itself.

Since the varied human responses that constitute holiness depend on the religious matrix of the subject, I will explore the significance of holiness cross-culturally. This approach comes from a life-long commitment to the study and teaching of the world's religions, and I am convinced of the profound wisdom and grace that has flourished in the religious history of humankind. It is something of this wisdom and grace that I wish to share in *Soulsong*. I was raised Catholic and have been formed in powerful ways by Jesuit spiritual and intellectual traditions, above all at Georgetown, as an undergraduate, and in the Jesuit community itself, where I spent four years, many years ago, but whose influence still shapes me today. And yet, my vision of things has been indelibly formed by my own encounter, in person and in practice, with the insight and teachings of non-Christian religions, especially the religions of India, the focus of my academic training. What one cannot help but discover in the world's religions is a powerful solidarity on the path of human flourishing. Communion is here—sisters and brothers and soulfriends, a great community of kinship. And this is an exquisite resource in a world thickened with grief and fear. A communion of saints—a communion of heart, mind, and will—transcends a host of cultural, ethnic, and religious differences. It is precisely this communion that we need to explore as a resource for human self-understanding, especially as our world continues to be shaken by a host of moral failures in politics, religion, and society.

This book considers the examples of others—and their religious impulse—as resources to investigate what it means to be human. The book then is an exploration of the epistemology of holiness; that is to say, what do we "know" through holiness, the holiness of others as well as our own? I maintain that in the end what we know through holiness is ourselves. While heroic examples of sanctity do provide "rumors of angels" (to borrow Peter Berger's phrase), decisive metaphysical conclusions based on the lives of the saints are at best inconclusive (though not by any means unimportant). What does one make, for example, of the nondualistic claims that follow the experience and teachings of Hindu saints such as Ramakrishna or Ramana Maharshi or Tibetan Dzogchen masters, especially as they contrast in striking ways with the claims and outcomes of holy persons from monotheistic traditions such as Mother Teresa or the great Muslim saints?

Still, the windows to the Supreme, which holy lives intimate, become, perhaps more significantly, windows to our own humanity. The two, it seems, are in some sense coextensive, as is suggested by Irenaeus, the second-century bishop of Lyons, "The glory of God is humanity fully alive," and Cyprian, the third-century bishop of Carthage, "Christ became human so humans could become God." Yet, such testimony to the intimate interface of the human and divine is hardly limited to any one tradition. Ramana Maharshi (1879-1950), for example, repeatedly insisted on the truth of the nondual Self; in keeping with his own experience of realization and the teaching that accorded with it, he called his disciples to access the divine within one's heart, refusing to engage in any fundamental separation of the human and the divine. Ramana's typical counsel was "After finding out who you are, you may know what God is." When we discover our truest selves, we discover God. We come home.

"God"

Before I go further, let me say a word about my use of the term "God." That term is highly problematic because of its conceptual overlays, developed in complex historical and cultural processes. This process is the usual course of things in history, but it occasionally has negative outcomes. Some of these overlays, representing cultural assumptions, are unhelpful or, worse, alienating, such as, for example, a kind of apotheosized masculinity or a sanctified sexism. When I use the term "God," it is as shorthand for the sacred, unconditioned, pervasive beneficent presence, grace at the heart of the universe. Occasionally, I will use the term "Holy One" to intimate this divine presence. My use of the word "God" may not satisfy those who favor conceptualizations of the divine perhaps more strict than mine, nor may it satisfy others for whom it implies a personal God with form; these persons, following nondualist traditions, may feel that the word unfortunately creates a gulf between the sacred and the profane. Rather than writing a book with the word "God" in scare quotes to flag caution constantly, however, let me flag it here. For me, then, "God" is shorthand for the divine presence and need not imply the heavy-duty monotheisms of the West. It is inclusive, embracing Eastern conceptualizations of the Holy and those found in indigenous traditions. This is not to deny or to ignore very important philosophical distinctions in the world's religions, nor is it to create what Thomas Merton once called a "mishmash of semi-religious verbiage." It would be dishonest to do the former and disingenuous to do the latter. Like Merton, however, I wish to engage the wisdom of the world's religions and pay close attention to the observable effects these wisdoms have produced in real lives. Witnessing the lives of the holy ones and listening to the wisdom that formed them angles the prism of reality in such a way as to reflect its rich hues. Part of that unfolding for me includes a truth that grace is here, compassion is here, the Holy One is here.

So, in my view, communion with the divine, no matter how that divine is construed, often facilitates a deep personal communion, an integration, one that issues in profound freedom and acceptance, both of self and others. The great Muslim poet Rumi writes, *"Touch my skin so I can be myself."* Contact with the Holy One, the Beloved, generates life and healing and wholeness. This issues in the deepest, truest expression of our lives, our own exquisite humanness. This is our soulsong, the song for which the universe has long waited. The examination of quality human presence and what we learn from it naturally becomes a reflection on what it means to be human, and this is the scope of this book. In a sense, this book is an extended essay on this one question alone, one that has long been compelling to me.

Peril and Promise of Religion

I wish to use the examples of others to illuminate this reflection. There is a pitfall in this strategy, however. When we examine the spiritual *virtuosi* of religious traditions, we see a clear reflection of what it means to be human, modeled exquisitely by persons committed in faith and practice. But this model too often marks the distance between regular people and the very human, though idealized, saint. By elevating the status of one human example, we run the risk of denigrating our own deeply embodied authenticity, the source of our own holiness. To speak of holiness is to reflect on the diversity of human responses in wisdom and love. By reflecting on this diversity we help to create the conditions for our own authentic becoming, the integrated weave of holiness in our lives. If anything, the holiness of the saints becomes a lens by which we examine the central question of our lives—what does it mean to human?—and the lens becomes a mirror by which we recognize ourselves, that is, we recognize key streams in our being. We see something in them that resonates in us, something that we need to actualize in our own path of becoming. Responding authentically, we gather our soulsong back to God, thereby creating yet another model of holiness, our own living and loving. Holiness becomes a window to the depth dimension of human being where, wonderfully and paradoxically, we meet both our truest selves and God.

One final point concerning the rationale for this book: the failure of religions. The disturbing contemporary developments—religious terrorism, an increasing interpenetration of ideology and religion, various forms of social oppression, and the abuse of power—point to the dark shadow of organized, institutionalized religion and its abject failures. I do not take an idealistic position or argue against organized religion. Religious institutions are human constructions (bracketing for the moment claims to a divine presence in them), and are therefore beset with any number of human flaws woven into its organizational structure. The crisis in the American Catholic Church concerning sexually abusive priests and the church's manner of dealing with them bears painful witness to institutional betrayal and its devastating impact on people's lives. Yet the oppressive tendencies in organized religion are hardly limited to the Catholic Church; nor are violent fringe groups limited to Islam.

September 11, 2001, however, revealed the demonic outcomes that ensue when religion is hijacked to serve political ends. But such events have their historical antecedents. Muslim conquerors in medieval India razed Hindu temples and Buddhist monasteries. Popes blessed Crusaders who slew the infidel in the name of Jesus Christ. The history of anti-Semitism, often countenanced and supported by religious teachers and teachings, has issued in a long and sorry record of persecution, continuing to this day with desperate people strapping on backpacks with bombs while dreaming of paradise. And in India, patriotism as genuine virtue has not escaped being co-opted by Hindu ideologues who marshal religious rhetoric to serve political ends. Instead, I wish to recall that religion first and foremost is about personal and social transformation. *Soulsong* aims to access the religious instinct, bearing witness to the lives of real people responding to their deepest instincts and inspirations. In so doing, it retrieves the raison d'être of the world's religions which too often are implicated by institutional dysfunction.

By examining and reflecting on holiness, we thus have an important resource in the rapprochement of religions. Witnessing extraordinary examples of these fruits—kindness, patience, self-control, compassion, joy, love, peace, goodness, gentleness—in persons of any faith tradition naturally arouses wonder, admiration, and gratitude for such outstanding human presence. While theologians and philosophers will continue to reflect on competing metaphysical claims, witnessing the extraordinary fruit of great saints is a happy provocation, that is, it pulls us close to the heart of another—and to the heart of another's tradition—resolving, for a time, philosophical differences into a communion of hearts. That these fruits have a divine source in various faith traditions suggests that meeting at the heart will not only inform our efforts in interfaith dialogue but even be a necessary requisite to it. The appeal of the saints and sages reveals a more basic and universal attraction to goodness and holiness. For if there is a sacred beyond mere social construction, then the serenity and calm modeled by saints may be a window to that realm. Moreover, by encountering the outstanding human presence in models of holiness, we are driven again to consider—and integrate—the prospects and possibilities of what it means to be human.

A Typology of Holiness

For now, I can do no more than name and outline a typology of holiness, and I will conclude with several comments on the approach of this book. Typologies are not natural, as if inscribed in the fabric of the universe; they are human constructs, heuristics created to stimulate reflection. I have chosen six categories in this typology; they are hardly exhaustive but nonetheless capture key patterns of living and loving. These in turn become cogent responses to the question of human being.

The first is the *holiness of fire.* Here I examine the radical call to justice and compassion embodied in the lives of activists from the Christian and Buddhist traditions, particularly the Jesuit priest John Dear and the Thai activist Sulak Sivaraksa. Above all, I wish to consider the movements of heart, mind, and will that have shaped the authenticities of these lives. What religious resources have served, fed, challenged, or led these activists? While the religious, cultural, and ethnic matrix of each is significantly different, these activists share a common inspiration: commitment to a world of justice and peace.

The second type is the *holiness of energy,* or the holiness of *action,* a model well served in Hinduism by its own call to karma yoga. The examples I choose here—the late Salesian priest Francis Schlooz and Mother Teresa—speak to an energetic and tireless commitment to service, almost relentlessly so. While the boundaries of the prophetic model and the service model are often (properly) blurred, the examples here illustrate the commitment and creativity required to make a difference in the lives of the poor in India. The classic method of karma yoga—action done without attachment to the fruits of action—is quintessentially found in the *Bhagavad Gita,* the Hindu classic which Gandhi, a karma yogi if ever there was one, called his "dictionary of daily reference."

The third type is the *holiness of calm,* or what might be called serenity within the storm. Here, I examine the impact of the inward path of insight and meditation, particularly as we confront the ubiquitous problem of suffering. While there is no shortage of academic discussion of mysticism, what practical outcomes from our religious matrices can we observe in the lives of real people? In this chapter I focus especially on the wisdom that has shaped the lives of Hindu and Buddhist holy ones such as Ramana Maharshi, the Dalai Lama, and Thich Nhat Hanh.

Next, I shall consider "letting go" as an ultimate act; this implies the *holiness of death.* Here I consider the meaning of "letting go" at the deepest levels of the mind and heart. Such a process can be seen in classical and contemporary expressions of religious wisdom. To this end I will consider various mechanisms developed in our religions to confront and to embrace death, perhaps the premier dynamic in our own holy unfolding. Living in surrender or "letting-go space" catalyzes our holiness, much as the crystal, in due course, flares out its exquisite beauty.

Next, I examine the *holiness of the everyday.* Holiness, as the process and outcome of deep integration, is a project hardly limited to professional religious. Here, I explore the reality of the ordinary with its host of opportunities to love well and live wisely. We all know persons who express exquisite humanness. They may be our grandparents, neighbors, teachers, or friends. They are not famous; no one surrounds them or acclaims them as gurus, masters, or avatars, but we nonetheless walk away from them feeling somehow affirmed or uplifted. We are in danger of idealizing holiness if we fail to consider the hidden holy ones in our own communities. They too bear witness to profound integration, wisdom, and love, and their example also becomes a window to the Supreme. With no clamor of the crowd and no grand stage, they exhibit an everyday holiness that embodies God.

The danger of idealization needs to be addressed further with yet another category, the *holiness of brokenness*. Here, I consider human weakness and imperfection as a central dynamic in our own authentic becoming. I have no interest in detailing the mistakes and flaws of others. Instead, we are all afflicted with weakness and limitation, and it marks the deepening of our own authenticity, the hallmark of our holiness, to accept this, embrace this, indeed to have the courage to be imperfect. In a real sense, the "fallen" serve by challenging our projections and constructions, stretching our categories, indeed stretching our capacities to love. This includes recognizing and internalizing the truth of our brokenness, too. Internalizing this truth, captured in a wider vision of love and value, deepens our humanity, helps to form our unique way of being in the world, and living this, in love and freedom, becomes *our* holiness.

It is my view that holiness is deeply embedded in authenticity, and authenticity itself is shaped by the wisdom of our religions, the examples of others, and our own bank of life experience. Holiness, then, is the process of our own deepening humanization. What we discover in the holiness of others is the discovery of ourselves. We gain a deep intuition of who we are and who we are called to be in full human flourishing. Such awareness catalyzes our own energies to embody it in a life lived well. That, in the end, is the deepest invitation of this book.

An Approach to *Soulsong*

Thomas Moore notes that we all are philosophers, if not by profession. And it is that impulse in all of us that I hope to quicken in *Soulsong*. We all, at one time or another, ask ourselves certain basic questions; we try, as best as we can, to answer them, thereby living out internally coherent cognitive structures. As we all are philosophers insofar as we aim to give rational coherence to our lives, however, so also are we all poets. And by this I mean that while we may be neither published poets or even persons who scribble a few lines from time to time, we nonetheless live the poetics of our lives, the dimension within us that touches and expresses *deeply felt conceptual truths*. This emerges in art, dance, song, music, and poetry, but also in the way we dance our lives, the way we live the mystery of our giftedness, the way we gather our soulsong back to God. The poetics of our lives thus comprehends the whole of our lives: our conversation, our play, the way we move and live, the way we gaze into the eyes of a child—all this is poetry, too; all this intimates communion.

To help in this foray into holiness, I will occasionally draw upon poetry in the hope of triggering or stimulating certain insight. Although trained in philosophy, I am a poet at heart. I've always been drawn to the poetry of mystics and seekers— this touches deep chords in me—and the poetic expression of truth sometimes captures it far more effectively than erudite philosophy. When I studied at Georgetown, a course taught by Leona Fisher, "Poetry of Meditation and Praise," made an indelible impression upon me. I remain very grateful for that course and for Leona's poetics of teaching—passionate, inquiring, alive, joyful. I still return to the poetry we read then—that of Gerard Manley Hopkins, John Donne, George Herbert, and T.S. Eliot—and have used some of their poetry in this book as well as in many of my courses.

But in my study of non-Christian traditions, I've discovered vast universes of passion and meaning in the poetry of saints and seekers, and so I draw also from Hindu, Muslim, and Buddhist poets. The Zen poet Hung-Tao writes, "What the poet does is this:/ Improve on a blank page./ Me, I doubt it's ever been done."[5] This sensibility suggests a caution in the use of words as any sort of ultimate handle or grasp on reality. Reality is already pristine, already complete, needs nothing added to it. Words become an overlay, once removed from reality, and, worse, become objects of attachment. Yet, even with this caution, the poet still scribbles a line to evoke this truth. And poets everywhere have uniquely expressed their own feints and sallies into life, love, God, presence, absence, darkness, and holiness. So, as I venture out on my own exploration into holiness, I use poetry, reflection, and personal narrative to make inroads into the premier question, What does it mean to be human? And this, for me, is another way of asking, What does it mean *to be here?*

The Gift

Just before I began writing this book, I suffered a painful personal crisis which fundamentally changed the trajectory of this book. That crisis opened up this book as it has opened up me. During the most difficult period of that time, however, working on the book was impossible; indeed, I felt overwhelmed with depression if not despair. My family, especially my mother and father, to whom this book is dedicated, offered me support that was profoundly helpful, often in surprising or striking ways. I learned things from them—equanimity, unflappability, and even an unanticipated flexibility. While my mother has always been supportive, I also heard from my father real wisdom that made a deep impression on me. One of things he said to me as I found myself slogging through my morass was a word of encouragement, "You have a gift, Tom, you have something to say, and it will help people."

I felt two things as I heard this, the most important being the relationship of a son to his father. We come into the world with such need—for love, for acceptance, for the sense of who we are. And our sense of our worth and value comes first from the loving embrace of our parents, the absence of which creates grave and ancient heartache. To feel my father's love, to discover his wisdom, and to feel his validation, all have been gifts emerging from crisis. While I am not one to do "warrior weekends" and I do not know very much about men's studies, I know that a son needs his father in a unique way. The encouragement and support of a father is soul food for the son. But there was more than just encouragement in my father's words. Self-knowledge is strengthened by the observations of those who are closest to us, those who know us well. It is the voice of others, the *knowing* of others, spoken freely, with compassion, which has the capacity to empower another. In this case, freedom "docks," and uniqueness unfolds. The insight of the other does not define or control but offers a mirror to behold one's own beauty and uniqueness, one's own special gift to the universe, replete with its wild streams of glory and pain, shadow and light, all of it a certain constellation that adds to the infinite richness of the universe.

That's all we have, in the end. It is our authentic person-hood that becomes our gift—to ourselves, to others, and to God. Deeply embracing this personhood begins the sacred weave of our unique holiness. Such encouragement is motivat-ing and brings with it the desire to offer something as gift to another, to all of us seeking wholeness, seeking communion, seeking peace, seeking love. And so I begin this book with a poem, "The Gift." It is my hope that this query into holiness helps to remind each of us of our own unique giftedness, our own exquisite humanness, our own soulful return to the Holy One. *Soulsong* expresses something of who I am; it is an expres-sion of my aspirations, inspirations, strengths, and weaknesses—something of what I've learned along the way. All of this becomes an expression of the gift of my life, which includes, as it does with all of us, the difficult, dark, and conflicted, too. The gift of our lives includes it all, the whole of it. Embracing that wholeness is a key step on the path of holiness.

It is my hope that this book becomes something of a gift to you who read it, perhaps offering a word or thought or insight or phrase here and there that becomes soul food, evokes some grace, some help along the way. For me the poem that begins this book names an intention and a conviction. May there be gift here to reawaken in some modest way the giftedness of life, the giftedness of our paths, the giftedness of being enveloped in love, the giftedness of *you*. The little haiku-like poem gently evokes the mystery of the divine, the mystery of the soulfulness, in our lives. Breath—life force, *prana*, *ruah*, *chi*—is often coterminous with the divine in many religious traditions. Our breath mingles with the divine breath, the kiss of God in our lives as we breathe, as we come home, as we settle into the unique solitude of our lives. And there we experience communion.

In the Christian tradition, Jesus invites disciples to come out into the deep—to discover the depths of life, the depths of our lives, the depths of God. But in setting out, the goal is to come home. And that is communion. All of us are on our own sacred journeys, with their exquisite uniqueness, great glory, and occasional piercing pain. We need help—inspiration, insight, conversation, silence—to keep courage and maintain heart. "The Gift" intends to remind us that somehow we are already home as we set out for home. Integrating the wisdom of our experience, of our traditions, and of our hearts—this is more than enough. Our circuitous lives, with their excesses and failings, are all gifts, all opportunities to come home: to ourselves, to others, to God. This is real presence, holy communion. It marks the sweet freedom of being here, stitches sinews of someone really *here*. The Japanese Zen poet Muso Soeki writes:

> Those times when I'm wandering
> and cannot find the road
> back the way I came,
> well,
> the road goes where it will
> and anywhere at all is home.

Holiness is about coming home. Freeing ourselves from the expectations of others, even from what counts as traditional holiness, and living an authentic life may be the most exquisite expression of holiness. Our authenticity, not our perfection, becomes our holiness, our gift to ourselves, to others, and to God. Then, as Desmond Tutu once said, we become that lovely triangle in the universal symphony that offers its simple, single note with great eloquence. Perhaps barely noticed amid the great cacophony of sound, the divine score is nonetheless incomplete without its voice. So it is my wish that these reflections help in some small way as each of us wends our way home, lives the poetics of our lives, gives voice to our cogent word. Gathering our soulsong back to God expresses our authentic *being* in the ongoing process of our *becoming*. This is our holiness, which in turn becomes gift for others.

2

The Holiness of Fire

THE FIRE OF LOSS AND THE FIRE-TENDERS

Standing in the Fire

Azariah sang a song of humility;
a cool wind soon encircled the young men,
fanning away flames fueled by hate and contempt.
Standing in their truth set them free.
Yet when truth is tinged with complexity
the fire of doubt begins to singe,
quickly fueled by the ire of the injured
and those who see only in black and white.
Grant us the healing cool wind,
and clear light for our seeing,
as we stand in the fire of our lives,
and stand in the truth of our being.

THIS CHAPTER CONSIDERS the radical call of justice and the commitment to live it prophetically, to bear witness to higher values than tribalism, consumerism, ethnicity, and competition. Persons from various religions are motivated by higher principles to put their lives on the line. In the poem at the beginning of this chapter, I make direct reference to the famous story of Azariah, Meshach, and Abednego, who refused to submit to idols in ancient Israel, and because of this, were to be executed by flames. The message here is both simple and not so simple. Jesus says the truth shall make you free. Of course, we might wonder, with Pilate, just what *is* truth after all? There could be many different answers to this question, depending on one's Christology, but I doubt that Jesus is indexing truth to a proposition: affirm me as Savior. Another way to interpret this is to affirm truth as a way of life, truth *indexed* to life. When Jesus says, "I am the Truth, the Way, and the Life," we can read it thus: live the way I have lived, learn what it means to live unconstricted by egotistic littleness, trust me, come out into the deep, live like this, and death shall have no hold on you, for you shall be free. Truth as indexed to life was Gandhi's method, and it was also the method of Albert Schweitzer (1875-1965), whose ethics of affirming life proceeded directly from his reverence for life. Here is his straightforward account,

> Let me give you a definition of ethics: It is good to maintain life and further life; it is bad to damage and destroy life. However much it struggles against it, ethics arrives at the religion of Jesus. It must recognize that it can discover no other relationship of love. Ethics is the maintaining of life at the highest point of development—my own life and other life—by devoting myself to it in help and love, and both these things are connected.[1]

Coming from a Christian tradition, Schweitzer clearly understood the call to be an *alter Christus*, another Christ. Living the way of Jesus is the truth we weave in the fabric of our lives, thereby discovering our full human flourishing. But living this way is hardly the province of Christianity alone. Indeed, this way—predicating one's behaviors on wisdom and compassion—is the method of many contemporary Buddhist activists, such as Thich Nhat Hanh and Sulak Sivaraksa. Indeed, in Buddhism, right action has less to do with rote conforming to external standards than with cultivating skillful habits of mind and heart that conduce to personal and social well-being. It also includes eliminating those habits that are unskillful and unwholesome. The reason for this method is basic: wise loving leads to peace; unwise living does not. What is implied in this approach, however, is process and self-acceptance. We work at this. We are imperfect. Sometimes we do this well. And sometimes we do not; the arcs of our loving do not hit the mark. In this case, we do ourselves a service to *practice*, that is, resolving once again to choose patterns of mind and will that generate life. It is not so much that practice makes perfect but that in the *practice* there is perfection. The practice itself—little acts of kindness, mindful breathing, incremental steps in a life of love—is the goal. In this case, there is no looking to outcomes, for the outcome is already achieved in the practice.

The three men in the story refused to worship idols. And although we might consider ourselves far too sophisticated to worship golden calves, most of us are afflicted with some form of idolatry, the evidence of which is the inordinate cultivation we give to the objects of our attention. Our idols might be wealth and status, or they might be something more subtle, such as the incessant need to be right, or habituated anger, or insecurity, or anxiety, or an ancient grievance that we hold onto but in fact it holds onto us. Whether these objects are external or internal, the outcome is the same: they take up an inordinate space in our consciousness, which in turn chokes our soulsong back to God.

For many, career might become an idol, what I called in a long-ago poem, the "idol of the unseen grail." It is unseen because it is always unrealized. When career ceases to be a creative form of self-expression and instead becomes an idol, no amount of success satisfies. Enough is never enough. This is not to minimize the many understandably attractive and appropriate benefits of success—a sense of accomplishment, material gain to meet family needs, an expression of passion and creativity, the praise of peers, the esteem of others; but all this can become overly gripping, and the intense discipline and focus required to make a name for oneself often comes at great cost. Woven into the very structure of achievement are the cracks and fissures that sometimes result in brokenness and loss. For some of us, the ascent can be a flameout; we crash, come back to earth, suffer our losses and failures—and, paradoxically, this suffering can become our calling card into our humanity. We discover what's really real for us, we recover new authenticity. While no one wants to suffer, suffering nevertheless can be a slingshot into new awareness, capacities, and freedoms. The Indian religious traditions are quite clear about this: there is a *telos* to suffering, which we might paraphrase idiosyncratically: the end of suffering is the end of suffering. That is, the objective or purpose of suffering is to end it; in other words, suffering arouses in us the resolve to enter the fiery space of renewal and authentic personhood. A genuine will, autonomous and unconditioned by fear, is born. Suffering therefore is *provocative*; it calls forth (*pro-voke*) the cogent word of our lives, a deeper, more complete humanity. Within suffering itself, therefore, are the seeds of freedom. We come to new places of authenticity, the central axis of our holiness.

The catalogue of our personal idols includes much more than material gain. Muslims are quite wise about this as they explain the concept of *shirk*, the flaw of associating anything with the status accorded only to Allah. So, in this sense any excessive self-preoccupation, unsurrendered to the sacred, is a form of idolatry. This could include anxiety over a job interview, or giving a presentation, or speaking the truth to someone dear to you, or suffering the acid of unmet longing. The root anguish associated with each of these examples is fear of loss or rejection or loneliness. If we are living in surrender, however, the job—or raise, or recognition, or book, or relationship, or neurosis—is, in a sense, none of our business. *Inshallah.* "If God wills." To surrender is *really* to surrender. To let go is *really* to let go. Most of us who have been raised with some sort of spiritual training know such language and the truth it expresses. But, as we also know, there are times when living this truth is unbearably difficult. This gap, and our inability to bridge it (revealed in our thoughts, words, and behaviors) may surprise us. Yet, there's no sense in judging ourselves for holding on where and if we need to hold on. We will let go when we are able to let go.

When the losses of life do visit us, as they will inevitably, we might consider the extravagant call to radical generosity seen in various religious traditions. For example, in the potlatch or "give-away" ceremonies of various Native American traditions, great honor is accorded the one who radically embraces newness and demonstrates this by literally giving away *everything*. Or, from the perspective of Buddhism, we might consider the example of Prince Vessantara in the penultimate lifetime of the Buddha. According to this mythology, Vessantara heroically modeled the premier Buddhist virtue of generosity—generosity is essential to the path because it purifies the mind of habituated selfishness and instantiates wisdom and compassion. In this case, Vessantara gave away *everything*—wealth of the kingdom, the royal elephant, even his beloved wife and children. This latter seems unbearably jarring—*he gave away his wife and children*? That's absurd, and it's not helped by the comment, "It's not that he disliked his children but that he loved omniscience more."[2] There is clearly a different scheme of values here than most of us are accustomed to, and it would be easy to write it off as absurd. However, according to the Danish philosopher Søren Kierkegaard, the founder of existentialism, it is precisely by virtue of the absurd that redemption occurs. But our anguish includes not knowing that as we make the leap of faith. In letting go, we do not hedge our bets: we *really* let go. We really allow for new futures to unfold. Moreover, those of us who are parents know well that we *do* need to let go of our children—for *their* sake—at key periods in their lives. Out of love, we let go of *our* need for them, and, because of that, we give them the space *they* need to fulfill their own destiny and authentic becoming. Can we therefore think differently about the inevitable losses in our lives, and, rather than dwelling on them and the pain they represent, be radically open to a new disposition toward them? Indeed, can we *give away* more than life takes away from us? This is living in surrender. This is living in letting-go space.

Buddhism would not use the language of idolatry in its analysis of human behavior. In its idiom, all forms of self-assertion reveal an addiction more basic than that of alcohol or drugs, namely, the addiction to *ourselves*. Our selfish preoccupations, our knee-jerk urges to justify ourselves, to prove ourselves, to do mental battle with our oppressors—all of these become expressions of self-addiction, perhaps the most egregious idolatry of all. And yet, the powerful energy we give to our ego-defenses also indicates the great potential we have for cultivation of heart and mind. The same energy we apply to nourish our idols, as it were, can be directed to more wholesome habits of mind and will. The Dalai Lama recognizes this potential in our unwholesome mental obsessions. The energy required to feed our distress or inner discord is highly concentrated and in effect is a kind of meditation. We have the capacity to change the object of our concentration, and in so doing, grow in the grace of surrender.

Perhaps surrender finally means less about letting go of persons or things than letting go of *ourselves* and our presumed needs. We may come to the humble awareness that we invest in others and things insofar as they bring us happiness or somehow reinforce our sense of identity. The hard truth is no one or no thing can make us happy, and our identity, in some sense always fluid and certainly complex, is our responsibility alone. We are on our own, as it were, masters of our own happiness, authors of our own destinies. Insofar as we predicate our happiness on external events or inordinately depend on others for our well-being or sense of self, this, too, from the Muslim perspective, could be *shirk*. In order to live in the holy space of our

discuss this
relate to Mara

authenticity, we need to surrender our hold on external markers of satisfaction and identity. Comfort, prestige, beauty, affirmation, money, success, wealth, and fear—all this is can be *shirk*. Even undue anxiety over anything, from the perspective of Muslim spirituality is *shirk*—it is not living a life of surrender, not living in "letting-go space." To live in surrender is, from the perspective of Islam, the first and greatest *jihad*, the striving (*jihad*) against self. Indeed, in some Sufi traditions, masters would deliberately invite ridicule and criticism to speed up the shattering of egotism and the grip of external praise or blame, the markers we often use to justify our sense of self, if not our existence. In this tradition, we are already beloved of the Beloved. To believe that, to breathe that, to live that, is to be free.

Just as an individual reveals habituated clinging, grasping, ego, and craving, so does a culture. Dominant cultural structures reflect and reinforce cultural tendencies to grasp and crave. Money, possessions, power, prestige, all this, insofar as we culture it, grow it, attend to it, becomes something bigger than us, often draining the life from us. As some contemporary thinkers have observed, borrowing from Buddhism, America could be considered the land of "hungry ghosts," those gaunt specters with enormous stomachs and needle-like mouths unable to take in the food they crave. Their hell is that their craving can never be fed. And neither can ours, yet the subterranean refrain that fuels it is *more*. More success, more publicity, more money, more prestige, more sex, more comforts, more affirmation, more, more, more. The fire of craving can only be cooled by the breath of the divine, however that divine is construed. The truth is this: living in surrender cools the flames, allows us to breathe. Coolness, then, is a kind of holiness. Indeed, in the early stilted translations of Buddhist texts, one stock comment of the Buddha is this: "I am become cool." While this phrase conjures an image of the Buddha in Ray-Ban sunglasses and a black leather jacket, it means that the Awakened One has cooled the flames of passion and craving. While the fire of agonizing loss can be conducive to holiness, so can coolness, which cools the fires of passion and craving. The coolness of equanimity leads to holiness, but so can the white-hot fire of loss.

The Fire of the Prophets

But there is another kind of fire, one that expresses holiness rather than leads to it. The holiness of fire in this case is the holiness of the prophets who call us to a vision of things that stretch us beyond the possible in the ways of love and life. These persons fan the flames to create a conflagration that consumes our cultural habits and patterns and attachments. They are the fire-tenders, as it were, calling us—as a culture—to pass through the fiery furnace and be purified of our cultural idolatry. And so here I wish to highlight the saints of fire. These are the persons who recognize an indisputable requirement for social transformation that must accompany any and all personal transformation. Specifically, I will address the examples of John Dear, S.J., and the Buddhist activist from Thailand, Sulak Sivaraksa, above all considering the religious wisdom and values that inform their authenticities.

There are many more, of course. From the Catholic tradition, perhaps the most well-known example of this model is Daniel Berrigan, who has lived the truth of the radical gospel ethic in a seamless weave throughout his long life. Kathy Kelly, nominated three times for the Nobel Peace Prize for her nonviolent activism in Iraq, is another extraordinary example of a life wholly committed to a gospel vision of justice and peace. And so is Thomas Gumbleton, auxiliary bishop of Detroit. Gumbleton, as a young priest, served in the parish of my youth, St. Alphonsus, in Dearborn, a suburb of Detroit. As I came to know him as an adult, I recall being deeply inspired by his resolute commitment to a gospel ethic, not to mention his commitment to making the pastoral letter of the bishops on peace as strong as possible; despite its limitations, that document remains a powerful witness to an ethic formed by Christian scriptures and tradition. For all his efforts, which included serv-

ing as president of Pax Christi, he was awarded the Oscar
Romero Award at Mercyhurst College, an award given each
year to one who embodies the call to faith and justice. And
while it had been many years since I heard Bishop Gumbleton
speak, the same powerful prophetic call to justice and peace
that I heard so many years before rang true once again when he
gave his address. Such resonance is a grace, a hint of who we
are or perhaps where we need to go in order to be more fully
ourselves. This resonance comes from listening to others, seeing
examples of lives lived well, and practicing, little by little, the
habits of wisdom and love.

But there are many others who give voice to truth, both well
known and perhaps not so well known. Joan Chittister and
Mary Lou Kownacki, Benedictines of Erie, Pennsylvania, have
each been recognized for their prophetic calls to justice and
peace. Indeed, my colleague, Mary Snyder, has edited a volume
honoring Joan Chittester's life, example, and profound contribution to the church and the world. Mary Lou Kownacki, also
a past president of Pax Christi, has done extraordinary work
that has been recognized publicly. She is also an accomplished
poet, whose words touch deep impulses of the human spirit. But
there are many other examples, equally resonant, who are less
known by the wider public. Dorothy Stoner, also a Benedictine
sister, is a colleague with a lucid vision of faith and justice, and
she lives this out, not only in her prayer life, in her teaching, and
in her community, but also by actively supporting programs and
actions that further embody that vision. Dorothy regularly
takes students to Georgia to protest at the School of the Americas (SOA), the institution that has trained many Central and
South American military leaders, including personnel who have
tortured or killed those struggling for human rights in their own
countries. To build upon these experiences, Dorothy has spon-
sored lectures at Mercyhurst delivered by Roy Bourgeois, the
well-known Maryknoll priest and activist who founded the
School of the Americas Watch, an organization that uses nonviolent civil disobedience in an effort to close the SOA. But
Dorothy, always thoughtful and collected, also has taken to the

streets in another way, namely, to pray for healing where murderous violence has occurred. In 2000, a young woman was slain in Erie, a rare occurrence here, but all the more disturbing since it was not far from our home. I happened upon Dorothy, who was part of a large crowd of people, and asked her what was going on. She and her community were praying for the young woman and for the man who killed her. In a sense, they were absorbing the violence that occurred on that spot, aiming to transform that rupture into a space of healing. It was a remarkable witness, an extraordinary adaptation of the Last Rites and even called to mind the Tibetan postmortem funerary traditions that oversee and facilitate the passage of the soul into wider space after death. These public or private acts of wisdom and compassion bear witness to ways of being in the world that authentically express truth and life. This is holiness, and it resonates with us.

There are others who similarly express compassion and wisdom in their local communities. The person who speaks up at a city council meeting. The one who organizes a letter-writing campaign to reinstate the ban on assault weapons. The colleagues who pour themselves out to green the campus. Anyone who speaks truth to the powerful. The latter is difficult, because it requires letting go, above all, of ourselves. And while speaking the truth to the powerful is difficult enough in society, it is no less difficult in our personal relationships. How can we speak truth without the need to win, without the knee-jerk need to defend ourselves? How can we peacefully stand our ground, stand in the fire of hostility and rejection, speak our truth in love, and let the chips fall where they may? Our personal relationships are often mere microcosms of broader cultural patterns of power and domination.

Standing in the fire means to put our bodies on the line, to trust so radically that our bodies—our comforts, our needs, our ways—are offered on the altar. We become a holocaust, a sacrifice. We ourselves become Isaacs. There could be no more powerful image of this than the Buddhist monks in Vietnam who offered their bodies as a visible symbol of what was happening in their country. They sat in the fiery furnace. They *were* the fiery furnace. Yet by their astonishing meditative equipoise, they were able to bear suffering without crying out, and in so doing bore profound witness to the horrific trauma happening in their country. While such a witness is stunning and, for most of us, incomprehensible, at issue is the call to bear witness to deeper truths and to be willing to suffer the consequences for doing it. The following persons, in my view, do this, and we profit from their example, learn something of the places where we are called to extend our projects of personal transformation into social change.

John Dear and El Salvador

John Dear is a Jesuit. When I was a Jesuit twenty years ago, John and I and three other scholastics worked as volunteers in refugee camps in El Salvador. It was 1985, just five years after the murders of Archbishop Oscar Romero and the four American church women. There have been only two times in my life that I fully expected a dire end on a trip abroad, and that was one of them. In the preceding years, beginning with ongoing conversion and deepening faith experiences at Georgetown, travel to India to work with missionaries, and my training with the Jesuits, I learned that a natural extension of personal transformation is to work for the transformation of the world. In the idiom of the gospel, we work to help usher in the reign of God—the reign of justice and peace and love and forgiveness. And this movement, springing first and best from intimacy with the divine, is demonstrated time and again in each of the great Abrahamic faiths. The call to action, the call to live prophetically, the call to live the holiness of God is a central dynamic in the Western religious traditions. However, it was also exemplified in an exquisite way by Mahatma Gandhi, who drew his inspiration of nonviolence not only from the Hindu, Buddhist, and Jain traditions of South Asia, but also from Tolstoy, a volcanic personality who, after his conversion, lived a radical gospel vision marked by pacifism and justice.

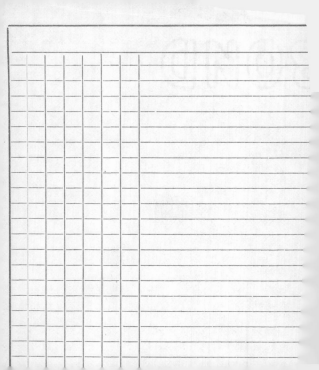

I felt the call increasingly to put my body on the line. And so I worked in offices and organizations dedicated to social change; I wrote a graduate thesis on nonviolence; I participated in protest demonstrations in New York and Chicago; I traveled to Offut Air Force Base in Nebraska to cross the line. Although all of these unfoldings felt true, other truths over time emerged, too, truths of intimacy, family, the mystical elements of religion, teaching, scholarship, poetry. But in the summer of 1985, I went to El Salvador and met and became friends with John. While coming to know ourselves is always an ongoing process, it takes on particular intensity at different periods of our lives, and the twenties seem to be a particularly vital time in which we explore questions of meaning, value, and purpose. I was struck by the decisive manner in which John responded to these questions. He utterly poured himself out in his commitment to Christ and the values of the gospel. The texture of the commitment was broadly shaped by his Jesuit background, but that is precisely what it was, background. He was given over to Christ first. And he understood this to mean a life of radical nonviolence. These things I believed—and believe—too, and I have tried to live them with integrity, despite my own limitations and flaws. But as I think about John's example in El Salvador and elsewhere, I would say, in an entirely nonevaluative way, that I, over the years, have allowed my experiences to shape my vision. John let his vision shape his experiences.

This was strikingly evident in El Salvador. In El Salvador we stayed at a camp called *Calle Real,* "Royal Way." It was not far from the capital but still ensconced in hills, with a long winding path leading up to it from a nearby highway. We lived with a small group of *desplazados* ("displaced"), and sometimes in the morning we could hear planes dropping bombs on guerrilla targets. In my view, we didn't do much, and, just as I had experienced as a lay volunteer in India years earlier, this sometimes caused frustration, perhaps being overly attached to achieving and accomplishing. But it was clear from the testimony of the refugees that our *presence* itself was more than sufficient, was more than good enough, above all because, as internationals, we afforded the refugees a greater sense of safety and security. Just *being there* was good enough. We can apply the lesson to our lives in our current here and now. Just *being here* is good enough. We are welcomed. We are valued. We have something to offer in virtue of our being. Accepting this allows us to "be here" with greater ease and simplicity and to be free—to be here for others.

John and I enjoyed each other's company, but I was profoundly struck by his laser-like resolve. He often wrote for long periods each day, and he made independent trips to various places in El Salvador, including Chalatenango, where the U.S. church women were murdered. We had long conversations, agreeing on so many premises and values, and yet I very much felt that John was always prepared to push the envelope, to take the extra step to *realize* his commitment. Two events illustrate this. One day he asked if I wanted to do an "action" with him at the U.S. embassy. I had participated at many protests at the Federal Building in Chicago and elsewhere, but this immediately felt different. This felt genuinely *dangerous*. And then it dawned on me: to live and to speak the truth in some circumstances *is* dangerous. I recalled the words of Jesuit theologian Jon Sobrino, who offered an informal lecture on liberation theology one afternoon during our first week in El Salvador. When we asked about the persecution of the church, he bluntly said, "The church had better be persecuted." That is, under egregious oppression, anything less than prophetic condemnation of rampant violence and degradation could only be viewed as tacit approval of that oppression. El Salvador was layered with violence: economic violence—a poverty that kills; political violence—with death squads; and military violence in the form of the professional military elite, trained in the United States. In the face of this overwhelming domination of death—"And God is a God of life"—"The church had better be persecuted."

I couldn't help but think of the courage—no matter how wrapped in fear, too—of all the leaders of the base communities, of every person in El Salvador who attempted to speak the truth or to live the truth, and of all the victims of violence, including the American women killed in 1980. Maura Clarke, Dorothy Kazel, Ita Ford, and Jeanne Donovan were killed for doing what many of us do as volunteers in our local parishes—distribute clothes, food, and medicine to those who need it. And Oscar Romero, the archbishop of San Salvador, murdered while celebrating the Eucharist, was killed for speaking the truth. He refused to let the violence and violations go unknown; instead, he identified the victims of violence, methodically naming them from his pulpit each week. Their suffering did not go unnoticed. One of the displaced persons in our camp expressed it in simple but profound words, *Decia la verdad* ("he told the truth"). And he was killed for doing it. When six Jesuits—and a housekeeper and her daughter—were murdered in 1989, the message was clear: you will be killed for speaking your voice—or for associating with those who do.

John and I talked about what kind of action we might do, and we settled on simply praying on the roundabout in front of the embassy. When we arrived there the next morning, I felt thick with fear. Soldiers were everywhere. And, although very much accustomed to the practice of prayer, I suddenly felt unmoored and unable to pray. But John and I began the Lord's Prayer, and instantly I felt tension melt away in its first words, "Our Father. . . ." It is not my place here to address the theological nuance of the fatherhood of God—indeed my colleague and good friend, David Livingston, is writing a book precisely on this topic. The relevant existential fact for me was the *surrender* implied in that prayer. May *your* kingdom come. May *your* will be done. On earth—here, now, in me, in you, in society, the world—as it is in heaven. Give us this day our daily bread—our food, everything that nourishes our physical and spiritual well-being. And forgive us our sins as we forgive those who sin against us.

This is the hard one. Forgive us *as we forgive*. Many of us find it difficult to forgive. In fact some psychologists argue that under certain circumstances, *not* to forgive may be an appropriate assertion of power and self-care for victims. But that is not the counsel contained in the Lord's Prayer. To pray "Forgive us as we forgive others" is haunting because, while it may be easy to forgive the little slights, the grave hurts feel daunting. And so we might say, *don't* forgive us as we forgive, because we don't forgive! Forgive us as *you* forgive. You are the Holy One, after all. But the call here is to steep deep the truth of love in our lives, and allow the holy process to unfold. We can forgive. We can let go. This, of course, doesn't mean forgetting the injury, but it means the injury no longer has a hold on our peace. We can arrive at the place of letting go, showing patience and compassion to ourselves as the healing unfolds organically in due course. The Lord's Prayer implies that we can do this, and living it might be one of the greater miracles of which Jesus spoke. Christ left us but did not abandon us. We have the capacity to arrive at love even in the crucible of loss and heartache. Jean Vanier, the founder of the L'Arche community and yet another example of exquisite humanness, said, in a recent address at Gannon University, "We say we want peace. But if we want peace, are we willing to work for justice? And if we want justice, are we prepared to work for forgiveness?" Healing isn't complete with polices alone. Healing is complete with communion. This sensibility has long fueled the efforts of Desmond Tutu, the title of whose latest book makes this clear: *No Future without Forgiveness*. And it was a principal insight of Mahatma Gandhi and Martin Luther King, Jr., whose goals were not complete until the enemy became a friend.

As John and I did our action—a simple prayer—I felt peace, and I understood something about surrender, perhaps above all that to be able to let go is a grace, but we have to be willing to let go, too. We have to want to let go, even as our fingers betray us, still clutching tightly to that which must be surrendered. But in the fire of our lives, can we say, "Our Father" (or "Our Mother," or "Our Beloved," or "Our God"), and let go, and really allow all bets to be off? To live in surrender, to live in letting go—this is the place of freedom. We know this. We've heard this. We need to pray for this. Why? Because our biological and social and psychological conditioning predispose us to the old song of defense, assertion, and self-protection.

John and I decided to practice this once again, making a pilgrimage to Aguilares, the town where Rutilio Grande, S.J., served as pastor before he was murdered in 1977. Taking a bus to El Paisnal, Grande's hometown, we disembarked, quickly noticing that the plaza filled with National Guard. We nonetheless began walking to Aguilares, knowing that somewhere on this path Grande and two others were murdered in a hail of gunfire. We walked in the summer heat, composed and reflective. Coming upon a massive cloud of butterflies, I wondered if that happened to be the site of the murders. And if not, I wondered if the butterflies, as in the mythology of Latin America, were the returning souls of the dead. At the very least, they were, and remain, a potent symbol of metamorphosis and transformation, and transformation requires a dying, a dissolution into primordial chaos. There, in the milky stew of renewal, we weave new threads of being and begin the alchemy of becoming. But this requires a dying, a radical letting go. We need to *dissolve* in order to *resolve*.

John and I made it to Aguilares, went to the church and prayed, bought a soda in a little shop. In that shop an armed young man loaded a gunny sack with staples. I am not certain of this—as I did not ask him—but it struck me that he might have been a *muchacho*, one of the "boys," the guerrillas, because Aguilares was close to an area that they controlled. It was disorienting to be surrounded by National Guard earlier and now, perhaps, to be in the world of the *muchacho*. Later, when it seemed that we were followed by someone on the way back to El Paisnal, we wondered if we were taken to be CIA agents. We made it back, unmolested, our brief pilgrimage complete.

There is a tightness that comes with fear, and this fear, at its root, is fear of death. We do not need to be in war zones to feel this fear; many of us feel it in our homes, at work, and in our relationships, when conflict and rejection strike a primordial dread. Once, when I left *Calle Real* and headed down the path toward the highway, I was met by the camp agronomist who urged me to be alert, since over a hundred soldiers of the Salvadoran army were on the path ahead. Again, I felt fear and

tried to let go, and, in fact, I drew strength from the words of
scripture that I had just read that morning, "Lord, you esteem
the rank of no one." There is a profound self-possession in that
passage, one that emerges in virtue of self-knowledge. Many of
us might be intimidated by certain people or certain personalities, and part of the curriculum in being who we are—the hallmark of our holiness—is relaxing in the face of pressure, not
caving in to fear. "You esteem the rank of no one." And yet, I
am sure that Jesus knew fear, too. But the key element in his life
or Gandhi's or Mother Teresa's or anyone who lives truth is not
to be immobilized by fear. They carry on, push through, do not
flee. And so can we.

In our humanness, we might recognize—list, write down,
reflect on—the times when we were afraid—to take a new job, to
call a friend, to volunteer in some capacity, to stand up to someone's hostility, to say yes when we want to say no, and to say no
when we want to say yes, to let go of something or someone we
love. Most of our difficult encounters are in the end encounters
with ourselves; these are opportunities, in the face of fear, to
instantiate authenticity. Since the fear of rejection so often unconsciously dominates our habituated ways of being, we may come
to a haunting question, Is my authenticity good enough for me?
The hidden fear is this: will my way of being me—being who I
am—be rejected? And the answer, of course, is, yes, sometimes.
In order to avoid the pain of rejection and defend against it, however, we might let go inappropriately. In this case, we might let go
of the truth of our experience, inappropriately surrendering who
we are in a specific moment in time, therefore losing the greatest
gift to ourselves and to others, our authenticity. This does not
mean that we are required to thump our chests like gorillas to win
a debate or to make a point. But do we surrender too much in
order to be accepted? Do we slowly let our soul slip through our
hands because we can't stand the heat of reactivity or rejection?
Our worst-case scenario, of which we may not be conscious, is
the fear of abandonment. The truth is, there is nothing to lose if
we are ourselves, for even if we are abandoned by others, we have
not abandoned our soul.

Our enemy in the end is ourselves. Those who are hostile to us are mere occasions for the deeper battle within each of us. Our external enemy merely triggers deeper, more primordial fears, our real enemy. It is for this reason that so many spiritual adepts from the world's religious traditions count the enemy as our finest teacher, for paradoxically we come to know deeper places of wisdom and compassion. In the struggle experienced by Tibetans in the face of Chinese aggression, an often-told story recounts the words of a monk who was asked what he feared the most in his torture: "Losing compassion for my jailers." Our enemies can be difficult teachers. Can we love them as our greatest teachers? Indeed, these words of Geshe Lang-ri Tang-pa's Tibetan hymn, "Eight Verses for Training the Mind," call us to rethink radically our relationship to the enemy.

When I see beings of a negative disposition
or those oppressed by negativity or pain,
may I, as if finding a treasure,
consider them precious, for they are rarely met.

Whenever others, due to their jealousy,
revile and treat me in other unjust ways,
may I accept this defeat myself,
and offer victory to the others.

When someone whom I have helped
or in whom I have placed great hope
harms me with great injustice,
may I see that one as a sacred friend.

This is by no means easy.

It is difficult to imagine living completely beyond fear. It is part of the human condition. Overcoming fear, however, may not necessarily mean eradicating it but pressing forward despite it. As we practice new habits of mind and heart, we develop new strengths and capacities. As we dance with fear, which, at root, is the fear of death, we may ask ourselves, how can we befriend our dying *now*. How can we "die before we die," as Muhammad enjoined? In this case, every loss, every limitation, every heartache becomes the training ground for the great letting go.

After our summer in El Salvador, John and I returned to the United States and to our respective Jesuit programs. I left the Jesuits in 1986, married in 1987, had three children with Therese, taught in high schools, returned to India several times, completed a Ph.D., and now teach as an associate professor of religious studies at Mercyhurst College in Erie. John has continued to let his vision shape his experiences, writing many books on nonviolence, being arrested many times for acts of civil disobedience, and indeed, serving in federal prison for nearly a year for attempting to disable an Air Force bomber in an action by Ploughshares. In 2002, the religious studies department at Mercyhurst conferred on him the Oscar Romero award, as we had done earlier with Tom Gumbleton. It was a joy to see John after nearly twenty years. We talked long and compared stories and memories. And yet, I was struck again by the same resolute conviction and drive that I had seen many years earlier in El Salvador. Although much had changed since, one thing did not: John was being John. In one sense, he hadn't changed at all. He was being who he was, and is, and this is the essence of *his* holiness. From his being—his authenticity formed by wisdom and value—his doing flowed. Our holiness begins with being ourselves, our authenticities formed by the wisdom and value of our lives; in being ourselves, our doing flows creatively and spontaneously, and thereby becomes a gift to ourselves, to others, and to God.

What is clear in the work of so many faith-based activists is the conviction that personal transformation must catalyze social transformation. It is not enough simply to "get one's act together" when the very conditions of our lives, in the West, are afflicted with injustice and social ill. For example, Americans, while representing about 6 percent of the world's population, consume 60 percent of its resources. And it is not the case that

America is endowed with the happy fortune that allows it to enjoy extravagant privilege. Instead, we are fortunate because of the misfortune of others. We are rich because others are poor. It is always appropriate to give thanks for the benefits we enjoy. It is also appropriate to support policies that provide generous assistance to the global village and to support other policies that fundamentally restructure the distribution of scarce resources. The world needs the Mother Teresas, who pick up, one by one, the sick and the dying, and reveal to them, in the luminous exchange of sight, their dignity and value which no sickness or poverty can steal. This is the work of the heart, or in classic Christian terms, charity. The world also needs its prophets, the fire-tenders who call for justice and who are willing to stand in the fire of personal attack. Charity meets immediate needs, addressing the empirical fact of poverty; justice examines its causes and aims to restructure social systems accordingly. Those who sound the clarion call for justice critique institutional sin— for example, inequitable policies, laws, customs, and trade relationships—which becomes woven into the fabric of society and only creates a wider gulf between the powerful and the marginalized.

Sulak Sivaraksa and Socially Engaged Buddhism

In 1999, I had the privilege of being invited to a conference held in Dharamsala, convened by His Holiness the Dalai Lama. There, for whatever reason—my own readiness, conversations I had with Tibetan monks, witnessing their example—I had a glimpse of the spiritual power of the doctrine of emptiness, the cardinal concept in Mahayana Buddhism. I will say more about this in following chapters, but for now let me suggest that emptiness—the fact of being empty, empty, that is, of a separate, independent existence—is held to be the direct antidote of the self-grasping mind, the mind afflicted with ego. For Buddhists, the notion of a fixed self inevitably leads to selfishness. The path of holiness in Buddhism traditionally has been the path of meditation, best realized in monasteries, or the path of the bodhisattva, who embodies wisdom in compassionate action. What is new to contemporary Buddhism is the social analysis of selfishness and the call for social transformation, not just personal transformation. This call, at the conference, was lucidly—and for me, refreshingly—made by the Thai Buddhist Sulak Sivaraksa.

Religion begins with personal transformation, calling the subject to become aware of one's finitude, especially that imposed by death, and aims, by diverse means, to rewire one's consciousness or align one's heart with the truth of reality in its most complete context. This truth, expressed variously in the world's religions, transcends our ontological poverty, our inherent limitation; accessing or internalizing this truth is freeing. Without entering into debate about the nature of this truth, we might say that the terms God, Buddha-nature, *Shakti,* the Beloved, Allah, and so on point to this truth. In other words, these terms identify some transcendent, ultimate state or way or being that relativizes all our longing and limitation, brings healing of one's heart and the hearts of others. Living this truth is holy communion.

But the premises and logic of most religions do not remain at the level of personal transformation alone. This is seen, for example, in the great Abrahamic faiths by the testimony of the Hebrew prophets, the teaching and example of Jesus, and the social assistance required of all Muslims in the "poor tax" (*zakat*) the third pillar of faith in Islam. It is also seen in the life and teaching of Mahatma Gandhi (1869-1948), Vinoba Bhave (1895-1982), B. R. Ambedkar (1891-1956) in India, as well as that of contemporary Hindu physicist and activist Vandana Shiva. In 1993 Shiva won the international Right Livelihood Award, which recognizes extraordinary effort in the work for justice and peace.

Sivaraksa, nominated twice for the Nobel Peace Prize and also a Right Livelihood Award winner (1995), and Thich Nhat Hanh, another the Nobel Peace Prize candidate, are perhaps the best-known Buddhist activists weaving together the dynamic of personal and social transformation, drawing from the first principles of Buddhism itself. But there are many others, such as Nobel Peace Prize winner Aung San Suu Kyi in Burma, Maha Ghosananda in Cambodia, and the late Nichidatsu Fuji (1885-1985), the founder of Nipponzan Myohoji, the peace-making order begun in Japan after World War II.

When I listened to Sivaraksa speak at the conference, I was encouraged, in part because his words resonated with the call to justice that is found in all religious traditions. The awareness and specific expression of this call unfolds in history. Christians today, after all, no longer endorse slavery as an acceptable social institution as some did two hundred years ago. The call to justice might be implicit in our religious traditions, but it is made explicit when we consider all relevant conditions, above all the central dynamics of our faiths. This is the process that fueled Gandhi's heroic efforts, and one that is seen in the work of other Hindu activists as well. It is the same process that also gave rise to the great body of Catholic social teaching. The implications of the gospel *require* social justice. Anything less undermines or erodes the premier gospel value, namely, the dignity and worth of human beings. Sivaraksa, in no uncertain terms, gave voice to a cardinal truth, namely, the requirement for social transformation in consort with personal transformation. While he did this in the idiom of Buddhism, it nonetheless resonated with my training and experience in Catholic social thought and faith-based activism.

Moreover, as a practicing Buddhist, Sivaraksa was in a unique position to challenge even the Dalai Lama, which he did, bluntly suggesting that His Holiness' teaching itself remained overly focused on personal transformation. Indeed, while the Dalai Lama's teaching does resonate with profound truth, I tend to agree with Sivaraksa. On occasion the Dalai Lama appears not to apply the logic of his rigorous metaphysical analysis to a broader social context. If he did, he might pull fewer punches and call for a radical change in social structures and policies. For example, in the introduction to *An Open Heart*, he offers counsel that seems almost naïve, encouraging the rich to share and the poor to work hard and to exercise self-confidence in all their efforts.[3] But such counsel appears to forget a singular principle of Buddhist metaphysics: the fact of relatedness. In this case, the plight of the poor is in part the result of broader social and economic forces over which they have little control. So the counsel to work hard and be confident in the face of terrible poverty is, at the very least, insufficient, and, at worst, patronizing. Instead, the broader truth, so well captured by the Buddhist doctrine of dependent origination or interbeing, is the web of relationships woven into global, as well as personal, dynamics. These social dynamics, when harmful, must be addressed, confronted, and changed as part of the program of healing and transformation.

Let me add a further comment. The fact that the Dalai Lama does not forcefully press the social truth implied in Buddhist metaphysics, say, in the manner of Sivaraksa or Nhat Hanh, is not really a criticism of him but is the reason why we need Sivaraksa and Nhat Hanh. They, and others from the perspective of Buddhism, angle the prism of holiness to reflect different hues, new ways of seeing things that reveal brightness and color. We see the invisible enfolded in the visible, refracted in crystalline fashion. These plural ways of wise living reflect key streams of human being and becoming. Similarly, the fact that Mother Teresa says, in the Petrie film, "We don't mix up in politics," is not so much grounds for criticism as the reason why we also need John Dear and Kathy Kelly, the extraordinary Chicagoan dedicated to justice and peace in Iraq since the first Gulf war. These holy ones are holy precisely because they are themselves, their authenticities informed by their spiritual commitments. With laser-like resolve, they embody a vision of love and wisdom generated by the central dynamics of their traditions. Mother Teresa's holiness is hers. In being Mother Teresa, she becomes a mirror to our own becoming. And so, too, the activists from every religious tradition who address the requirements of justice as well as charity. There are as many models of holiness as there are people, but one dynamic is clear: personal transformation somehow must include social transformation, even if this process, embodied in ourselves and in society, is best done slowly, as yeast surely makes the bread rise.

Much outstanding scholarship has been done on developing trends in contemporary Buddhism. These include new models of leadership, the role of women in the Western *sangha*, greater awareness of ecological needs, and the development of socially engaged Buddhism. These trends are paralleled in other religions, reflecting broader cross-cultural patterns in the religious response to the modern world. The parallel of socially engaged Buddhism and Christianity is evident, and it may be the case that the program of social analysis in Christian theology served as a model for similar analyses in contemporary Buddhism. Whether or not this is the case, the fact remains that many contemporary Buddhists, like many contemporary Christians, are not satisfied with transformation that remains only personal. Personal transformation must be accompanied by social transformation. In the idiom of Christianity, sin is not just selfish, hurtful, actions, but also something greater than our personal flaws, and often far more serious, too. Consumerism, crass capitalism, globalization, militarism, these are social patterns woven systemically into culture in the form of policies, tax cuts, laws, customs, trade relationships, and multinational corporate growth. These produce a host of negative outcomes, including bleak disparities in wealth, education, social and health services, not to mention the political tensions that emerge from such disparities. Unresolved political tensions around the globe often generate resentment and sadly lead to violence. Economic violence often leads to political violence, which in turn escalates into full-scale military violence, the terrible cycle addressed by Oscar Romero, Dom Helder Camara, and many others.

The argument for social transformation from a Buddhist perspective follows directly from its premises, especially the doctrines of no soul and dependent origination. The former suggests that the idea of a permanent substrate of personality—some fixed notion of "me"—inevitably leads to selfishness. Our uncritical, habituated way of being in the world is typically governed by afflictive emotions of greed and anger, which themselves can only emerge by some notion of "me" or a sense of self. For Buddhists, from "self" comes "selfishness," which in turn issues in myriad personal conflicts. If we all operate out of the misguided premise of self, then we inevitably cast ourselves into competition and anxiety, for we are surrounded by others also operating from the same misguided premise. We, therefore, battle, in the face of limitation, to accumulate more and to protect our score. This conflict, while empirically real, is, in the Buddhist view, caused by a fundamental delusion, namely, the fixed notion of self. When we live self-lessness, we are free of fear, because separation and isolation dissolve in a broader configuration of identity. We have nothing to lose, because the redefinition of self now includes the whole of everything. And this is spelled out in the doctrine of dependent origination, a technical term that really means relatedness. Everything and everyone are woven together in a great dance of connectedness, some events more proximate than others, but all of them affecting everything else. Thich Nhat Hanh coined the term "interbeing" to intimate the relatedness woven into all events.

Socially engaged Buddhists, like Thich Nhat Hanh and Sivaraksa, apply these insights to broader social and political patterns. First, it is not the case that selfishness itself remains purely a personal phenomenon, but cultural and social identities—tribe or nation—also become fixed in a group self-understanding, and this often issues in group selfishness in the form of ethnocentrism, tribalism, fascism, and imperialism. Here, once again, sin is far greater than our personal moralities and often more dangerous, as evidenced by the Holocaust, the Killing Fields of Cambodia, and the tribal slaughter in Rwanda. The same afflictive emotions—greed, craving, hatred, anger—sometimes govern social and political choices, often with disastrous consequences. Similarly, while the doctrine of dependent origination originally accounted for one's personal causal history, it was reconstrued more broadly in later Buddhism as the doctrine of emptiness, which underscores the relatedness of all phenomena. These insights are the inspiration of socially engaged Buddhists. The phenomenon of selfishness is an empirical fact; according to Buddhist teaching, it serves our best interests to lead a life free of selfish craving. Our well-being depends on the cultivation of habits of mind, speech, and action that conduce to wholesomeness and erode those that do not. Through a variety of mechanisms, above all meditation, Buddhist practice aims to rewire consciousness with new grooves of compassion and wisdom. At the same time, socially engaged Buddhism aims to rewire social consciousness with new habits governed by wisdom and compassion, too. These habits take the form of constructive policies that reflect awareness of a broader set of needs and values, rather than the narrow concerns of a privileged elite. The doctrine of dependent origination means that we are all related to one another, whether we live in Bangkok, Burma, or Boise. While empirically this may not be evident, the increasingly shrinking global village bears this out. We are tied to one another in a complex weave. Global economics, trans-national policies and programs, ecological effects, and political conflicts reveal this increasingly intimate weave. In Mahayana Buddhism, the bodhisattva is the archetypal hero who returns to help all sentient beings attain nirvana. The assumption in this model is the same found in socially engaged Buddhism: either we all go together, or none of us goes.

Sivaraksa, Thailand's most prominent social critic and activist, is a lawyer, teacher, publisher, the author of over sixty publications, and the founder of numerous organizations dedicated to justice and peace. In all his work, he has spearheaded the call for global reform, a drive fueled by the social analysis implied in Buddhist metaphysics. He has been jailed for defaming the Thai monarchy; he has lived in exile; and he has indefatigably worked for nonviolent social change. The central engine of all his efforts is the awareness of the requirement for personal and social transformation. This principle is made clear in the many organizations founded by him:

To reduce suffering in the world, we must also awaken
to the structural causes of suffering. These work hand
in hand with the causes from within. Personal change
and structural transformation are invariably linked.
One without the other is similar to a bird trying to fly
with one wing.[4]

Thich Nhat Hanh has lived this vision as well, and, in fact,
it was he who coined the term "engaged Buddhism." The same
principles have been operative in all his work, beginning with
his opposition to the Vietnam War. In Sivaraksa and Thich
Nhat Hanh from the Buddhist tradition and in John Dear and
Kathy Kelly from the Christian tradition, we see the prism of
holiness reveal its rich hues. We see a revelation of what it
means to be human, and the differences in their linguistic idiom
matters far less than what is shared in their common vision for
human community. These persons have plumbed, by the mechanisms of their traditions, a depth dimension to reality and
human experience. In doing so, they have discovered something
exquisite, something profoundly holy woven in very fabric of
humanness. Because of this, they *cannot not do* what they do,
prophetically bearing witness to truths that extend far beyond
instrumental needs.

These prophets enter the fiery furnace because they cannot
do otherwise and still remain true to themselves. What do they
reveal to us? They show us how to walk into the fire *of our
lives*, to stand in the truth of our being, to be who we are, our
authenticities often formed in searing initiations. Being willing
to stand in the fire can mean many things—suffering the fire of
personal loss, suffering the fires of ecological devastation, suffering the fire of criticism and attack. Standing in the fire is
required to lay claim to our authentic humanness, to learn that
being true is a key to *being human* too. Indeed, the title of
Sivaraksa's autobiography is informative: *Loyalty Demands
Dissent*. Loyalty requires being true, being willing to challenge
injustice, speak truth to power, stand in the fire of attack, and
offer compassion to our jailers. To do this requires the courage

of bearing the fire of rejection, attack, and loss. The fire is indeed hot, and our suffering is real, but we *can* "catch courage from others," as Kathy Kelly has said.[5] We *can* stand in the fire of our lives, bearing witness to deep truths of our being, and these truths themselves become the cool wind fanning away flames of hate. The holy ones, always, by being who they are, show us something about ourselves. We see something in them that resonates within, and so we gain a hint of where to go in our story of becoming. We see that we too can take the brave steps in our holy unfolding, and, in doing so, gather our soul-song back to God.

3

The Holiness of Energy

THE ELEGANT DANCE
OF BEING AND BECOMING

Today the Lepers Came

Today the lepers came,
in their sad parade of sunken faces and barbed hearts,
wearing tattered dhotis, torn saris, dirt.

Today the lepers came,
to Sacred Heart, home of Christ Crucified,
who, too, wore a barbed heart.

And wears it now.

Today the lepers came, old and young,
branded by their painless pain:
toes, fingers, palms, and nose. None.

Today the lepers came, this sunny day,
and children sang and children played,

and they touch your heart
and so does the leper.

Maybe you feel one of his thorns.

Today the lepers came
and are ten rupees richer for receiving their sulfur.

Maybe you feel one of their thorns.

Today the lepers came
and went.
I do not know where they will go.
But one thing is certain.
The barbs still dig.

Polur, India
1981

I BEGIN THIS CHAPTER with a poem that I wrote nearly twenty-five years ago. I did not know much about writing poetry then, so it perhaps rings of sentimentality. Still, the poem attempts to give voice to potent experiences I had when I served as a volunteer in India after graduating from Georgetown in 1980. I wanted to use the year as an opportunity to *give*, offering whatever I could to others. A subtext of this agenda was to determine the best way for me to live out my authentic expression of spirit and creativity. Put in the simplest terms, what was my call? Was I called to priestly life? To the life of a missionary? How would I live out my authentic self-expression, enfolded within the context of Christian commitment? It was only later that I understood vocation to be far deeper than specific contexts, and this was—and is—the vocation of being human. This comes first, and context, which serves the holy unfolding of one's authentic personhood, comes second.

My primary motivation was to serve, to give back after having received so much in those formative years at Georgetown. Having always felt a mysterious draw to India, I sought to go there and to work with a church-related program, thereby giving me the opportunity to live and express certain values that were important to me. I thereby bypassed important nonsectarian service programs such as the Peace Corps and decided to work with a Catholic missionary, Father Francis Schlooz, a Salesian of Don Bosco. My parents had known Father Schlooz for many years, regularly sending him donations to support his work in South India. Father Schlooz, from Holland, had been serving as a tireless missionary for nearly fifty years, and I can recall his visits to our home when I was a child. I was struck then by his unbridled enthusiasm and humor. He was diminutive, energetic, endowed with a long white beard, a vision that easily evoked Santa Claus.

The Value of Leaving

When I was a senior at Georgetown, I wrote to Father Schlooz and asked if I could volunteer in his mission. I wanted to serve. I wanted to give back. In my youthful idealism, I wanted to help usher in, in whatever way possible, the breakthrough of God's reign. I recall a postcard from one of my best friends, who wrote that she imagined me riding on an elephant to preach the Word in the furthest reaches of India. I no doubt felt a certain romanticism about going to India, one that India rapidly shatters not long after I landed on the tarmac. But in addition to these motivations, there was another: I felt a powerful, inchoate need to leave what was familiar, comfortable, and safe for me and to separate myself from culture, family, friends, and even from my religion. While the other motivations were there, this one, perhaps the deepest, seemed to call for distance in order to gain greater self-knowledge and freedom, a spiritual pedagogy, incidentally, that may be needed more than once in one's life. Separation and distance are key elements in any human unfolding, perhaps paradigmatically seen in the growth to adulthood of children, not to mention the growth in adult love relationships. "Leaving" or separating, when undertaken with the aim of conscious growth, can be a powerful vehicle for transformation, however difficult. My year in India, though very difficult in many respects, changed my life, planting the seeds of experience that bore fruit in many ways, including deciding to join the Jesuits, discovering an astonishing connection with Therese (who also volunteered in India), to be so intrigued by Hinduism that I wanted to teach and write about it, and later bringing my children there, which in turn impacted them in visible and invisible ways. Essentially, my year away was a pilgrimage, both in a literal sense—I visited holy places and stayed in ashrams and monasteries—and in a figurative sense—the entire year was a journey of discovery. And yet at the end of the year, I came home. T.S. Eliot's words rang through me:

> We shall not cease from exploration
> And the end of all our exploring
> Will be to arrive where we started
> And know the place for the first time.[1]

Holiness—wholeness, health—is about integration, creating a circuit between the mind and heart that is unconstricted and dynamic. But to integrate, sometimes we need to disintegrate. To discover ourselves, we need to lose ourselves. To find out who we are we need to suffer the loss of who we are—our assumed roles and identifications.

To develop deeper authenticity, unconstricted by social expectations or the demands of others, we need to discover—and love—who we are as we are, undetermined by our roles, our personas, the opinions and expectations of others. These may be useful guides as we negotiate our uncharted inner life; however, while they can be helpful and informative, they can also drain away the soul when their impact outweighs our sense of self. The growth of authentic personhood, the source of holiness, requires us first and foremost to be ourselves, to be who we are, able to stand alone and to stand in the fire if need be. But getting to the real me sometimes requires a way of reversal, perhaps going against the cultural tide or countering standard operating personal or cultural assumptions.

Most religious traditions address the requirement to lose oneself as central to the process of transformation, and certain "crazy wisdom" traditions deliberately shatter social conventions to reveal their artificiality and arbitrariness. At a conventional level, categories and expectations are appropriate and required, but there is always something deeper, more real, more authentic, and sometimes accessing this requires a crazy space of reversal. It is crazy because it counters habituated, automatic patterns that become soulless and conformative. To live reversal, for a time, upsets the status quo, whether in religion, society, or relationship. And to mitigate the anxiety of ambiguity and the distress over change, people sometimes label as "crazy" those who destabilize the status quo. But life requires, sometimes, the path of reversal, which is really a version of the path of leaving, and both are part of the process of coming home to deeper authenticity, deeper communion, a deeper sense of identity. Such a process, of course, recalls Arnold van Gennep's work on rites of passage, sacred rituals which cultivate spiritual growth in three stages, separation, the liminal space of transition, and reunion or coming home, endowed with a new sense of identity and purpose.

So, to come home, we sometimes need to leave our actual homes along with the comfort zones of our cultural, relational, and conceptual systems. Genuine intimacy and authentic personhood sometimes require separation, distance being the precondition to communion. This is not easy for many of us, and the strain of separation and distance is a key theme in the astonishing poetry of Hindu and Muslim saints, not to mention the Christian mystics in fifteenth-century Europe. In the great devotional poetry of Bengali Vaishnavism, leaving social duties under the powerful spell of devotion is abundantly evident. In this tradition, Krishna, the Divine, is utterly entrancing, capturing the hearts of devotees, especially his beloved Radha, who is, after all, married. In one stanza the requirement of leaving and being willing to enter the dark to find God is clear:

> When the sound of your flute reaches my ears
> it compels me to leave my home, my friends,
> it draws me into the dark toward you.[2]

Leaving is sometimes required to discover one's authentic personhood, but authentic personhood, in the religions of the world, is fundamentally realized by intimacy with the sacred. The two should not be seen as mutually exclusive, but instead be viewed as converging streams to the path of wholeness. And stepping onto this path—courageously entering the dark—sometimes requires a leaving or separation. The irony is that while some of us may feel impelled to leave in a literal sense, this dynamic happens everyday, for separation and union, presence and absence, are fundamental existential dynamics found paradigmatically in relationship. Leaving can occur as simply as voicing an opinion that counters the opinion of those whom you respect and being willing to accept the consequences of being who you are, even if that means rejection. Integrating the weave of separation and union into the weave of our lives is a key theme in our being here. To be able to dance in this tension, without caving in to fear or to need or to the clamor of nay-sayers, is the hallmark of authentic personhood, the source of our holiness.

So even as a young adult, I was aware of deliberately leaving, separating myself from the standard markers of my identity in order to discover deeper streams of identity. To do this, I worked in a grocery warehouse for six months to earn money for the trip. A characteristic of my personality, no doubt influenced by my parents' middle-class work ethic, is a do-it-yourself mentality. If you want something, work hard to earn it. When I wanted to study in France as a high school student, I earned the money to pay for the program. When I wanted to go to Washington, D.C. for a high school civics seminar, I earned a scholarship. When I went to Georgetown, I paid for as much as I could by my summer work. There is value to the earn-your-way mentality, but there is also an inner flaw to it, if held too tightly. Not everything has to be hard. Grace, luck, happenstance, or karma can lighten the load. And so can asking for help. Projects need not to be taken up in isolation; everyone benefits from the input of friends and clear thinkers. Moreover, working hard to earn your keep can come perilously close to working hard to earn your salvation, the failure of which is all too evident in our distressing flaws and limitations. But even this becomes a vehicle, for the breakdown of achieving can yield the breakthrough of healing.

Standing Alone, Standing Together

In any case, it never even dawned on me to ask others for help to go to India. I worked in the warehouse, saved money for the flight, saved additional funds to donate to the mission and to provide for my needs for a year abroad. One year later, I walked the last few miles home with less than ten dollars in my pocket. Although I am still very much a hard worker with the same do-it-yourself tendencies, I'm much less attached to going it alone, an experience deepened by suffering and loss. Moreover, I'm far more aware of resources out there to help meet one's needs, and this I teach my students and my children. The dialectic between depending on oneself and depending on others is a tension neatly captured in the debates over faith and works in Christianity, self-help and other-help practices in East Asian Buddhism, and by the evocative metaphor of the monkey-and-cat schools in South Indian Hinduism. One South Indian tradition holds that the devotee is required to exert some effort—to cling to God as a baby monkey clings to its mother; a related tradition holds that the devotee's work is surrender—the devotee is carried by God as the kitten is carried by its mother. While philosophically loaded, these paradigms are rich with psychological insight germane to our own holy unfolding.

For example, excessive self-dependence has its limitations, including isolation. We are social entities and we need others. This is transparent in the mundane functions of our everyday living. But it's much more than this. It is our loss if we do not or cannot express our need to others. Revealing that soft spot is the calling card to our humanity. To reveal it to another is a gift, for to say, "I need help," validates the other's capacity to express wisdom and compassion; in fact, it offers the other an opportunity to embody his or her humanity and to actualize key streams in that person's being. Excessive dependence on others, however, misses this opportunity: developing the ability to cultivate skills and strengths that gives birth to competence, creativity, and resourcefulness. This applies, above all, to one's inner life. There are times, particularly in crisis, when the presence and support of friends become essential not only for wellbeing but for survival. But when the chaos calms, we need to develop the skills to be able to stand alone. We are not served by turning to our friends to discharge every single stress in difficult inner processes. If we do so, we inadvertently use our friends to avoid the hard work—and genuine suffering—of arriving at something ourselves. There is a parallel to the solitude required for any creative project. Any effort—whether it's learning another language, writing an essay, producing a report at work, or establishing a career—requires solitude as a condition for creativity, and this solitude sometimes becomes a particular kind of suffering, the hard work of effort, the fruit of which is one's authentic self-expression. It doesn't matter whether it is lucid, or smooth, or elegant: it is yours. It is you. Relying too much on others enervates the "muscle" of independence. However, in the end, we need to stand alone *and* we need to stand together. This is another dance, not always learned easily.

India and Father Schlooz

I remember the enthusiasm I felt about going to India, filled with images from Kipling. I also remember, with a smile, that on the day I left for a ten-thousand-mile trip to South Asia, my mother packed a lunch for me, a memory that I still find endearing. More importantly, I have vividly pressed in my mind the grizzled old man in Bombay, hands folded, asking for money when I had finally arrived in India after a long and exhausting trip. While I did not yet have any rupees, I handed him the orange that my mother included in my lunch. He opened his hands, received the orange, and brought it to his forehead in a gesture of gratitude. What does it mean, in the recesses of memory, that an image of a gaunt old man bringing an orange to his forehead remains indelible? For me, it speaks to the humility found in that exchange, a mutual reverence, a felt presence of the divine in a sudden and strange encounter. Indeed, a gloss of the *namaste* gesture, hands folded before another, as in prayer, is informative. While literally meaning "salutations to you" and typically used as a colloquial greeting, it may be interpreted in another way: I bow to the divine in you; I bow to that place where God meets God, the site of the Supreme, the realization of which can only mean the communion of hearts, holy communion. And while at that time I had no knowledge of the Buddhist doctrine of interdependence, the sense of connection was nonetheless clear to me: my mother's kindness now became a kindness to another. The orange, grown in California, bought in Detroit, packed in a brown bag by an Irish Catholic American mom, was gratefully received by a graceful old man in Bombay.

I found my way to Sacred Heart Church in Polur, a village in the North Arcot district in the state of Tamil Nadu. Father Schlooz, who had created a massive mission complex in Madras, which fed five thousand people each day and included numerous self-help industries, schools, and a leper colony, had now been transferred five hours west of Madras to a rather desolate mission compound. But there he began his work anew, developing programs in the various villages to help the marginalized, while also ministering to the spiritual needs of Indian Catholics by celebrating the Eucharist in a dozen or so villages. Although I was only twenty-two, I had a hard time keeping up with him. He was more than forty years older than I, and yet he was a whirlwind of energy and commitment, a kinetic master always involved in another project, another scheme, another program to help others.

This kind of energetic holiness merits close scrutiny. There are people—we all know them—who are endowed with a certain current of energy that must be expressed for them to be who they are. They are creative, dynamic, passionate in *their* way, and they can be awesome multitaskers for good. These people cannot *not* do what they do, and they shouldn't be expected to do otherwise. Their passion, devotion, and will become a unified expression of their nature; their flow then produces flow. To express themselves otherwise means being someone they are not; if that happens, *their* soul drains away. This is the central current in holiness: being who you are in a unified, authentic expression of *your* humanity. And in Father Schlooz's case, an enormous outpouring of creative service was the testament of his life. Among other things, he had established schools, infirmaries, clinics, self-help programs, and leper colonies, all with an indefatigable energy that was both dazzling and exhausting to witness. The source of my exhaustion lay in the misguided notion that I needed to keep up with Father Schlooz or be like him when his way was *his* way, not mine. *Our* holiness is the authentic expression of *our* nature. We can prosper from the examples of others, but in the end we are called to be ourselves. There is no exhaustion when we let others be who they are and allow ourselves the permission to be who we are.

While being who we are is the key element of our holiness, being who we are does not mean being perfect. I'm not suggesting that living with someone whose being and doing are unified is easy or without frustration. It actually was rather difficult to live with Father Schlooz, but this was largely a factor of my needs and desires. Father Schlooz very much struck me as someone deeply in love with God, and this was the key to his unflagging energy and devotion. In terms of his personality, he was naturally energetic and enthusiastic, and perhaps overwhelmingly so. Whatever the mix of his personal history and temperament, this much was clear: he was soulful and content and utterly dedicated to God, the source of his inspiration. While temperamentally quite different, Mother Teresa struck me the same way, though I never had the privilege of meeting her in person. Quieter, more soft-spoken, a woman of few words, she nonetheless possessed the same unflagging drive, fueled, as it were, by her surrender. I do not imagine that living with Mother Teresa was always easy, and I could understand how her determined resoluteness could be seen as stubborn or unyielding. But her vise-like resolve was reflective of her fundamental option: she had voiced her yes to the Holy One, and this determined every choice and every decision she made thereafter. This same intensity is characteristic of many saints, East and West. In my view, Father Schlooz shared this fundamental orientation, every practical question answered by a primary criterion: maximizing the growth of God's reign on earth.

Although inspired by Father Schlooz, I sometimes felt a gap in our theologies, and although I took numerous courses in theology at Georgetown, this gap was more visceral than discursive. For example, at dinner one evening he expressed satisfaction that, while visiting a patient at hospital, he leaned over a crib in the maternity ward and furtively said, "I baptize you, Don Bosco, in the name of the Father, Son, and Holy Spirit! There, Lord, I got one for you!" I was startled by this, for even then I had a different vision of the mystery of universal communion, no doubt informed by my course work at Georgetown. After all, I had studied Karl Rahner's theory of the anonymous Christian, not to mention *Nostra Aetate*, an official church document that affirms the living pulse at the heart of all religions. While I occasionally felt a theological disconnect, however, I also felt another gap, a longing for something from him—something more personal than the robust persona he projected. Occasionally, this did happen. After midnight Mass, we talked over glasses of unrefrigerated beer, and he offered me a thick packet of letters from home, which he had collected over the preceding several weeks. And at other times, his high energy would slow, and he would speak softly, deeply moved by the suffering of his people, very aware of their humanity. When I shared my frustration over real-world limitations—the bus driver stealing from parish funds, the office manager doing the same, the coffee shop vendors following our milk distribution to buy the milk powder from the mothers to whom we gave it— he was remarkably calm and nonjudgmental, adding, "If we were in their situation, we would do worse things."

My most enduring memory of Father Schlooz was stopping by his bedroom at night, to say goodnight. He used the night to correspond with his many benefactors, brewing a cup of coffee, creaming it with sweetened condensed milk. Once a week, following the example of his beloved Don Bosco, he would work through the night, responding to friends and benefactors from around the world. I was amazed by his dedication, passion, commitment, and resolve. He had a laser-like awareness of exactly who he was and what he was here for. And everything else after that was mere detail. Whether he was established in Madras, or Polur, or elsewhere in Tamil Nadu, or on his trips back to Europe or America, there was a yogi-like focus on one thing, and one thing alone: God.

While I was there, however, I desperately tried to find my niche, but I felt profoundly limited, too. I didn't speak Tamil, and I felt utterly ill-equipped to learn it in any systematic way. I didn't have the real program of service, say, of trained Peace Corps volunteers. I taught children, I did some minor first aid, I distributed medicines and milk powder to those who needed it. But overall, I felt woefully inadequate. The sense of inadequacy, however, is very much the product of an attachment to doing, predicating our worth and value by what we achieve. To be sure, a central truth of our lives is that we all have something to offer, and not to know this or not to share this is a genuine suffering. The way we live our "being here" is the gift we give to ourselves, to others, and to God; indeed, it is our soulsong back to God. Unfortunately, we sometimes layer our lives with artificial expectations: we count insofar as we do. This is the conditioning reinforced by every corporate bottom line, every effort we've ever made, beginning with the ancient affirmation (or lack thereof) of our parents and the little stars we received on our kindergarten worksheets.

There is an elegant dance between being and becoming, a dance in which being and becoming are one. Doing flows from our being. Integrating this is the path of wholeness, and wholeness always reveals holiness. When doing is aligned with our being, the hold of ego is released, and our doing becomes a bit more smooth, more natural to us; there is a hint or intimation of effortlessness, the actionless action, creative and free, of which Taoism speaks. From the perspective of Buddhism, action springing from egolessness is spontaneous and skillful, becoming just the right thing to do or say in a given moment, rightness having nothing to do with juridical duty, but that which is useful and wholesome.

When the hidden hold of ego tightens, however, strain and suffering emerge. True enough, to feel that we have something to give, something to contribute, is a deep human need; not doing this or perceiving that we do not have something to offer produces the silent suffering of self-depreciation or estrangement. But when self-worth is inordinately predicated on doing and achieving, ego takes hold, and pain inevitably follows, for an unbridled ego becomes a cavernous hole, impossible to fill. In India, as a recent and successful college graduate, I felt utterly humbled by the fact that I would not make any significant quantifiable impact in my year of service; the haunting lesson, hard to believe, is this: simply *being there* was more than enough, and sometimes *being here* is all there is anyway. Indeed, the way I phrased this reveals its American flaw: impact need not be quantitative; impact can be qualitative. What did I do in India? I played soccer with children. And haplessly at that, my tender, bare feet no match for the rocky pitch. But the children enjoyed my efforts, and the villagers came to speak fondly of me as "Mr. Tom, the American boy." Mere presence is sometimes more important than number crunching. And yet, as Mother Teresa so powerfully taught us, "It's not how much you do that matters, it's how much love you put in the doing that matters"—little things done with great love. And once the action, expressed in love, is completed, it becomes infinite.

This is the lesson of doing which is woven into being. Being is our essence, our at-home-ness, our profound self-acceptance for who we are in the world and how we are in the world. This need not issue in a rigid notion of soul, for whether there is a soul, as in Hinduism or in the Abrahamic faiths, or no-soul, as in Buddhism, it is empirically true that who we are at a given moment reflects both continuities and change in the matrix of our lives. Accepting the whole of this, embracing it, issues in the sweet freedom of being here. Despite Father Schlooz's tornado-like activity, which felt overwhelming to me, he seemed at his best, at least for me, when his robust persona softened in the quiet of night. Once, when I shared with him my confusion over vocation, he offered this age-old advice, speaking with conviction that empowers the uncertain, "Pray, and give it to God, then let go. You will know. And always remember, God writes straight on crooked lines." This homespun advice, simple but sure, is a key to our being here in freedom. This is its truth: all the events of our lives in some strange way conspire to bring us to deeper intimacy with ourselves, with others, and with God. Cooperating with this process leads to deeper authenticity, the freedom to be who we are in every context of our lives. Weaving our being and becoming *authentically* is our unique path of holiness. And to get there includes embracing the entire fabric of our lives—the exquisite ways in which we've loved as well as our failures in love, the pain we've suffered and the pain we've caused. There are lessons to be learned in all of it, but it helps profoundly to know that a presence wraps us round, stills the agitation and confusion, and says, "I want *you*. I want your heart. I am not interested in your accomplishments, nor in your failures. I am interested in you. Feel our love, feel our kiss." If we say yes—and perhaps even if we don't—life sometimes suffers us into receiving the kiss of God.

Mother Teresa

Mother Teresa shared the single-minded focus of Father Schlooz. And while Schlooz did not have the universal recognition of Mother Teresa, to me he seemed to be cut from the same cloth, endowed with the same dynamism, the same single-minded concentration, the same resolute faith and devotion. Both were magnetic and charismatic, although their personalities could not have been more different. Father Schlooz had a high-energy personality, robust and engaging; Mother Teresa, although endowed with an indomitable will, struck me as more soft spoken, prone to use as few words as possible. But she shared a trait with Father Schlooz: she refused to use her time for anything other than bringing forth the reign of God.

Mother Teresa's story is well known, so I won't recount it in detail here, but there are several key things to note about her path as we consider holiness. First, we might speak of the holiness of Mother Teresa above all by recognizing her profound authenticity, an authenticity formed, of course, within the values of Catholicism. Mother Teresa knew who she was—a servant of the Divine—and knew therefore what she was about: service. Done. Decided. She was as clear about her fundamental option as John Dear, or Kathy Kelly, or Mahatma Gandhi, or Sulak Sivaraksa. And her resolve, it must be underscored, emerged from her intimate relationship with Jesus, not from a commitment to an ideology or abstraction. Sometimes, in the vast pool of ideas and experience—we forget that we are not alone, however much we may feel intensely alone. All religions testify that we are not alone: the Holy—however we may construe it—is *here* with us, indeed within us. We can *communicate* with this real presence here and now. And communion is not to be restricted to a liturgical ritual; communion is always available, always here. Mother Teresa's holiness begins with Mother Teresa being no one but Mother Teresa, applying the whole of herself—gifts and weaknesses, strengths and limitations—to the yes she said on the train to Darjeeling at age thirty-eight when she heard the call to leave the Sisters of Loreto and found the Missionaries of Charity. She didn't hesitate. Her tireless efforts to provide care and dignity to the sick and dying of Calcutta had far more to do with responding to the personal presence of

Christ than with the desire to erect a massive social service program. Owing to this existential premise, her service became a mystical path.

By allowing herself to be transparent to the transcendent, Mother Teresa became a clear window to the Supreme, revealing God in her doing. And neither God nor love is abstract. God is enfleshed in love and compassion. Both God and love need to be embodied, and this begins with physical touch, the absence of which can be an occasion of genuine suffering. Mother Teresa clearly provided an example of this in her work and in her instructions for caring for the dying destitute. Those who died, died with dignity, and others who recovered were restored to life by human touch. The lesson is clear. Touch heals. Touch generates life. Touch itself leads to communion. Concerning the premise and motivation of Mother Teresa, one could say that Mother Teresa disappeared and God met God in her work. *Namaste.* The Holy, animating her heart and inspiring her will, used her to attend to the broken Christ in the dying and the destitute.

In the Christian vision of things, Christ identifies himself with the disenfranchised, the poor, the broken, the lonely. Christ reveals this identification in his practice—he heals lepers, he associates with the marginalized, he does not judge the woman caught in adultery, he deliberately befriends Samaritans, the pariahs of Jewish culture. Not only does he do this, he chooses the full scope of human *being*—including the real human experience of heartache, loss, and conflict. But this is not all: he chooses to suffer humiliation, torture, and death to reveal his unconditional yes to humanity. "I am here, with you. I know what you experience. I know your suffering. I am here." And this is the timeless revelation for Christians, timeless because it is always present, always current. The revelation in ancient Palestine becomes, for Christians, the clearest window to God, far transcending its local context. As Kierkegaard argued, there is a radical contemporaneity to the gospel, which applies to all time and cultures. We could construe the message a number of ways but this might be part of it: "I am here, with you. You are beloved to me. Let me show you the way. Live like this. You will live. Do not worry. Do not fear."

In the case of Mother Teresa, a particular kind of mysticism is operative, one in which Mother Teresa's transparency allows God to love God, and, in getting out of the way, Mother Teresa actualizes or realizes her own divinity. While some contemporary pop psychologies and New Age spiritualities occasionally seem self-serving or narcissistic, the message of the gospel is clear: if you die, you will live; if you let go of yourself, you will find yourself. If you live in letting-go space you cannot die, for all the assumptions associated with death are nullified. You've come home. You dwell in the eternal now. This is why Jesus speaks of eternal life *now*. There's no need to wait. Communion is here.

On the other hand, if we hold tightly to the assumptions to which we cling—our private, self-centered agenda, our sense of self-protection and territoriality—we will lose our life, but losing shouldn't be understood as yet another competitive ego contest. Instead, the counsel is to lose our ego, and get on with the program of living the radical selflessness of Jesus, the Buddha, the bodhisattvas, and saints. It is perhaps easier, and probably more constructive, to say this: selfishness will cause suffering to the one who is selfish; unregulated ego really does lead to death—in the form of tightness, tension, stress, and estrangement. It takes enormous effort to maintain ego defenses, and it comes with great cost. But the life of Mother Teresa eloquently speaks the cogent word of selflessness. Victor Frankl, the psychologist who founded logotherapy, a therapeutic process less concerned with resolving neurotic drives than discovering what is meaningful for someone at a given period of life, argued that self-actualization is a by-product of self-transcendence. In colloquial terms, we find ourselves by going beyond ourselves, and, this is done exquisitely in loving service. This affirms a central truth found in all religious traditions: we are built for others, we are made to care for others; to resist this impulse in a habituated pattern is perilous; our universe constricts and so does our humanity. I recall the words of a philosophy professor in graduate school who once lamented the adolescent egocentrism of his son. He decried the lack of an unselfing mechanism in his son's life, something to loosen the hold of self-centeredness thereby discovering richer hues of his own humanity. This entails no injunction or requirement to become a Mother Teresa or Father Schlooz or Mahatma Gandhi. The only requirement is to be ourselves as we cooperate with the grace that allows us to give ourselves to others.

This rationale is found in the many service programs that now are standard curriculum at many colleges and high schools across the country. And indeed, many years ago, Therese and I created a community service program at the Latin School of Chicago, an outstanding, albeit highly privileged, independent school not far from Chicago's Michigan Avenue and its prestigious Magnificent Mile. The objective for such programs often includes a learning component that considers and reflects upon the causes of poverty and homelessness, the inequitable distribution of social benefits, and the disenfranchisement and demoralization in neighborhoods which, among other issues, give rise to destructive organizations such as gangs. Such reflection is substantive, real, and necessary as part of teaching students to think critically about social policy. But there is also a more obvious spiritual truth operative, one that Therese and I both learned in India and in the homes of our youth: we find more of ourselves when we give of ourselves. Something in our nature is expressed, resonates, and we feel more ourselves.

The way I explained this dynamic to my students was by the use of a Venn diagram of two intersecting circles: the student's world—wealth, privilege, outstanding education—and the world of need—the homeless, the indigent, the disenfranchised. These two apparently different worlds intersect after all: something is shared that dissolves estrangement. What my students learned was communion—a communion of hearts in which the stranger becomes a friend. People who look different or sound different or smell different are different in circumstances but the same at heart: bottom line, people are people are people. And yet, to leave one's comfort zone to know this experientially is often frightening. Moving into unknown territory often provokes discomfort, but it is only by *acting* that discomfort itself dissolves. Very often I would volunteer with students at soup kitchens, both to mitigate their anxiety and to model confidence, ease, and, not insignificantly, joy. I did this not from duty alone but to activate that same stream in me where estrangement dissolves in the communion of hearts. I needed to go to the soup kitchen for me, too. Indeed, even in graduate school, I regularly served at the same overnight shelter where I and various tenth graders volunteered years earlier. I still volunteer with students at a local soup kitchen here in Erie. It is almost a truism that one often gets back more from those whom we serve than what we, in all our gift and power, give. And that, of course, is the point. When we die to ourselves, we live.

While I still have excerpts from students' papers that testify to this dynamic, of the many conversations I had with students back then, I can only remember one very honest comment by a student who felt profound discomfort when I suggested that he sit and visit with some of the homeless over dinner. I was in the kitchen cooking. He blanched, then blurted, "Mr. Forsthoefel, you've lived your life already! *I'm still young*! *You* go out there. *I'll* cook." While we both laughed at the histrionic plea, the assumption in it was clear: he would die if he sat out there. And, of course, he was right, but not in the way he imagined. We all are invited to die to ourselves in the many micromoments of our lives, that is, to surrender our armored defenses, our easy answers and quick judgments, our comfort zones, our need to win, our need to be right. This *is* dangerous to old ways of being. I don't remember if he finally gathered his courage and visited with the women. And, of course, just *being there* was good enough. He already left his comfort zone by being at the shelter, and, entering the world of the homeless, he could not *not* be affected intellectually: why are there homeless people? Do the structures of society and social policy have anything to do with poverty? What would a just society look like? More-over, he could not *not* be affected spiritually. Most persons, in the presence of suffering, are moved to compassion, and com-passion calls for action. Mother Teresa, in my view, was very astute about this: when people clamored around her asking for information about her programs, she usually replied, "Come and see." To "come and see," as my students learned, cannot help but affect us intellectually and spiritually. And then, with new data entering our field, we are now faced with critical ques-tions: What will I do? How will I respond? *How shall I be in my being here?*

Service

Service is a key theme in our being here. It is an expression of a key stream in our being. It is an element in our wholeness and therefore our holiness. We suffer if we do not express it, and we gain if we do: we discover that we have something to offer; we are connected; we are part of the human condition; we are not isolated territories requiring endless defensiveness. And this connection, this communion, provides a deep contentment: we feel ourselves, more at home here. This is why the Dalai Lama speaks of an ethics of altruism that transcends religion and cul-ture. In blunt terms, we get something by showing kindness and compassion. We feel better about ourselves, and this outcome is profoundly informative; it tells us something important about our being, namely, that we are built for others. We become more who we are in our acts of kindness and love. The Buddhist notion of interdependence, however, implies a wider sense of identity: helping the other is helping me, for the other *is* me. We might say that there is only one body out there and the whole of humanity, indeed all sentient reality, constitutes that body. So, just as suffering in any part of my physical body is my suf-fering—my hand instinctively drops to rub my scraped knee— so suffering in any part of the wider body is my suffering too. In this view, hypernationalism or political chauvinism is merely selfishness writ large whose outcome only produces negative consequences to the greater body. When we ignore the wider reality of suffering and its causes, we should not be surprised by the slippery slope of political hatred and aggression, bitterly revealed in terrorist attacks. We are one body. Caring for others is caring for the body of which we are members. We might say that an ethic of wisdom and compassion on local and global scales is good politics because it is constructive, sewing life into the fabric of global relationships. This is, of course, the political viewpoint of Gandhi, and it certainly was the fundamental ethical option of Albert Schweitzer. And it has been well articulated, from the Buddhist perspective, by the Dalai Lama and Thich Nhat Hanh.

The Dalai Lama has written much about the need for compassionate action, while humbly noting his own limitations. In *An Open Heart*, he nimbly teaches the intricate weave of wisdom and compassion, yet he writes, "However, I often tell people, 'My compassion is empty words. The late Mother Teresa really implemented compassion.'"[3] Such humility is endearing, but perhaps the Dalai Lama underestimates the value of his own example, different and distinct from everyone else on the planet. So perhaps his comment reveals an untoward comparison which, while self-effacing and charming, really is beside the point. Mother Teresa's holiness is holy because it is *hers*. The Dalai Lama's holiness is *his* unique way of living and expressing wisdom and compassion. In authentically being the Dalai Lama, he is a saint. He expresses wisdom and compassion, which for Buddhists is the truth of reality as it is. The concept that best captures this truth is emptiness. Rather than being a blank, negative nothing, emptiness is, in fact, personified, in Tibetan Buddhism, as Mother, for the free space of egolessness generates life. In the idiom of Buddhism, as in the gospel and other traditions, this is the truth of selflessness: when you lose yourself you find yourself.

In Buddhism, the false notion of a self, an ego that isolates itself against other egos in a competitive, contentious world, is the fundamental cause of suffering, more so than even desire, for to have a desire one must first have a sense of self: *I* want this. But this self becomes a hardened, constricted, tight space in one's chest. Indeed, in some cases, heart attacks might be viewed less as physical malfunctions than as spiritual malfunctions, a lifetime of tightness triggering an inward implosion. From the Buddhist perspective, there is vast spaciousness within our chest, within our body, within every cell, within every element in the universe. There is nothing but space, and while interstellar space has the capacity to hold galaxies too numerous to count, intersoul space has the capacity to hold oneself and others with compassion and kindness, infused with the grace of letting be. Living like this, in Buddhism, is seeing things as they are, a standard formulation for nirvana. And nirvana, the supreme "cool," is precisely the end of selfishness. To attain this is to attain the deathless, the immortal. When you lose yourself, you find yourself. When you live like this, death has no hold, becomes irrelevant, for you already live eternity now.

This is what Mother Teresa lived, though her spiritual and conceptual framework was, of course, Christian. She was given. She made her fundamental option. She chose to be transparent to the transcendent. She allowed herself to be a vehicle for spirit. Responding to the call of the Holy, she ministered to Jesus in the lowly. She offered self-less love to the dying, but in the dying she saw Jesus. It was as if Mother Teresa fundamentally got out of the way and allowed God to love God, as if the Spirit, which is always here and in our heart, motivating and empowering, tended to Jesus in the broken. God loving God, and by allowing herself to be an open circuit in this flow, she became Mother Teresa, the extraordinary saint. But this holiness is special because it is hers. She was no one but herself. By losing herself, she found herself. By surrendering, she flourished. And then, her being and becoming became one.

There are several things to note here. First, Mother Teresa heard the call to minister to the dying at age thirty-eight, after twenty years as a Sister of Loreto, years in which she apparently did not show extraordinary signs of her destiny, though she was a beloved teacher. This is what we should take from this:

process. Everything becomes a training ground for the soulful yes of our lives, the moment or series of moments in which we affirm who we are and in doing so become more grounded, more founded, more established in the pivot of our souls. This is the impression I get of Mother Teresa, too. There was a pristine clarity to Mother Teresa's choices, a clarity obtained, first, by her fundamental option, and, second, by the priorities that followed. The fuel for both was faith and prayer. The clarity and power of her convictions no doubt were challenging for some. The laser-like quality of her resolve is notably seen in the Petrie film. In one case, the Guatemalan government rescinded an offer of land that was to be given to Mother Teresa for her work with the poor.[4] Mother Teresa, calm but displeased, gently persisted, unwilling to take no for an answer. When the flummoxed bureaucrat attempted to rationalize the government's decision on the basis of creating a city market, Mother Teresa quickly replied, "We have the best market, we are selling love." The look on the face of the bureaucrat is that of painful dismay, as if she desperately wondered what on earth she would say to her boss. In the end, the land was granted. The lesson, according to Mother Teresa, is to pray and pray and pray, for "God makes known what he wants by the fruit."

Resolve

This same energy is seen in the Petrie film during the bombing of Lebanon by Israel. Mother Teresa, motivated only by the needs of others, consulted several priests about going into West Beirut to rescue developmentally disabled children who had been abandoned. One priest who is visibly uncomfortable with executing such an operation during a war admitted that the idea was good, if ill-advised. Mother Teresa quickly replied, "it's not an idea, it's our duty." When she refused to be intimidated by the news that priests were killed earlier, she simply said, "all for Jesus." This was a woman in love; she was relentless, prepared to go any lengths for her Beloved. The conative aspect of her fundamental option was resolve, also a key virtue in Buddhism, for it is the arrow that pierces doubt, the instability of emotion, and the limited conditions of circumstances. Resolve is the power that makes things happen in uncanny ways. It is an empowering energy that flows from commitment.

I once had the privilege of listening to the late actor and film director Christopher Reeve (1952-2004), who suffered his personal tragedy, a devastating spinal cord injury, and rose above it with heroic efforts for personal and social change. One could not listen to him without being profoundly inspired by his words and example. He urged us in the audience to get beyond our limitations as we press toward our respective goals, and the phrase that remains most vivid for me is: "Ignore your emotions." Such a stance is certainly at the heart of yoga and Buddhist philosophies, not to mention certain cognitive therapies that draw on rational frameworks to guide behavior rather than rely too heavily on feelings, which are inherently unstable. If resolve or commitment is determined entirely by feeling, anything of lasting effort and achievement would never be realized, because very often we don't feel like doing difficult things. The best scenario occurs when the head and heart—reason and emotion—come together to form a lucid, clear, cogent resolve. When this happens, miracles happen; this is seen in exemplary lives, including that of Christopher Reeve. The impact of the last nine years of his life on so many people—the disabled, the able bodied, researchers, politicians—perhaps transcends his many other noteworthy accomplishments. He said yes to life, pushing through terrible loss and limitation, refusing to allow it to paralyze his will. This is the cogent word of his heroic example: live with resolve. It makes a difference not only in our lives but in the lives of many others. Like the stone dropped in the middle of a pond, whose waves ripple to the banks, so our actions, formed by our intentions and embodied in our resolve, ripple outward, impacting others.

In the case of Mother Teresa, many anecdotes address her determination and resolve. With this resolve, uncanny things do sometimes happen. The land is given, supplies arrive, or a cease-fire occurs to allow volunteers to rescue abandoned children. Mother Teresa was quite blunt about asking Mary, venerated by many Catholics, for a cease-fire to rescue children the next day, the day of the feast of the Immaculate Conception. The priest narrating this story recounted the startled comment of U.S. Ambassador Philip Habib, "Mother, I believe in prayer and I am a man of prayer, but you're dealing with Prime Minister Begin; don't you think the timeline is a bit narrow?"

The cease-fire occurred the next day.

Nevertheless, the director of the Red Cross registered his misgivings, "I was not sure a saint is what I needed most." Such a comment, however, reveals an unnuanced notion of sainthood. Mother Teresa was not pious nor was she perfect. In this case, she mobilized rapidly, and the children were soon taken to safety. Mother Teresa loved well. Her way of being was fueled by her own experience of communion, the place where she knew the kiss of God in her life. From that communion, everything changed.

I wish to underscore that this transparency, this communion, first of all was a sequence in a life of becoming—in this case, everything becomes curriculum in the path of love. And second, the sacred intimacy that she experienced eventually required a leaving, too. For her sake, for her soulsong back to God, Mother Teresa had to follow the call she received on the train to Darjeeling. She had to leave the Sisters of Loreto, a community with a long history of service, but one whose structures and vision no longer matched that of Mother Teresa. To be herself, to fulfill her destiny, Mother Teresa had to leave. And it did not matter that no great banners portended her success as she established the Missionaries of Charity. Mother Teresa was true. She responded according to her deepest impulses. She did what was right for herself, and, this being the case, the Missionaries of Charity already were a success, even if no one ever heard of Mother Teresa or her community. By being true, she allowed "Mother Teresa" to be born. But this unfolding, formed within intimate communion with the sacred, occurred in and through lucid resolve, the endless yes by which she spoke her life.

In this laser-like resolve, Mother Teresa clearly evokes the archetype of the bodhisattva in Buddhism. The bodhisattva is the one who sees selflessness as the essence of reality, and, therefore, applies this wisdom to compassionate acts in lifetime after lifetime of service. The meditative training of the bodhisattva in effect rewires the circuitry of his or her perceiving. No longer seeing discreet things out there, the bodhisattva no longer sees solidity that is actually not there. The so-called solidity of things is dissolved—there is only movement and flow, a mass of vibration, a dance. This intellectual therapy is called emptiness, and its ethical outcome is compassion, for if there is only flow, there is no isolation. Instead, we are connected, living in a grand dance of mutuality and interdependence. The idea that we are separate selves who therefore fear loss and require strategies of self-protection is fundamentally misguided, according to Buddhism. In living in letting-go space, there is nothing to lose except the misguided notion of self, which, for Buddhism, is the root of suffering. If you lose your self, you will find it. In fact, identity is reconfigured on a far vaster scale: everything is you, and you are everything; the cosmos itself becomes a sacred matrix of interbeing. This is also sweetly seen in the famous Native American myth of the rough-faced girl, a version of the Cinderella story. A poor young woman, of pure heart, was the lone woman of the village who could see the Beloved in nature, and, because of this, she alone could marry him. To see the sanctity of the cosmos reveals the wisdom of relatedness. The ethical outcome of this wisdom is compassion. Your suffering is my suffering, because there is no you nor I; there is only suffering, and suffering anywhere in the body of the cosmos is the suffering of all. And so the bodhisattva labors to eliminate the suffering of all sentient creatures. The energy that drives this vision is *bodhicitta*, the resolve for enlightenment. It is resolve or determination, one's fundamental option, that carries one through difficulty and grants the power to negotiate every challenge and obstacle.

This was the strength of Mother Teresa, Father Schlooz, Albert Schweitzer, and many others, including, I would add, Christopher Reeve, for in his heroic resolve, he too spoke the cogent word of his life. Resolve also was one of the strengths of Gandhi, who lived the program of energetic action taking his inspiration from the *Bhagavad Gita.* Gandhi interpreted the cataclysmic battle in the *Gita* to be a metaphor for the inner battle to overcome congenital selfishness, an inner battle captured also by Jain, Zoroastrian, and Muslim metaphors for self-transcendence.

What are the lessons we learn from Father Schlooz and Mother Teresa and others like them? They express an energetic holiness, fueled by resolve. They were most definitely *doers.* But their doing was a lucid expression of their being. In this sense, they were artists, for they emptied themselves in their dazzling energy and creativity. Their doing and being became one, and their lives, in choice after choice, spoke the cogent word of their being. Fueled by resolve, they could not *not* do these things. Not to pour out their service and to create their great works would have jeopardized their souls, not in a moralistic way but existentially—they *had* to do these things to express their being. They were not looking to be heroic, or great, or Nobel Prize winners. They were looking to be who they were, and loving service became the lucid expression of their lives. Their doing flowed from their being, and their lives then became a cogent word far more powerful than any litany of words.

We all know examples of those who *do*, selflessly, and with great energy and resolve. And in these examples, something resonates. A chord in our soul is struck. And we know something more of how to be here: that chord is a key note in our soulsong back to God. We are not required to contort ourselves and become something other than we are. No one is asking us to be Mother Teresa or Father Schlooz or Mahatma Gandhi. But we can allow ourselves to be enriched by the examples of others, and let it strike the chord in our soul that we need to harmonize with every other note in our soulsong.

In this case, we are called to serve. Service is an aspect of our soul; it is a key stream in our being, and so it must be expressed that we may be more who we are. We come to know ourselves in many ways—in the eyes of our beloved, in self-reflection, in prayer and meditation—but also in what we do and, more importantly, how we do it. And the latter is key. Because when we *do* with thought of accomplishment and gain and stature and status, we reinforce an identity overly predicated by external markers, such as praise and blame, success and failure. In that case, we are doomed to ride a roller coaster of emotion, because external markers are inherently unstable. When wrapped in achieving and the fear of loss, we may feel our souls slip away from us, because our actions begin with the pivot askew. Tinged with ego, they are not free. As Gandhi often counseled, taking his cue from the *Gita,* ours is the right to action, not to the fruit of action. Let us take care of the means, and let God take care of the ends.

Everything we do can become service, an expression of our soulfulness, and it does not matter in the least if no one knows about it. In fact, it is often better if the actions remain unknown, for ego surely can be woven into good works, too. Our motivation helps to make everything we do become service. Right intention—not moralism but the good heart—takes the edge off our doing. Fueled by the grace of surrender, doing already has its effect—above all on us. So, where is the call to service in our lives? Our work, certainly; our volunteer efforts, yes. But everything else too: the way we speak to our children, the way we cook, the way we give voice to truth, the way we jog, the way we greet the stranger on the street, the way we wait, the way we listen, the way we suffer.

Gandhi spoke of experiments in truth. All actions, from local to grand, became laboratories of life and love. We might engage our own experiments in truth, that is, seeing what happens when we cultivate life in the little ways that each day offers us, extending the arcs of our loving in the myriad choices before us. The hard and the dark in our lives can become service, too, by the manner in which we suffer them and in the measure of wisdom and compassion that ensues. Everyone suffers. No one is spared. Anguish, sorrow, loneliness, despair, longing: these are ours, too. Perhaps counter-intuitively, the titanic struggles of our hearts become service in the intention and resolve, somehow, to allow our suffering to help others. Then, like the rock dropped in the middle of the pond, our actions ripple outward, not only in our lives but in the lives of those we know well, those we don't know well, and those we don't know at all.

4

The Holiness of Calm

SERENITY WITHIN THE STORM

Ocean of Compassion

Waters lap softly,
gently cresting,
a graceful eternal fall,
a pace which issues from eternity.
Airy foam slaps the packed sand,
and a billion white fingers knuckle forward,
slipping into endless tiny crevices,
dissolving an ancient pulse of love.

ALL RELIGIONS WORTH THEIR SALT must honestly face the problem of suffering. Humans are marvelously equipped to avoid pain, and indeed the avoidance of pain is a useful, even necessary, coping mechanism—for a while. But there comes a time when we allow our defenses to drop, the armor falls away, and our core humanity lies exposed; at this point we can do only one thing: drink the bitter cup, stand in the pain, feel it through. Yet the message of all religions is that pain does not have the last word. Religions offer messages, counsel, a kind of distance, not to avoid the pain but to generate the capacity to stand in it. Religions do not remove suffering; they help us to bear it. For religions to be real, relevant, and valuable, they must offer mechanisms to relativize suffering, to mitigate it effectively without dishonoring it with superficial piety or, perhaps worse, developing structures—intellectual or social—that demonstrate power and control. An instance of the former might be a well-meaning but nonetheless offensive comment in the face of loss. "It was meant to be." "It could have been worse." "They're in a better place now." "It's karma." These platitudes superficially draw from concepts in religion and, in fact, trivialize suffering, somehow robbing the other of his or her authentic experience at a time in which distress is at its peak.

Few people consciously desire to suffer pain, to enjoy swimming in endless self-pity. When we find ourselves hyperfocused on our pain, owing to trauma, the histories and inner structures of our psyche actually make it quite difficult to "let go and let God," the bumper-sticker spirituality that nonetheless does offer a measure of truth. In fact, it may be true that all spirituality can be summed up in two words: let go. Yet, for most of us truths are easier spoken than lived. Even Jesus wept tears of blood the night before his ultimate surrender. Encoding these truths in a felt, embodied manner—rendering them real in our lived experience—may be the Mount Everest of our mind and heart. Indeed, Jesus lived his surrender *first* in his mind, and only then was he able to live it the following day.

Instances of the second misuse of religion are all too common; militant fundamentalism that issues in death-producing terrorism is perhaps the central geopolitical problem of our day. But also problematic are institutional patterns of control and domination that are, unfortunately, on the same continuum whose most extreme edge is religious terrorism. Hierarchy, patriarchy, and sexism all factor in here, and their untoward effects are seen not only in the control and transmission of power but also in the development and transmission of knowledge. A problem in institutions—and in relationships—is the absence of the keen listening, mutuality, and empathy that is required for genuine community, whether microcosmic (relationships), or macrocosmic (institutions, nations). Defining the other, setting the terms of conversation, and determining what counts as valid experience all factor here, and all reflect hierarchical patterns of relating governed by power. The absence of listening issues in monologue not dialogue. Monologue in turn reveals nonmutuality and disparity in power, for the one who speaks usually commands power. Such a condition in the end dehumanizes both parties. Discounting the lived experience of the other renders the other as a nonperson, a particularly offensive, however subtle, form of oppression.

There is no shortage of dysfunction in religion, but there is also no shortage of virtue. Perhaps its most important concerns the problem of suffering. Religion must relativize suffering. It must offer a view of reality that honors the suffering—does not deny it, does not drain it of every drop of pain—but nonetheless somehow puts it in its place. Most of us are familiar with the overwhelming nature of intense suffering. Not only is the suffering itself painful, but its immediacy dominates our consciousness and we often become hyperfocused on it—our world shrinks. Catastrophic loss—death of a loved one, betrayal, divorce, bankruptcy, imprisonment—all tend to dominate our consciousness. We may feel overwhelmed by and fixated on our crisis. If we have some self-awareness, we may actually also feel embarrassed, recognizing how transparent, needy, and self-absorbed we are by our pain. We may know that self-reflection is a requisite for growth, but we see little calm in our inner spirals.

Mind Control

Religions offer mechanisms to access calm, to find serenity in the storm. But we need to be compassionate with ourselves and recognize that even our endless rumination is not only understandable but in some sense necessary; we need to "pop" every grief and worry and loss, so as to let them bear the fruit of genuine renewal. The Indian yoga tradition spells this out in its philosophy—certain seeds bubbling up from the depths of our consciousness do indeed need to pop, their lives terminated by our sustained mental focus. Buddhist meditation recognizes this too by the call to give bare awareness to our minds, "taming the puppy" by returning one's focus to the breath while not being tossed about by mental chaos. Instead, the call is to be honest with ourselves and honor our "little" truth—"this is an instance of fear (worry, lust, anger, jealousy, etc.)," giving it its due, without slipping into the operatic drama of our minds. I remember the droll comment of my scripture professor in college, a Jesuit priest; he told the story of a witty confessor who responded to a penitent worried about "impure" thoughts— "Are you entertaining them, or are they entertaining you?" While the comment may make us smile, the truth is that often we are not really here, instead identified with our mental dramas. The best instincts in religion help us to be here, present to ourselves, to others, to the Holy One. Living this authentically is the seed of our holiness, our soulsong back to God.

Religions properly recognize the immediacy of suffering and mental chaos that cloud the "blue-sky" mind of calm. The Eastern traditions remind us that rather than being subjects who think thoughts, too often thoughts think us. That is, without appropriate mind control—not some zombie-like Svengali trance but reasonable direction of our mental flux—we are at the mercy of our minds, because our minds constitutionally attach to objects. Our mental world shapes who we are, creates habits, tendencies, patterns—cognitive and affective—and these cannot but condition our will. Mind control does not imply a trick by the Amazing Kreskin or a Uri Geller-like bending of the fork; it means exercising certain mental muscles that allow us to drop the drama, thus creating a space for calm as well as for wisdom. The message in the antidrug campaign, "a mind is a terrible thing to waste," might be modified more simply to "the mind is a terrible thing to control." For whether we are drug addicts or not, our minds often are buffeted about, forming habituated tendencies to certain stimuli. Substance addictions are outward manifestations of inner pain. But other patterned responses can also become habit forming, including reactive anger, depression, and even grief. These mental states produce suffering, yet the irony is that we sometimes become attached to them. Our minds become grooved, like a record, and we typically slip into our old songs of reactivity. The goal is to change our tune, to rewire our consciousness; this allows for a new song to emerge, one more expressive of our authentic selves. This is our soulsong.

But the mind at times is recalcitrant and unyielding. This empirical observation is testified to by the world's religious traditions. For example, the two great exoteric texts of India, the *Bhagavad Gita* and the *Dhammapada,* share the same observation of mental obstinacy, the former within the ambit of Hinduism, the latter, that of Buddhism. The *Dhammapada* declares, "The mind is wavering and restless, difficult to guard and restrain: let the wise man straighten his mind as a maker of arrows makes his arrows straight."[1] And the *Gita* weighs in similarly, "The mind is faltering, violent, strong, and stubborn; I find it difficult to hold as the wind."[2] So mind control, no matter how that is construed (meditative equipoise, surrender, dropping into the love of God), is a requisite for the spiritual life. This agenda is consciously cultivated in the meditative and contemplative traditions in all religions. By internalizing the cardinal truths of religion, we rewire consciousness, allowing for greater spaciousness, becoming less fixed on our private needs. We might recall the words of St. Paul, "be transformed by a renewal of your mind." The cardinal truth of Christianity—love that surpasses death—allows us to change our tune, relax in the space of letting go. But this is often easier said than done. An acquaintance, suffering a traumatic separation from his children, told me that one afternoon he sat at his computer and five hours later hadn't moved or written a thing; he simply floated in his distress and mental chaos. And yet, floating in chaos, for a time, may be a necessary requisite for freedom, for dissolution is antecedent to resolution.

Religions invite us to float, but not willy-nilly; they invite us to drop down into a core aspect of experience in order to discover the seeds of transformation in and through the chaos itself. I've always valued the etymology of the Sanskrit word *mantra*, given to me by my beloved mentor in India, Dr. Mudumby Narasimharchary. The term has two components, *man* ("mind") and *tra* (from the verb "to protect"). So a mantra is "that which protects the mind." We might use certain verbal formulas to help rewire our consciousness, helping to generate space in the immediacy of our anguish. The promise of religions is this: there is a reality more immediate than even our pain. And this reality is named variously in the world's religions (Brahman, Buddha-nature, Krishna, Trinity, Yahweh, Allah, and so on) and more general terms might include the Infinite, the Holy, the Unconditioned, the Great Mystery. To access this reality, repeated verbal formulas may prove useful, for they help to override the conceptual mind, the locus of our endless rumination. The mantras help us to surrender. Examples might be the Jesus prayer ("Jesus Christ, Son of the living God, have mercy on me, a sinner"), a line from the Song of Songs ("I am my beloved's and my beloved is mine"), or the gospel ("Into your hands I commend my spirit"), or formulas invoking healing and strength from other traditions: these usually are in the indigenous language, for example, Sanskrit (*om namah shivaya* ["salutations to Shiva"]), Tibetan (*tayata om bay kan dzay bay kan dzay maha bay kan dzay radza samung gatay soha* [an invocation to the medicine Buddha]), Japanese (*namu amida butsu* ["salutations to Amitabha Buddha"]), or Arabic (*la ilaha illa allah Muhammad rasul allah* ["there is no God but Allah, and Muhammad is his messenger"]).

Sacred Ocean, Holy Waters

I began this chapter with a poem I wrote in a time of great conflict and struggle. In and through our struggles, it is useful to recall that we are suspended by something greater than us—this may be something as simple as the support of friends, something that is indeed mundane, but, in crisis, is utterly sublime. In this case, we do see God in the eyes of those who listen well. In those sacred encounters, we very much experience holy communion: we are touched by God, who becomes enfleshed in the compassion of another. But religions call us to remember the metaview—the reign of God, Buddha-nature, the Tao, Torah, Dharma, the supremacy of Allah—without however, bypassing the lurch and stumble through agonizing heartache and loss, in the end draining pain of every drop in order to pass through it.

Can we recall that some energy, some power, has called us forth? That we set out onto the ocean in our tiny skiff but that the ocean itself is God? That the ocean of compassion somehow knows us, calls us in and through our deepest intimacies, our glories and our failures—and perhaps especially by the failures? That this sacred presence, whether conceived of as personified or as an inner sense of Self or as a spacious awareness that sees the connectedness of all things, embraces us in unfathomable grace? That some divine intelligence is operative in our lives, and that every element that makes us whole, the light and the dark, becomes the gift of *us* to ourselves and to others?

I share the poem, not only because I believe there *is* an ocean of compassion that bears us up but also because of the evocative force of the symbolism of water. Water gives life. Both the earth and our bodies are largely composed of water. We are born in water. Water evokes birth and renewal. The historian of religion Mircea Eliade writes,

> In water everything is "dissolved," every "form" is broken up, everything that has happened ceases to exist; nothing that was before remains after immersion in water. . . . Immersion is the equivalent, at the human level, of death, and the cosmic level, of the cataclysm which periodically dissolves the world. . . . Breaking all forms, doing away with all the past, water possesses this power of purifying, of regenerating, of giving new birth, for what is immersed in it "dies," and rising again

from the water, is like a child without any sin or any past, able to . . . begin a new and real life.[3]

I had the opportunity to visit Lourdes on my way back from India after volunteering with Father Schlooz. My time in India had been difficult—in some ways quite isolating and lonely, no matter how much I enjoyed the villagers, especially the children (who were utterly adorable). Father Schlooz once encouraged me to go to Lourdes if I ever had the chance, a suggestion that I kept in mind in my travels. On my way back to the United States, I disembarked in Rome, discontinuing the return trip to New York. After a series of adventures, first in Israel, then back in Rome, I bought a ticket to Lourdes. After a night with some Americans from Santa Suzanna Church (and after perhaps a bit too much wine), I walked to the train station late at night to take a morning express to Lourdes. I fell asleep and awoke to find not only my backpack slashed and emptied, but the pockets on my jeans as well. Passport, travelers checks, money, everything was gone. Except my train ticket to Lourdes. Eventually, after a magical stay in Assisi at a guest hostel run by French Poor Clare Colletines, I arrived in Lourdes.

Lourdes represents a traditional kind of Catholic piety marked by a strong Marian devotionalism. Intriguingly, Lourdes in recent years has become a site of pilgrimage for Hindus, too, whose "polytheistic imagination," to borrow Diana Eck's phrase, lends itself to a deep appreciation of the spiritual power and value of other religious traditions. At that time, the focus of my spirituality was Christ, though I did pray the rosary, too. But as with all good Marian piety, the Marian inspiration of Lourdes quickly orients one to Christ. The symbolic power of the baths at Lourdes is both remarkable and profoundly efficacious. One enters a special hall, disrobes, wraps a towel around the waist, waits, prays, then is invited to step into the baths. The assistant then instructs, *Descendez.* Go down. Descend. Go under. Submerge. Die. The ritual symbolic clearly evokes the watery grace of baptism, aligning our lives with the life and death of Christ. The question is, as we float in the chaos of our lives, can we understand ourselves as being suspended by some greater power—grace, love, the Christ, Allah, Buddha-nature—such that we actually become empowered to let go of ourselves, let go of our ego strivings, let go of our protective strategies, and do something unimaginable . . . trust? An inner intelligence to our lives, our soul, God, the Tao, Buddha-nature . . . somehow holds us, somehow leads us home.

At some point, no matter our heartaches, one is faced with a choice whether to fund the difficulty or to give it its due—real time for process and reflection—but then unplugging from it for one's more complete sense of self and history to have its impact as well. Religion must deftly create a distance from our suffering without minimizing it or denying it. It must put it in its place. The suffering *feels* absolute, but religion says it is not absolute; relative suffering does not have the last word. It is encompassed in a broader, more inclusive, and finally, more compassionate reality, one that embraces our suffering, and in that embrace, transcends and transforms it.

The Complexity of Suffering

The Buddha said that he taught only two things, the fact of suffering and the means to escape it. Here he does indeed offer a metaphysic, but hardly the kind of metaphysic seen in New Age bookstores with shelves of books on the power planets, angel guides, the secret weavings of tarot, and how-to sessions on shamanism. "Metaphysic" means an understanding of reality in its most complete context. And this the Buddha offers in the First Noble Truth: *everything* is suffering. And unless Buddhists are unbearably dour (which I have not witnessed) such a statement can only make sense not by the fact of impermanence but by our typical resistance to it. "Everything" means what it means. So, not only are flu, cancer, destructive typhoons, divorce, and death instances of suffering, but so are Thanksgiving holidays, sexual delights, romantic dinners, and much more. These are instances of suffering precisely because they are impermanent; they inevitably pass, and, what's more, they create longings that cause suffering, too. Our joys and attachments are fleeting. And worse, a kind of spiritual algorithm is at work here: precisely the amount of positive affect that we invest in certain experiences is directly proportional to the negative affect that we will experience when it ends. One can cite statistics on divorce to speak to the painful end of relationships that begin with such joy and inspiration. And yet, even a happy marriage is not spared ample doses of heartache and pain. And if that's not enough, we know that one of the partners in happy marriages will die first, leaving the other with terrible grief. The prescription for this is not a robot-like affect (although equanimity, a goal of meditation, does mean "balance of affect") but a calm acceptance of the facts of life. The truth of suffering, however, points to the truth of liberation. This is included in the Eightfold Path, a program of inner renewal, which includes wisdom, morality, and meditation.

I find it interesting that the Buddha felt required to teach the *fact* of suffering. One would think that for most people suffering is all too self-evident. Yet, most of us become experts in denial. Suffering is, after all, unpleasant, uncomfortable, distressing, often provoking further anxiety or primordial fears of abandonment in addition to the immediate pain, emotional or physical. So, owing to such discomfort, we tend to marshal various strategies to escape disquieting or painful feelings or experiences. Some are well known—the self-medication of substance abuse, for example, and the various addictions we use to avoid feelings of despair or emptiness. Others are also fairly obvious but still slightly more discreet or at least civil—busyness, over-work, entertainment, even relationships can all be buffers to difficult feelings of emptiness or distress. While we might not drown our sorrows in pints of gin, we may choose other more subtle patterns to avoid pain—procrastination, for example. "Don't put off tomorrow what you can do today" is a healthy maxim to live by, but maxims by themselves usually don't have the power to shift our will.

I had a brief conversation many years ago with one of my best friends. Both of us were in graduate school in Chicago. I called him one Sunday afternoon and was surprised, when I asked him how he was doing, to hear him say, "I'm miserable." Why? I asked. "Because I have twenty-page paper due on Tuesday and a twenty-five page paper due on Friday." Wow, that's a lot, I said. What are you doing?

"I'm watching the Bears game."

We procrastinate, avoiding the suffering of hard work, but this, in its own peculiar fashion, actually increases our suffering. But procrastination, a subset of the broader problem of denial, is just one tool in our workshop used to deflect discomfort and pain. Other strategies include hypersensitivity, self-defensiveness, blame, projection, anger, passivity, and anxiety. We can be very creative in our defensiveness, and so our strategies for self-protection can be rather vast indeed. How do we react when someone justly or unjustly criticizes us? What does that feel like? What is our immediate response to it?

And the root of many of these strategies is fear. Fear of being rejected, fear of failure, fear of success, fear of suffering, fear of being alone. The root of this branching weed of fear is fear of death. It is this fear that religions must face honestly, and to do so religions establish a model or archetype of being here in the lives of founders and saints. Religions wake us up to the fact of death in our lives, inviting us to integrate the whole of our lives, the light and the dark, into a pattern of wholeness and health. This, to be sure, does not and ought not to be a program of perfection, because this will always devolve into frustration. But it involves integrating it all, the light and the dark, into a weave of deep acceptance of ourselves and others.

What does one who is integrated look like?

In the *Bhagavad Gita,* this question is directly posed to Krishna, the supreme deity posing (as it were) as a charioteer. In the text, Arjuna, the hero, undergoes a profoundly marginalizing experience. Every shred of Arjuna's self-understanding was destroyed as he was compelled, as a warrior, to wage war against his cousins, friends, uncles, and teachers. Krishna offers a teaching to clarify Arjuna's confusion. This he does, offering the famous Hindu teachings on the soul, the *atman*, while speaking to certain qualities in a person who is integrated, the one "established in wisdom" (*sthitha-prajna*). Arjuna asks the question that we might ask: How would one describe such a person? How does he or she speak? How does he or she sit? How does he or she walk?

Being "Established in Wisdom"

And so I'd like to offer several examples of those who are "established in wisdom," and of the wisdom that leads to integration. This is the holiness of calm. Before doing this, I draw attention to the impact of an integrated one in classical Buddhist texts. Something seems to happen in the very cells of an awakened one that transforms him or her, a transformation that becomes visually compelling to those disposed to behold it. Two stories will illustrate this. When Siddhartha Gautama entered the path of salvation, he first joined a group of ascetics. He eventually left this community—its harsh asceticism nearly killed him and generated no enduring peace. He took food from a servant; and, when his former colleagues saw this, they disparaged him as a backslider. After Buddha's "night journey"— entering the darkness of night to encounter his own darkness—he awoke to the light, the truth of reality as it is, not colored by selfish predispositions or cravings. He was transformed.

After this experience he emanated a striking aura. We don't know exactly what this means. But the writer of these early Buddhist texts wished to convey some truth about transformation, that is, one's appearance or disposition or deportment somehow is changed by the spiritual path. This does not necessarily imply massive, fundamental, structural changes—a radical soul makeover, as it were. This usually does not happen, nor is it desirable: our holiness begins above all with profound self-acceptance. We are who we are after all; coming to accept and love ourselves as we are, not as we'd like to be or as others want us to be, is essential to our own path of integration. Nevertheless, stories of radical conversion *and* profound transformation are found in contemporary culture as well as in religious traditions. In the case of the Buddha, he in all likelihood *already* was a fairly calm and sedate person before attaining the ultimate cool of nirvana. A Brahmin who saw him walking down a path was startled by the quality of presence of this person—a radiant glow emanated from him. The Brahmin asked if he was a human or a god. The Buddha answered that he was neither. He was a buddha, a different species, as it were. If we typically dance between the poles of kindness and selfishness, our actions often motivated by unspoken and often unconscious selfishness, a buddha *cannot not* act with kindness and wisdom. A buddha is, *sui generis*, unique. If the tautology may be forgiven, a buddha is, well, a buddha.[4]

As he emerged from his meditation, he used his spiritual eye to see who might be disposed to his teaching. He saw his former companions, and he moved toward them. At first, they scoffed, remaining seated, an insulting gesture, given the ritual symbolics of the culture. Yet as he approached them, they were taken aback—this was not the same fellow of earlier days. He was changed. Something happened to him, and they knew it. What was this? Imagine the people in your life who made this impression on you: those persons who were—or are—calm, forbearing, clear, self-possessed, not tossed by extremes, but neither are they robotic. These are the calm ones, and they often trigger something in us, mirror something we need but find difficult to access in our habituated dance with the frantic. The contemporary spiritual teacher Eckhart Tolle was once introduced to give a talk, and after the audience offered its ovation, he did not say one word for five full minutes.[5] Even though his audience was composed largely of spiritual seekers who no doubt had experience in meditation, that gesture still made many people uncomfortable, because they, as we, often cannot stand the silence, cannot bear the innate calm. Culturally, silence is overwhelmed by endless stimuli. We constantly look to the next thing—the next relationship, the next job, the next program, the next achievement, the next event, the next new thing. For most of us, the abode of calm found in the *now* is not quite enough after all. And the cultural gestalt with its ethos of immediacy secretly insinuates itself into our consciousness, and we are left with a vague but constant unease.

A second example occurs later in Buddhist history.[6] Two ascetics, later named Shariputra and Mogallana, the important leaders of the early *sangha*, are struck by the deportment of a holy one, a saint. Upatishya (i.e., Shariputra) happened to glance at a monk, the venerable Ashvajit, "whose way of moving and looking about, of wearing his robes and holding his bowl, was strikingly serene." Upatishya thought, "there are many accomplished renunciants dwelling here, but I have never seen anyone whose deportment is like this one's." So he asked Ashvajit about the Buddha and the Buddha's teaching. Upatishya "had little dust on his eyes"—he already was quite close to enlightenment, so it merely took the gist of the Buddha's teaching for him to get it and become enlightened himself. When he now wandered forth, Kolita (i.e., Moggallana), noticed him, "Venerable One, your senses are serene, your face is at peace, and the complexion of your skin utterly pure. Did you reach the deathless state?"

"I reached it, friend."

What does it take to be able to answer yes to such a question? Above all, a certain confidence born of experience. Also, an honest admission of a truth in which no ego is found. No kicking up the heels, "I made it! I made it! Hoo-rah!" No crossing the line at the end of the marathon, collapsing in tears for the suffering and joy such an *accomplishment* produces. An admission, a recognition, a truth, but with no conceit or attachment.

These two examples suggest a visible, physical fruit to holiness, and the compelling attraction it generates. This is seen in the career of the Buddha himself, who, in a previous lifetime, as the young man Sumati, met the Buddha Dipankara, and that encounter awakened the resolve for enlightenment (*bodhicitta*).

Bearing witness to a holy one is a mirror of our own becoming. We, as Sumati, see someone composed, calm, serene, and some primal aspiration wells within: "I want that, too." This is the efficacious power of the holy ones. A holy life issues in calm, serenity, and has profound value to those who are disposed to it, at least inchoately. But in the Buddhist tradition, the exalted goal of nirvana itself cannot be an object of craving any more than anything else, because that too is predicated on certain assumptions of self that Buddhist realization deconstructs. For Buddhists, the first step on the path is a life of virtue, and this in turn issues in an anxiety-free life, even serenity within the storm. While this is not nirvana, it is, for most of us, as good as it gets. But "as good as it gets" is pretty good after all.

What about our candidates here?

I wish to examine briefly the holiness of calm as embodied in the wisdom of several important Eastern spiritual leaders, namely, Ramana Maharshi, Thich Nhat Hanh, and His Holiness the Dalai Lama.

Ramana Maharshi

Ramana Maharshi was one of the foremost holy ones from India in recent memory. My interest in Ramana stems from a very felt visceral experience at the ashram in which he lived for many years. In the summer of 1995, when I was studying Sanskrit and philosophy in India on a graduate fellowship, I stayed at Aikiya Alayam, the Jesuit center on interfaith dialogue in Madras. While I was there, the venerable elderly Jesuit Ignatius Hirudayam, a priest who embodied a lifetime of prayer and virtue, encouraged me to go to the ashram of the "Hindu saint," Ramana Maharshi. Hirudayam, in his eighties, endowed with clear eyes, long white beard, and calm deportment, emanated the serenity of a life lived well, faithful and loving. As I spoke with him, I couldn't help but feel I was in the presence of another Indian saint. I took his suggestion to heart. I remembered the name of Ramana Maharshi from an ancient text on world religions that I had studied many years earlier before for going to India to volunteer with Father Schlooz. I now found it striking that his ashram was in a regional district called South Arcot, and Father Schlooz's mission in North Arcot had not been not far away at all. In a peculiar way, I felt an immediate connection with Ramana that somehow felt very, very old.

I went to the ashram in Tiruvannamalai and must admit that that connection came alive vividly and viscerally. In some inchoate, inarticulate way, I felt I had come home. I felt a calm, a peace, an ability to relax my mind, and with it all, I gained a deeper understanding of the truth of nondualism, which Ramana had lived and taught. According to Hindu nondualism, phenomenal appearances are not substantially real. This is not to say that the world is evil or fundamentally flawed. Every microreality, including our personalities, borrows, as it were, or builds from, the ultimate reality, which is the supreme Brahman, or the divine Self. It would be a mistake to imagine the divine Self as merely a sanctified *personality*, the identification of who we are as man, woman, American, European, African, heterosexual, homosexual, professor, student, parent, or plumber. Ramana offered no ecstatic trances, no formal programs of devotion, but only insisted on a faithful, persistent inquiry, Who am I? To answer this question requires recognizing that we can advance a host of descriptions but never discover something final or decisive in them, except for the ground or the consciousness from which all these constructions emerge. This ground is the deathless spirit, the Holy or the Supreme, called Brahman in Hinduism.

To access this truth reveals the connectedness and unity of reality, the divinity of every phenomenal event. In this particular Hindu tradition, called Advaita Vedanta (nondual Vedanta), the entire universe is permeated by the Supreme; we, being part of the universe, are therefore permeated by the Supreme. Realizing this frees us from fear and delivers us from death, because it accesses the transcendent reality not subject to change or limitation. By accessing this truth, one realizes one's nature and destiny *now*. One tastes immortality now, because one is no longer identified with and therefore subject to limiting constructs: limitations dissolve; a truer identity is known; one comes home. As some historians of religion have observed, we emerge from our mother's womb, wherein we first knew non-separation in a visceral, embodied way. It is as if we spend the rest of our lives somehow seeking or rediscovering that home—a sense of oneness, integration, wholeness, holiness. When this search remains at the level of the unconscious, it becomes difficult, poignantly seen in relationships: we project all sorts of hopes, needs, and ideals onto others, especially our closest intimates, in the end burdening not only them but ourselves.

But Ramana counsels dropping the entire matrix of the personality altogether, calling the ego the "formless ghost," which, when known, flees. Instead, discover who it is that fears. Who is it that resists challenge? Who is it that is jealous? Lustful? Who dies? For Ramana, this is the ego. For him, the abiding truth of reality was the deathless spirit, which, when acknowledged, renders us deathless. But this is no soul makeover; this *is* your soul. It is ignorance to think otherwise. Ramana's counsel: remember who you are.

When I went to the ashram, I felt I had a whiff of *moksha*, a felt, if fleeting, sense of nondualism, taught in India ever since the time of the Upanishads (ca. sixth century B.C.E.). In fact, I'd been teaching this as *philosophy* in my courses, but now I "got it," at least experientially and if only briefly. And how I got it had less to do with reading yet another book than with being at this ashram, where—and I regret that this sounds awfully New Age—a presence or a vibration seems to permeate. A spirit of sanctity can be felt there, especially in Virupaksha cave on the sacred hill Arunachala, at the base of which is the ashram. Virupaksha cave is the site where Ramana deepened his own immersion into nondual truth, and to enter that cave and sit for a while is to allow one's own mind to be calmed by a sacred calm.

I left the ashram genuinely feeling blessed. When I returned to Chicago, I began to notice comments about Ramana in scholarship on India. The great Indologist, Klaus Klostermaier, for example, considers him to be "among the greatest and deepest spiritual influences coming from India in recent years," and notes that even after his death, the ashram "is somehow

charged with spiritual power emanating from him."[7] Carl Jung
wrote effusive praise about Ramana in 1944, "In India he is the
whitest spot in a white space."[8] And while his tone is hyper-
bolic, it is clear that he too recognized the spiritual potency and
merit of Ramana. Other scholars and spiritual figures—Age-
hananda Bharati, Thomas Merton, Bede Griffiths, and Henri Le
Saux—also recognized the merit of Ramana's life and example.
The point here is that lay persons, scholars, and Christian spiritual teachers all have seemed to pick up on the life and teaching of Ramana. They resonated and seemed to speak to
something true about reality, that somehow, despite the roiling
waves on the surface of phenomenal reality, we already are in a
great ocean—wisdom, love, compassion, the divine essence.
Many spiritual teachers in India use the image of someone
standing waist deep in a sacred lake, crying out for water to
quench a terrible thirst. Grace is here. Grace is active. Grace is
not separate from God. For Ramana, God, guru, and grace are
one. Rumi, intimating nonseparation, writes,

> Late, by myself, in the boat of myself,
> no light and no land anywhere,
> cloudcover thick. I try to stay
> just above the surface, yet I'm already under
> and living within the ocean.[9]

It seems improbable and impossible that somehow our reality,
including our trauma, when seen in a particular light, is all right
just as it is. That, in some peculiar way, being adrift is also being
held. The ocean about which we're tossed is holy. The ocean is
God.

The Dalai Lama and Thich Nhat Hanh

The notion of God as ocean is developed with great compassion
and acuity by Buddhists, although God here cannot be construed either in terms of monotheism or Hindu soul theory.

Here I shall discuss the wisdom that has shaped the holiness of two great contemporary Buddhists, the Vietnamese monk Thich Nhat Hanh and His Holiness the Dalai Lama. While I have never formally met Thich Nhat Hanh or the Dalai Lama, I have attended talks they've given, read their works, and, in the case of the Dalai Lama, was privileged to attend a private audience. Indeed, at the end of the audience, the Dalai Lama held my hands and gazed into my eyes, and in that exchange of sight, in seeing and being seen, there was a micro-moment of holiness, sacred communion. In those eyes, I somehow saw both God and myself. Something extraordinary happened in that exchange, however much I later characterized it, perhaps flippantly, as being "zapped by the Dalai Lama's mojo." But even that snap comment suggests that something does happen in the exchange of sight, in the sacred gaze, of a holy one. The eyes have it; they are, after all, the windows to the soul. Indeed, this intuition was recognized in the film by Martin Scorcese about the Dalai Lama, *Kundun*. In the film, when the young Dalai Lama finally arrived at the Indian border after fleeing the Chinese, a guard asked if he was indeed the Dalai Lama. The young monk responded, "I think I am a reflection, like the moon on water. When you see me, and I try to be a good man, you see yourself." This is what occurs in the eyes of the saints—as well as in the eyes of our beloved; we see both God and ourselves, we recognize our own belovedness in the eyes of the beloved. We see the mirror in which being and becoming are one. However we construe God—as the matrix of life, supreme compassion, transcendent awareness, or a personal deity—something powerful is exchanged in the eyes of real people who love well and live wisely. This becomes holy communion, the experience of hearts opening to kindness and compassion.

The Dalai Lama and Thich Nhat Hanh belong to the Mahayana tradition of Buddhism. This tradition is sometimes called the vehicle of the bodhisattva, the hero who extends himself or herself in selfless compassion for the sake of all sentient beings. The path of the bodhisattva begins with the resolve to attain enlightenment for the good of all sentient creatures. Eon after eon, the bodhisattva perfects certain qualities—generosity, morality, patience, effort, meditation, and wisdom. This extraordinary evolution may have a cosmic analogy. In the vast reaches of outer space, with its 100 million galaxies, each with millions of stars, there is a spectacular galaxy called the Eagle Nebula. This galaxy is a 35-trillion-mile band of space dust. With its own ghostly beauty, the galaxy seems to float, with all its microelements engaged in an endless dance with one another. But in this massive galaxy, flared horns reveal the beginnings of a bright light. In some parts of this galaxy, the dust is drawn together, impacts, fuses, and begins to ignite. These distant horns are the formations of stars that eventually break off and float away, on new missions to cast light in the dark. The Eagle Nebula is, in the words of Ursula Goodenough, a vast star factory.

Let me make a parallel to the bodhisattva. Eon after eon (or if the paradigm of endless rebirths is not useful, perhaps we might restrict time to this lifetime, and say, day after day, moment by moment), the bodhisattva cultivates focus, concentrates effort, gradually becoming more and more luminous. The bodhisattva becomes a being of light, a light in the dark space of life. The persons whom I recount in this book are bodhisattvas, compassionate beings dedicated to the good of others, with few or no self-serving tendencies. In Buddhism, the manner by which we perfect the virtues is the application of wisdom. And wisdom here, once again, is not book knowledge or a graduate degree, some urbane command of concepts, no matter how cleverly spun. Wisdom, in this tradition, is the wisdom of emptiness.

Emptiness

Although emptiness (*shunyata*) is the cardinal concept of Mahayana Buddhism, we must be quick not to impute any negative emotional judgment to it. Most of us feel quite uncomfortable when we feel empty, and the notion that emptiness is where it's at may feel distressing. An early translation of *shun-*

yata was "the void," and the prospect of standing before the void as some bleak, dark, negative nothing would be distressing indeed. But, for the Mahayana, to internalize the truth of emptiness is freedom and joy, so the question remains, just what do Buddhists mean by emptiness?

The Dalai Lama and Thich Nhat Hanh have elucidated this in many books. Emptiness might be better rendered as the state or fact of being empty, since the term emptiness is an abstract noun, and nouns freeze reality into discreet, solid things. Such a project is entirely at odds with a Buddhist view of reality, which sees flow and continuity rather than fixed stuff out there. "Being empty" means being empty of an independent, separate, or essential nature, empty of the possibility of existing apart from everything else, as if isolated entities have a life of their own, separate from their embodied careers. But, given our perceptual and mental matrix, we tend to carve out bits and pieces of the universe, populating it with things; but, in this view, there are no *things* out there, just a streaming mass of ever-changing phenomena. What is the spiritual significance of such a view? Presumably, greater comfort with "what is"—"what is" being mere phenomena, mental or physical. And the truth of phenomena is that they change. Buddhism eloquently calls us to attend to this truth, genuinely to sink into it, and so know freedom.

The early Mahayana philosopher Nagarjuna argued that there was not one iota of difference between nirvana and *samsara*. There is no nirvana as a supramundane reality apart from the physical world—a really real, metaphysical world over and above the physical world. Nirvana is not different from *samsara*. Nirvana is not over there, won secretly in one's hermitage, peeling away this vile world in order finally to stagger and collapse across the finish line. The perceived difference between nirvana and *samsara* is a feature of the perceiver, not a statement about something out there. Reality is one. Reality *is*. And it is either nirvana or *samsara*, depending on the pull of our egotistical impulses, our selfish grasping for our little corner of the universe. Buddhism aims to deconstruct the self, to dissolve our islands of selfhood in order to know a deeper comfort of nonseparation. We are not isolated entities in jeopardy of losing anything at all. We have it all already. We are not cut off. We are not abandoned. We belong to the universe. We *are* the universe. We are part of its magic and mystery, and every bit of us, our glory and shadow, contributes to its beauty and wonder. Peeling away the notion of an independent, separate self is the objective of the doctrine of emptiness.

This is letting go. Letting go of who we think we are as well as letting go of our tendencies to marshal and manipulate the data of our lives to justify our sense of identity. This, according to Buddhism, is the fundamental neurosis, not issues of anxiety, depression, or anger. These, in Buddhist terms, would be symptoms of a deeper flaw, a false construal of the way things are. In this case, in Buddhism the cardinal flaw is not mere desire, but a profound ignorance, and ignorance here is not a neutral nonknowing (such as being ignorant whether the population of Mexico City is greater than that of New York City) but an *active* nonknowing. This pro-active wrong-headedness inevitably eventuates in massive chest thumping and endless self-justification, usually spiraling into discord and contention, desperate measures to preserve our corner of the universe. But life usually humbles everyone. As Robert Thurman once noted, "It's you against the universe, and we know who's going to lose that one." Buddhism invites us to surrender, to drop the melodrama and all the urgent librettos of our lives in which we assert self on an operatic scale. Surrendering here intends to free us from our addiction to ourselves.

Emptiness is the direct antidote to this addiction, which Buddhists call the self-grasping mind. Zen masters might echo Jesus' words, "unless you become as a child, you cannot enter the reign of God." The words of the gospel call us to internalize the innocent wholehearted trust of a child. The Zen master may go further and say, unless you become *as a baby*, you cannot attain freedom. A baby is free of conceptualization and the host of objects generated by it—me, you, book, chair, new car (don't scratch it!), expensive vase (don't break it!). To speak of objects is necessary for social interaction but their use comes with a price—we impute permanence where there is no permanence, and we feel distressed when the truth of impermanence reveals itself to us. The vase breaks, the car gets scratched, the flight is canceled, the relationship ends. None of these things are frozen, static objects, inscribed in stone as it were. They are empty, that is, they are empty of independent, permanent existence somehow separate from everything else, as if things in the universe are islands unto themselves. Things exist, but they exist in organic, living, flowing relationships. From the Buddhist perspective, reality is a stream of events, but we chop up reality into discrete bits and pieces, freezing them here and there and usually finding ourselves distressed when they don't stay put. They change, they move, they flow, they die, and even in death, the movement continues: they become something else. This is the nature of reality. It's as if we perceive things so slowly that we miss the flow altogether. We say "flower" and perhaps give passing nod to seed, sprout, bloom, decay. But if we saw reality as it is, it might be like replacing our stop-action method of seeing with time-lapse photography. We would then see *only* flow and movement from seed to sprout to bloom and thus we would behold something extraordinary: the exquisite, unfathomable *dance.* Seed blows from bloom, swept away by the wind, lands within a secret universe of insects and soil—sprout, shaft, bloom, beauty, decay . . . all a dance, all embraced in wider set of relationships, all *one.* From the Buddhist perspective, there is only unity and flow. Everything is related to everything else. There is no separation into islands of self.

This is the appeal to the baby by the Zen master. A baby is nondifferentiated from his environment. And this is sometimes humorously witnessed when a baby brings his hand to his face and is quite startled by it, not realizing that the hand is his. The baby is empty. Empty of a separate self, a limited identity. Mahayana Buddhism invites us to the greatest compassion; by dropping our urgent claims to a fixed identity (self invariably issues in selfishness), becoming fluid, moveable, flexible, our limited identity expands to include the entire range of reality, for each of us is connected to everything else. Separation is a delusion. Nonseparation is freedom. Buddhism asks us to weave a mystery of profound acceptance in our lives, to see reality as it is, freed of the distortions imposed by our intellect or emotion. "Seeing things as they are" means letting go, allowing every phenomena to be, without judgment, malice, posturing, or chest thumping. We all know our strategies for preserving our sense of self, our little corners of the universe, so well protected and defended. We can marshal hosts of theories to reinforce who we think we are or, equally problematic, who we think *you* are. In any case, Buddhism invites us to meditate on emptiness as the antidote that loosens our grip on our conceptualizations, all of which tend to freeze fluid and relational identities, imputing permanence where, empirically, there is only change. Our intake valves take in the stream of data of our lives—perceptual and emotional stimuli. More often than not we function out of a default mode—this is a cup, that is tree, this is right, this is wrong, this is you, this is me, and so on. These labels become an automatic cognitive default but are grooved with the emotion that marks our personal investment in them. But to deliver truth from perception may be the Everest of our minds. Why? Perception is conditioned by our default mechanisms, the organizing schema of our minds and the host of emotions associated with it. The promise of religion is to rewire consciousness, train us to see differently, and thereby override our cognitive and emotional defaults with something freer, less tight, less constrained, more spacious, more humane. Our emotional and perceptual habits trigger automatic responses, and these often are not particularly helpful or constructive.

Buddhism begins with simple awareness of where we are, with lavish self-compassion. No judgment, no inner belittling, no swimming in guilt or negativity. Buddhist teachers such as Thich Nhat Hanh and the Dalai Lama often counsel giving bare awareness to each phenomenon, with the recognition that as everything changes, so do our mental states, including our darkest moods and deepest sadness. These change, as everything else does. Moods and mental states are not absolute, even if they feel absolute in the immediacy of pain. They will pass, and they will visit again. Better to befriend our visitors rather than do galactic battle with them. So, rather than clinging to a truth beyond our *felt* experience (the sun reigns, God loves me), simply befriending ourselves, allowing every phenomenon simply to be, is the first step to inner peace. We then are more comfortable in our skin, more able to be here. Then, by befriending ourselves, we are more equipped to befriend others. Thus our darkest experience of ourselves is no longer grotesque, a horrible circus sideshow, but somehow configures with everything else in our lives into our own exquisite humanness.

The upshot of this line of thought may be expressed by the fourteenth-century Sufi mystic Hafiz,

> This is the time
> For you to deeply compute the impossibility
> That there is anything
> But Grace.
>
> Now is the season to know
> That everything you do
> Is sacred.[10]

But Hafiz, pouring out his poetry from his intimacy with the Beloved, reminds us that somehow everything we do—the wise, the unwise, the healthy, the unhealthy, our entrenched habits—all can be seen, needs to be seen, as the grace and grist of our lives, gently stretching our filmy selves into greater bearers of being. Somehow, it is all enough as it is, and it is good. In the end, our finite sense of self dissolves, but we discover the Beloved. The Muslim mystics spoke of *fana*, the dissolution of a separate self into the Beloved, as the moth flies into the flame. In this case, the Muslim pronouncement "there is no God but God," becomes something far more radical: there is *no reality but God*. Letting go, surrendering into this, is freedom. Hafiz's earlier contemporary, Rumi, intimates this invitation to deepest love:

Essence is emptiness.
Everything else, accidental.

Emptiness brings peace to your loving.
Everything else, disease.

In this world of trickery emptiness
Is what your soul wants.[11]

This is not the place to decide whether or not Rumi's notion
of emptiness (in the backdrop of Muslim philosophy influenced
by Greek thought) is the same as Buddhist emptiness. Rather
than explore their conceptual distinctions, I suggest that Sufi
fana and Buddhist *shunyata* (emptiness) both intimate a sacred
space of profound surrender. This space is by no means easy to
access or internalize; all we need to bear witness to this difficulty is to listen to our inner litanies of grief and heartache in
the sting of loss and change. Daniel Ladinsky's lively translation
of another poem of Hafiz helps us to see a wider view of reality, one encompassed by the Divine. Stepping into this reality
helps us to let go, helps us to be in the dance and become a great
artwork of God;

Understanding the physics of God,
His indivisible Nature,

Makes every universe and atom confess:

I am just a helpless puppet that cannot dance
Without the movement of His hand.

Dear ones,
This curriculum tonight is for the advanced
And will

Get all the blame straight,

End the mental

Lawsuits

That

Clog

The

Brain—

Hallelujah

Baby![12]

Religions call us to radical surrender. Indeed, *Islam* means surrender. But *islam* is also related to the word *salaam* (*shalom*), "peace," and so also implies the peace that obtains upon surrender. Christian scripture speaks of the "peace that surpasses understanding," which comes from knowing our value in the sight of God. This counsel is lucidly taught in Jesus' words, "Consider the lilies of the field, they neither toil nor spin, but Solomon in all his regalia was not arrayed as these . . . do not worry, little ones." The *Bhagavad Gita,* in the Hindu tradition, also calls us to drop into divine trust. Krishna, the divine teacher, counsels Arjuna, the conflicted hero, "Having surrendered all actions to me, make me your only refuge. I will free you from all sins. Do not grieve." In turn, the Buddhist mechanism to free us from the cycle of anguish and attachment is emptiness, the direct antidote to selfishness, which imagines the universe as discreet, separate things. Thich Nhat Hanh and the Dalai Lama lucidly address the truth of nonseparation and causal connectedness in their works.

Being Related

Think of the impossible and infinite host of causes and relationships that are implied in reading this book. As Thich Nhat Hanh explains in his commentary on the Heart Sutra, the sheet of paper contains the entire universe—the trees, the sun, the water, the earth, the logger, and we might add, the truck driver, the paper mill operators, the publisher, the marketing director, the editors, the printers, the author of the book.[13] And this still only names a fraction of the set of relationships that are contained on the page of a book. In this case, I've shared reflections on holiness, value, and certain relationships important in my unfolding, and this may trigger similar reflection appropriate to the constellation of your becoming. And we could trace the weave of relationships even further. You are equipped with the capacity to read what I have written. This is because you are endowed with intelligence. This, in turn, is the effect of the genetic contribution of your parents and the nurture they offered you. (If your mother had been severely alcoholic while you were in her womb, you would not be reading this book.) You can trace things back further and further, until you get the astonishing realization of the *dance*, the cosmic weaving of cause and effect, the cosmic weaving of relatedness. Nothing stays the same. Everything changes. There is only movement and flow. Everything impacts everything else.

Recall the intimacy of this truth with the so-called butterfly effect. Little changes have big effects. It is as if the entire universe, in its unfathomable sequence of cause and effect, has dovetailed into forming you. It is as if the entire universe is a Great Mother bearing you forth, pouring out every element of nature and chance and family history and social history to help shape you in your unfathomable uniqueness. It is as if the compassionate wisdom of the universe—God—is saying, "there is no one like you, you are important to me, you are enough, you are valuable." The ethical consequence of this train of thought is clear. If everything in the universe has contributed, in a massively intricate stream of cause and effect, to impact *you*, you in turn impact the universe. You contribute to the ongoing evolution of the universe. To make this real, we might observe the effects our words and behaviors have on others. We know, in our micro-cosmos, that kindness tends to generate kindness, and hostility tends to breed resentment and contention. This is one of those "let's-do-the-math" moments on the spiritual path.

As the rock tossed in the middle of the pond creates waves that inevitably extend to the banks, so our actions make waves that have their own reverberations. And we should not assume that this always implies or requires aggressive social action, nor that social action is free from the chokehold of egotism and contention. I've worked with community organizers who seemed to me to be as gripped by their version of the bottom line—numbers of people at a march or the amount of publicity for their cause—as those in business are concerned with theirs. Moreover, if there is a "great reverb" emerging from our intentions and meditations, then there is a great stream of grace pouring from monasteries, ashrams, quiet homes, and even from cars on crowded highways that impacts in subtle ways the course of things.

This premise is held by the Dalai Lama and Thich Nhat Hanh, and it was Ramana's view, too. When asked why he didn't attempt to impact India during the struggle for independence, Ramana answered, "How do you know that I'm not?" At the same time, we ought never to assume that monastic life is universally required, because we bring ourselves wherever we go. For Ramana, ego is as easily found in the monastery as it is anywhere else. The call is the same, whether in ashram or home, namely, to drop the ego, surrender, to die to the "little self." Doing so accesses a wider vision of reality that sees the interconnectedness of all phenomena, that sees eternity *now*. What would it be like to live like this? What would it be like to set sail onto the ocean and to realize that the ocean is God? This often requires a shift in consciousness, one that implies taking leave of concepts that no longer work or patterns of living that no longer bear fruit. And "taking leave" implies death, the greatest challenge of all, and so it is to the holiness of death that I now turn.

5

The Holiness of Death

INTO THY HANDS . . .

_____

Bardo

Hovering in the in-between
of death and life,
mindful of the tractor beam pull
back to the familiar,
the safety of straight-jacket habits
and the supposed comfort of the old,
never mind its ghostly hold and
icy chill.

Go slow.
Let blood fill your cells
and the crisp cold air of December
kiss your lungs.
Let the swirling current of blood and breath
renew your heart
letting you finally die this death
and surrender to the sacred dark,

the fertile womb in which you knit
new life.

THE BRUTE FACT of death confronts us with intense challenges, and these the best instincts in religion meet with courage and compassion. There is a clear connection here to the previous chapter, since suffering is a kind of death too, a minideath, as it were. Suffering comprehends in microcosm the same issues as our confrontation with death: limitation, loss, anxiety, fear. The question in this chapter is how to retrain our minds in order to engage the way of reversal. Not fleeing death out of terror but moving *toward* death—not recklessly, but in calm awareness. Is it possible not only to befriend death but in some peculiar way even to *cherish* death, as we would cherish an old friend who returns to visit and walks with us into the new?

The Need for Meaning, the Value of Chaos

Some professors of religion have used effectively the enormously successful book by sports writer Mitch Albom, *Tuesdays with Morrie*. That little book speaks volumes on the psychological—indeed spiritual—value of actively embracing the fact of death in our lives. While not outwardly religious (though there are numerous themes from religious traditions), the book resonates with the importance of finding meaning and value in life. In this regard, Morrie, Mitch's beloved mentor and former professor of sociology, clearly draws much of his inspiration from Victor Frankl, whose therapeutic program of logotherapy is less directed at healing ancient traumas than at clarifying one's choices in the present. In his book *Man's Search for Meaning*, Frankl succinctly states that we are endowed with a will to meaning far stronger and far more important than either the will to power or the will to pleasure. The absence of meaning provokes a genuine crisis, an existential distress, and logotherapy offers the client the context in which to reexamine or redefine meaning. *Logos,* of course, is the Greek term for "word"; it also means "reason." When used by Frankl, it implies a rational examination to discover meaning and purpose. I frame it this way: we are called to be human, to discover how to be here in full flourishing. To do this appropriately, that is, *as ourselves,* implies authenticity, and authenticity in turn implies self-awareness, meaning, value, and commitment. To live this is holiness, whether or not one is formally or consciously aligned with religious institutions, though religious wisdom does profoundly and positively inform our authenticities. By our authentic human *being,* that is, our authentic way of being human, we speak the cogent word of our lives, just as Jesus' authentic humanity becomes the cogent word of God, divinity enfleshed.

The absence of meaning and vitality creates painful inner discord. And such discord, while wrenching, is actually healthy, for it invites us to reevaluate our priorities and commitments in the face of new experience. Although Frankl holds that meaning making is an unfathomably unique program, he nonetheless argues for three general patterns whereby we discover meaning: in love, in creative work, and in our attitude toward suffering. It is often the case that facing our mortality, through our own health crises or the loss of loved ones, is the premier occasion for an existential crisis, which seems to sweep away, either slowly or rapidly, the structures that heretofore generated meaning in our lives.

Peter Berger approaches the same premise from the perspective of sociology. For Berger, we are congenitally disposed to find meaning, though this is usually shaped by social roles and expectations, the entire host of values and presuppositions that we breathe simply because we are part of a culture. But, for Berger, there are periods in our lives when we are forced to reevaluate radically our standard operating assumptions about ourselves, our country, and even our religion. The experiences that trigger these periods are called marginal experiences because they propel us to the limit or margin of our structured, meaningful universe. Beyond the margin is another universe, marked by chaos and discomfort. To be propelled into chaos demands the hard work of recreating a universe of meaning in our lives. To launch our boat for the new world, that is, new vistas of meaning, requires courage, but we do well to remember that the word "courage" is related to the French word *coeur*, "heart." To make such a voyage requires great heart. Cinematically, this is skillfully captured in the film *The Truman Show*. Here, the entire universe of meaning is wholly artificial and arbitrary, the constructed world of a movie director. Truman's world is, quite literally, a movie set, and for most of his life, Truman is unaware that he is a mere player in someone else's drama. Gradually, however, he becomes aware that the world in which he lived was false; this dawning awareness was, understandably, disturbing for Truman, for it shattered the assumptions he held about his identity and his place in the community. Truman comes to realize that he was playing a role, not living a life. To lay claim to his authentic personhood, he needed to leave the relative safety and comfort of his bubble and set sail across stormy waters. In his boat, appropriately named the *Santa Maria*, Truman journeys to discover a new world of meaning and value appropriate to him.

Grappling with questions of meaning, purpose, and identity are basic to what it means to be an authentic human being, and authenticity, informed by values, experience, and commitment, is intimately related to holiness. Religion, when free of the tendency to control, contributes wisdom and compassion, which create a space for authentic human unfolding. But there are times in our lives, provoked by internal shifts or external events or both, that call into question every assumption of our lives, including our religious assumptions. For many of us, this is profoundly disorienting. For Berger, death is the premier event that shatters our bubble—our neatly organized universe, the organization itself providing a certain safety and security. Death propels us to the margins of our lives, where what makes sense to us is undermined by chaos and confusion, where security becomes insecurity and stability becomes instability. These are times of terrible distress, made worse by feeling alone or even abandoned, but they are, in a peculiar way, our calling card into humanity, our own authentic unfolding, indeed our own holiness. These dark times, catalyzed by death, are a premier curriculum in becoming a real human person, one whose beliefs and values are tested, tempered, and transformed by the fire of adversity. And death is the greatest adversity of all, even for believers. As a bishop from Detroit once dryly commented to me, "Everyone wants to go to heaven—except when it's time for them to go."

The Awareness of Death

Religions aim to confront death, prepare for death, to welcome death into our consciousness. Through various practices, the goal is to befriend death, as the late Joseph Cardinal Bernardin of Chicago said of his terminal battle with pancreatic cancer. Focusing on death need not breed gloom and despair, but plants seeds for freedom to be here, even if that being here may finally be lived only in the last moments of life. Reflecting on death relativizes it, frames it in such a way so as to lose its sting and grip on our psyches. John Donne's famous sonnet captures this well:

> Death be not proud, though some have called thee
> Mighty and dreadfull, for, thou art not soe,
> For, those, whom thou think'st, thou dost overthrow,
> Die not, poore death, nor yet canst thou kill mee. . . .
> One short sleepe past, wee wake eternally,
> And death shall be no more; death, thou shalt die.[1]

Such reflections do not minimize the loss that every death spells; they contextualize it within a broader framework that loosens our grip, frees us to breathe, feel peace, to say "thank you"—for all of it—and to offer our breath back to God. Meditations on death in every religious tradition intend to generate value and meaning in the here and now. Death allows one to galvanize one's mental and physical resources in order to embrace, in the words of Mary Oliver, this one wild and precious life. The last lines of her great poem "When Death Comes" address the value of *this* life, this here and now;

> When it's over, I want to say: all my life
> I was a bride married to amazement.
> I was the bridegroom, taking the world into my arms.
>
> When it's over, I don't want to wonder
> if I have made of my life something particular, and real.
> I don't want to find myself sighing and frightened,
> or full of argument.
>
> I don't want to end up simply having visited this world.[2]

Reflecting on death crystallizes life, helps us to be here lucidly, allowing us to speak the cogent word of our lives. Moreover, by embracing death *now*, we stimulate the impulse of compassion, for we realize, recalling the *Dhammapada,* that death comes to all, and all tremble before it. At same time, we are also endowed with a great capacity for denial. Reflecting on death is natural to the human constitution and has occurred in all cultures in all times. Klaus Klostermaier recounts a particularly vivid story from the *Mahabharata,* the great Sanskrit epic of India.[3] In this massive, sprawling epic, an intriguing encounter occurs between Yudhisthira, the king of Dharma, and a water spirit. The water spirit had tricked and killed Yudhisthira's brothers, and the task now fell on the king to answer correctly a series of questions in order to restore his brothers to life. The many questions become a kind of oral exam: what saves a man from danger? Courage. Who is swifter than the wind? The mind. Who is the traveler's friend? The willingness to learn. What makes one popular by abandoning it? Pride. Which loss brings joy, not mourning? Anger, for if we give up anger, we are no longer subject to suffering. But one of the most striking questions is among the last, "What is the most surprising thing in the world?"

Yudhisthira answers, "Every day people see other creatures leave for the abode of the dead, yet those that remain behind behave as if they were going to live forever. This really is the most astonishing thing in the world."

This text is perhaps two thousand years old, and yet that last answer speaks so realistically about the human drive to deny death. By bringing death into our consciousness *now*, however, we more easily can be here, less attached to our private agenda and host of needs. Moreover, as we experience our poignant finitude, we cannot but feel greater compassion for others. Knowing our own pain and heartache in letting go, we understand the same in others. And the natural outcome of this understanding is compassion.

In Buddhism, an important practice in facing mortality is the vivid mental descent into death. This occurs in all Buddhist traditions, beginning with the early practices to meditate on the various kinds of corpses (freshly dead, bloated with gas, partially gnawed by dogs, a skeleton whose bones are bleached white by the sun, and so on) to later practices, such as the Tibetan "Mind of Transcendence" or "Transcendent Renunciation." In this case, the adept immediately transcends the litany of daily grievances by dropping into death in a moment's notice. To live each moment with the immediacy of death mitigates the sting of endless annoyances. Robert Thurman once made the wry observation that Atisha, the great eleventh-century Indian monk, gave the world's shortest marriage counseling session to a newly betrothed couple: "Husband and wife will each soon be dead! Be nice to each other!" Death is the horizon of our lives, yet most of us ignore it or forget it. By actively drawing that horizon to us, we bring a greater clarity to our efforts and actions. This notion is captured well by the famous words of Samuel Johnson, "the prospects of death wonderfully concentrate the mind." How so? We come to know in a crystalline way our deepest priorities.

Kabir, the great sixteenth-century North Indian saint, wrote much fiery devotional poetry, poetry to a formless god, as it were. Many of his poems speak to very real human issues and include attacks against the stony hypocrisy of organized religion. Others, such as the following, bluntly address the fact of mortality and our misguided infatuations:

> Why be so proud of this useless, used up body?
> One moment dead, and it's gone.
>
> How nicely you adorn it with sugar and butter and milk:
> Once the breath goes out, it's fit to burn.
>
> That head with its turban so artfully arranged
> Will soon be adorned with the jabbing beaks of crows.
>
> Bones: they burn like tinder.
> Hair: it burns like hay.
>
> And still, says Kabir, people won't wake up—
> Not until they feel death's club
>   inside their skulls.[4]

When I finish reading this poem to my students, I often pause, then add, "cue the sinister laugh!" I usually ask who in the class actually *likes* the poem. Typically, about half of the class likes the poem precisely for its blunt and relevant message. The rest find that it puts them off. Some students find Kabir to be self-righteous, condescending, or hypercritical. There is no question of Kabir's fiery statements and his diatribes (elsewhere) against encrusted religious practices. He most certainly launches attacks upon formalism in religion, but no more so than the Hebrew prophets—or Jesus for that matter. One could say that all the saints, past and present, whether on the great stage or hidden by the highways, remind us that life is short. The Spanish poet Antonio Machado writes,

> I love Jesus, who said to us:
> Heaven and earth will pass away.

When heaven and earth have passed away,
my word will remain.
What was your word, Jesus?
Love? Affection? Forgiveness?
All your words were
one word: Wakeup.[5]

"Wakeup" seems to be the clarion call of Kabir, too. The students in my class who like the poem often say that Kabir tells it like it is, and his bald-faced honesty is the reason for the poem's appeal. This speaks to the universal relevance of Kabir's poetry, for although this meditation on the body's fading beauty is five hundred years old, it speaks to our contemporary culture as well, with its endless attention to the body, nipping this, tucking that, coloring hair, tanning skin, enhancing this, enhancing that, removing skin, draining fat, botoxing lips, and, finally, even airbrushing perfection for the bodily best among us, the supermodels. The upshot of such objectification is really depersonalization, which reinforces the neurosis that we are simply not good enough as we are. We're not tall enough, trim enough, slim enough, big enough, blonde enough—and those are only our physical features. How about smart enough, handy enough, funny enough, wise enough, creative enough, and so on? And of course we know that the hyperfocus on the body breeds serious issues of self-image and self-esteem, the worst of which are disorders such as bulimia and anorexia. Death and loss force us to confront ourselves, in all our humanity, and discover that we are enough after all.

In Hinduism and Buddhism, the hyperattention to physical form is called "infatuation with the body," and we see no shortage of this in our contemporary culture with the marketing of sex in nearly every glossy supermarket magazine, endless innuendo in television sitcoms, and the explosion of pornography on the Web. Kabir and other South Asian poets aim to neutralize the infatuation with the body by meditations on death. This could take place in any number of forms, including meditating in graveyards or being entombed for a night with a corpse in order vividly to drive home the fact of the death and the inevitable end to sensual pleasures. In India (as I heard someone once recount) walking through cemeteries, with corpses buried just below the surface, in the steamy humid nights, one may hear disturbing popping sounds, the sounds of corpses swelling with gas and ripping apart. In India, the fact of death is transparent, far more so than in our sanitized culture. That transparency allows us to see reality as it is, even if reality is sometimes hard to take. Interestingly, the Buddhist formula for nirvana is rather simple: to see things as they are. But most of us cloud our perceptions by our emotional attachments, our investments in our egos, and even our conceptualizations—these too can be planks in the program of ego.

Our lives become estranged from reality. We are actually cut off from reality, that is, from the way things actually are, by our self-centered agenda. Suffering and loss cast off the cloak of invisibility and baptize us into the real. For most Americans, the catastrophe of September 11, 2001 shattered an illusion of safety and protection, the false bubble of safety in our comfortable lives. But in India, there are daily 9/11s, with disastrous truck and bus accidents (there was never a time when I traveled in India that I did not at some point witness the aftermath of catastrophic highway crashes), typhoons, fires and floods, and the wreck of disease. The rawness of suffering is very visible in India; it is in your face and you are asked, what are you going to do about it? When I first was in India, I recall a time when an elderly man, afflicted with leprosy, came to the rectory where I was staying. Most of the man's fingers were gone, and he pointed to a wound on his ankle. A gaping hole, thick with pus and maggots, needed attention. I cleaned the wound, gave him some rupees, and he left, folding his palms in the *namaste* gesture, the gesture of benediction. I then went upstairs, my face drained and grey, lay down, and tried very hard not to vomit. Cleaning thick pus-filled sores would not have been within the scope of my experience in suburban Detroit.

Later, when my family lived in India, we happened to live close to a temple and to the beach. With some frequency, a parade of mourners would carry a corpse—well dressed and garlanded with bougainvillea—on a wooden bier, blasting firecrackers and dancing along the way, sending the soul out with a bang, as it were. One section of the beach actually was a cemetery; over the months more and more burial mounds populated that part of the beach. It was jarring. For most of us, the beach is a place of relaxation and offers a connection with beauty and nature. And now, with anonymous mounds resting on the beach, a different connection to nature was established—and the realization that death is indeed just below the surface. Death is deeply enfolded with life and, indeed, is of the essence of life. The bittersweet secret is that death is the mother of life, for it is only by passing through it that newness is born. Indeed, ancient Buddhist texts remind us that death is the invariable companion to birth: "As a budding mushroom always shoots upward carrying soil on its head, so beings from their birth onwards carry decay and death along with them."[6] Moreover, disciples were sometimes instructed to consider the deaths that are already occurring in the body itself, namely, the deaths of endless microbes, viruses, and parasites. The disciple is reminded that these parasites are born, grow old, and die in the body; the body is their birth clinic and their burial place, and through the upsetting of these creatures, the body itself can be brought to death.

We live in the proverbial blink of an eye. And so do the little critters within us who call our body home.

So religions bring the horizon of death closer to our consciousness, call us to integrate death, our inevitable companion. And death, of course, must not be limited to mere (!) physical death. Death must be also be construed as painful loss and the required passage into newness. A new phase of life, the ending of a relationship, the loss of a job, and more—little embarrassments or big humiliations, or the mental and emotional habits that we may (or may not) be aware of, and yet we find constrictive and limiting. All these events are variations on a theme: death and its call to the new.

Every limitation is a kind of death, for it closes the door on possibility. But endless possibility is enervating to the soul, diffusing the arrow-like power of resolve. While our ego takes affront at any limitation, limits paradoxically are the condition for freedom. Proper ethical limits maximize harmony and minimize harm. Proper limits in parenting provide a secure space for children, facilitating their awareness of self and others. Knowing limits in intimate relationships provides self-awareness and indicates appropriate self-respect and self-care. Limits provide the space for genuine freedom and creativity. And death, as the ultimate limitation, provides the space for ultimate freedom. Every decision, every choice, invites the dance of life and death, but death is always the condition for new life.

Surrender

The act of surrender is the vehicle that facilitates the passage into new life. Most of us typically associate surrender with failure. Surrender is a defeat, an assault to ego. Yet the Muslims— and Christians, and Buddhists, and Hindus, and conscious seekers of every tradition—have it right. Dropping, letting go, gradually peeling our fingers back from our clenched grip, brings freedom. But surrender is not the same thing as resignation. Resignation is a slump-shouldered passivity. Surrender, on the other hand, is an act of the will, implies conscious choice, involves courage and trust, embraces reality as it is. Yet for most of us, reality, at one point or another, is hard to take, and as T.S. Eliot reminds us in *Four Quartets*, "Humankind cannot bear much reality." Still, letting go is often the most unbearable call. And, we may discover, the intensity of our suffering is usually proportionate to the intensity of our clenched hold. But the call is to let go, to surrender to the mystery of loss, the depth of whose wisdom usually extends beyond what can be articulated. The last lines of "In the Blackwater Woods" by Mary Oliver call us to this wisdom:

> Every year
> everything
> I have ever learned

in my lifetime
leads to this: the fires
and black river of loss
whose other side
is salvation,
whose meaning
none of us will ever know.

To live in this world

you must be able
to do three things:
to love what is mortal;
to hold it

against your bones knowing
your own life depends on it;
and, when the time comes to let it go,
to let it go.[7]

One task, when the inevitable losses of life visit us, is to befriend the process, to see loss and gain, death and life, as the inevitable companions of life and the ineluctable ground of our existence. For most of us, even those professionally trained in religious life, this is not easy, so we need to offer ourselves—and others—great measures of compassion too. When death visits us, we have an opportunity to gain profound wisdom, the likes of which could never be possible otherwise. This then becomes gift to others who suffer the death rattle of painful loss.

Moreover, the next time loss and trauma occur in our lives, our automatic defaults will likely be more tempered, causing less harm to ourselves and to others. The territory of death, at first so alien and frightening, will now be more familiar, less threatening, because we have learned the bittersweet secret, that death is the mother of life, a different life, to be sure, but life nonetheless, unexpected, bearing new fruit and new beauty. Knowing this experientially, and thereby becoming familiar with death in the guise of every loss, creates greater internal space for freedom and compassion, and this, once again, becomes gift to ourselves and to others. Internalizing the lessons that death offers is an opportunity to become more real, more soft, more free, more humble, and this is holiness.

Poverty at the Heart of Our Being

We all suffer the crises and irregularities of our lives, our heartache and pain, our losses, our encounters with death. Painful though they are, they carry seeds of new meaning. When I was a Jesuit novice over twenty years ago, our director scheduled numerous experiments for us—placing us in certain ministerial and community settings in order to gain more information about ourselves, affectively, spiritually, academically, and pastorally. So we did the hospital experiment, academic experiment, summer experiment, long experiment, and so on. On two occasions, I lived in large, traditional Jesuit communities attached to academic institutions. In these communities lived aging Jesuits, many of them quite vital intellectually, but others suffering, physically, and sometimes emotionally, because of the effects of age and isolation. To some extent I saw this as the death experiment; these older Jesuits were learning in a most poignant manner the last lessons of their lives: aging well and dying with grace. Additionally, it was for me a mirror of my own becoming: I saw my destiny as human too, which Buddhists bluntly call the "decrepitude of old age." My question then was whether the context of my life as a celibate male in a men's religious order was the fitting environment to live out that destiny. The answer to that question was no. But living in such communities was informative, for I saw numerous Jesuits struggling valiantly with limitation and loss, the presence of death woven into life itself.

This cannot be easy, for, depending on one's temperament, there must be times of intense loneliness. And for this reason, living in those communities held up a mirror not just to my future but to my present as well. In other words, these men mirrored back to me my own aloneness, my own loneliness, death's cool kiss in life. We all have death experiments in our lives, and they are hardly the province of our golden years. Losses, missed opportunities, rejection, unmet longing, all these are opportunities: what do we do when our skin sizzles in our solitude? At that time, I could not bear it—while I knew much joy and a deep sense of purpose and vision, the celibate lifestyle felt in the end oppressive, the full expression of my soul not possible in the context of formal religious life. Despite much creative work and a deep commitment, my heart and body yearned for something more: intimate communion with another. And after much prayer and discernment, I made the difficult decision to leave the Jesuits. But, while one may have a sense of one's need for intimacy, the other companion, the inner poverty of affect, cannot be met fully by anyone, nor does it ever completely go away, for it is the mark of our condition, our existential poverty; it is our secret tattoo. I could put a heady spin on it and say that such poverty occasions the call to surrender to our lives, surrender to ourselves in all our complexity, and in doing so somehow we surrender to God—or Life, or Spirit, or the Supreme. While I believe this is true, it is often unbearably painful.

The goal is to befriend our anguish, not judge it, flee from it, or act it out, all of which are strategies to avoid the pain, avoid the death—of ego, of the childlike need to have someone else heal us, care for us, love us, nurture us—that these instances invite us to. This is not to prescribe a life of gloom but to remind us of a basic poverty at the heart of our being, a poverty that reveals itself in our limitations—fearful, anxious, driven, frantic, agitated, competitive, angry, depressed, even *cheery*, when the outer Pollyanna masks an inner inability to deal with negative emotions. It is a step toward freedom to embrace our poverty in its unique emotional constellation. It is *ours*. And, moreover, it is the place where we meet the Beloved.

In some counterintuitive way, we ought to take pride in our poverty, our dying, and our dark nights, because in our courageous embrace of the whole of it, *we* become whole, more real, more ourselves. And wholeness here does not mean perfection. It means the whole of us—our gifts and glories, absurdities and mistakes, passion and pain. This is who we are—wholesome, unwholesome, saint, sinner, lamb, lion. We become like the pearl in the deep, formed by soft, subtle pain, a perfect imperfection, a treasure beyond words. Still, our poverty is disempowering until we come to terms with it, until we embrace and accept it. And this soft spot or yearning or need is, in some strange fashion, a gift—though it feels like a curse at times—for it contains latent energies and opportunities for deeper healing and deeper freedom, new ways of being here. A mechanism to live our dying is to follow the breath, for breath is life, breath is calm, breath is coterminous with the Divine. Focused breathing, as the sages teach, brings freedom, for it allows us to be here, free of the grip of emotional reactivity. Breath befriends death, but to do this we need first to befriend ourselves. Finally, befriending ourselves may be the most important step in our path of holiness.

We need to remember two principles that seem evident in the spiritual traditions of the world: (1) we are called to a full life—joy, peace, consolation, laughter, healing—and (2) we are manifestly imperfect. That soft spot, that vulnerable, tender place, that is the site of the sacred, our secret tattoo. To have the courage to be imperfect may not mean taking wild, reckless risks, but flat-out struggling with agonizing choices that from one perspective may be terribly wrong. We are not omniscient, enlightened, or supremely free, and perhaps the best we can do is to drink from the well of our soul, learning as much as possible from fear and loss and thereby allowing space for little epiphanies. But the courage to be imperfect also means living courageously with our choices and their consequences. This is drinking the bitter cup of loss, bravely draining it of every drop. As we do this, can we love ourselves in our dying? Can we love ourselves with the very love that we would instinctively offer to another person suffering through loss? Can we forgive ourselves for our *humanity*? Indeed, can we come to a place of *gratitude*, not for the suffering itself but for what the suffering has birthed in us?

Our poverty, our dying, our grief and sorrow offer us the opportunity to drop, to surrender, to let go—"to die before we die," as Muhammad counseled. Rumi has written many poems addressing the heartfelt poignancy of this call. These are our death experiments, our cup of limitation and loss and heartache. In such poverty,

> Then you pray the prayer that is the essence
> of every ritual: *God,*
>
> *I have no hope. I am torn to shreds. You are my first and last and only refuge.*
>
> Don't do daily prayers like a bird pecking, moving its head up and down. Prayer is an egg.
>
> Hatch out the total helplessness inside.[8]

Can we allow ourselves the agony of being torn to shreds? Can we drop our pious platitudes and just be there, dead, alone, hopeless, shorn of our standard pieties of heaven, salvation, and anything else that distances us from our lived and felt catastrophes? Earlier I suggested that we all are required at times to stand in the fire of our lives, but to do this we must be willing, as the young men, to burn in the flames, become a holocaust in the micromoments of pain.

The cure for pain, writes Rumi, is in the pain. We are walking a delicate tightrope here, which the wisdom of religion treads with honesty and truth. We are called to radical letting go, somehow knowing that death does not have the last word, that death is the condition for the possibility for renewal, resurrection, rebirth. This is helpful, and to some extent allows us to let go; but insofar as it actually distances us from our felt experience, it is not helpful at all. Even Jesus' faith allowed him the desperate feeling of abandonment on the cross: "My God, my God, why have you forsaken me?" Can we allow space for darkness, such that God or angels or Buddha or any spiritual help is as gone and dead as anything else? And it is in these times that we meet our truest selves—freed from our self-

certitudes, our own self-congratulatory anointings. Freed of all
this, death enfolds us, rendering empty all our little and big jus-
tifications. There we finally meet God, hidden in the silence of
the deep, our unique pain, our secret tattoo. And perhaps, if
we listen well, we hear God whisper, "I'm not interested in
your accomplishments, your heroic sanctity, your small-
minded moralities. I'm interested in *you*." But to arrive at this
place we experience the dark night, the place of emptiness,
death itself. And that is terrifying.

We sometimes have minitastes of this. Before I started my
Ph.D. program at the University of Chicago, I had a frightening
dream of death (the university will do that to you). Years ago, I
described the image of death very much like the personification
of death in the Ingmar Bergman film *The Seventh Seal*. Now I
would describe the image of death in the manner of J. K. Row-
ling's Harry Potter series as a Dementor, the cloaked, faceless
entity that inexorably draws the soul into its facial cavern as if
by sinister tractor beam. I recall vividly that I could not run
away, that this creature indeed was coming for me, and there
was not one thing I could do about it. And holding on until I
could physically hold on no longer, I was then pulled into the
jaws of death and swirled round in darkness, screaming. I recall
thinking, even in the dream, that screaming was pointless. This
was indeed happening and nothing was going to change it, but
I let out the inward cry anyway. And then I fell onto the earth,
finding myself in a meadow with all sorts of contented picnick-
ers, where the sun was shining and students were studying, a
place of beauty and peace. Everything was just fine. There was
no death after all. I recall feeling abashed. I had just made a
horrific scene, and here we all were calm, composed, serene.

The dream revealed a deep anxiety over beginning graduate
studies. All transitions imply a death of some sort, and graduate school is no exception. It calls for a death, manifested as the
real suffering a Ph.D. program exacts—physical exhaustion,
emotional strain, and domestic hardship. To face this or any
great creative task amounts to facing one's fears (will I fail?)
and one's insecurities (am I smart enough for this?), and sur-

rendering those fears is a kind of death. For entering that process—and anything new that deeply engages one's soul—actively instigates change, and this in turn is nothing other than the death of comfortable ways of being and the transition into the new. To do this at critical junctures of one's life is to embrace one's destiny. It is not ego, but self-knowledge and self-love that says, "Here I am, this is me, this is what I bring—to the field, to the company, to the board, to the college, to the family, to the marriage." Accepting oneself—not just in our imperfections but in the giftedness we bring to the world—far from being an act of ego is actually an act of humility; it is our soulsong back to God and the beginning of new freedom.

There are passages in our lives when the inexorable pull of death demands its reckoning. We can marshal all our defenses and denials—and these are quite useful for a time, for we are psychologically structured to handle only so much trauma. But in due time, when we are ready, perhaps spent with exhaustion, we hear the call of death and finally say, "Yes, I'm ready now. I will walk with you. I will let go. Today is a good day to die." In the end, of course, there is no escape. We can go kicking and screaming or we can go in peace. We may need to kick and scream for a time or even until the end; it does no good to create yet another ideal to live up to and to judge ourselves for falling short. Still, the deaths in our life—loss on every front—present us with our death experiments which prepare us for the ultimate passage, offering our breath back to God.

Bardo

In Tibetan Buddhism, the in-between space, called the *bardo*, occurs most powerfully in a postmortem state. But there are many *bardos* in our lives, liminal spaces of not-knowing, where we are called to let go of the old and prepare for the new.

For Tibetans, an "in-between" occurs in the postmortem state, and the invitation, in that tradition, is to realize the "truth body" of the Buddha, that is to realize the compassionate wisdom of enlightenment is one's true nature, as it were, and this, according to this view, is the nature of reality itself. But most souls, say the tradition, shrink from this, unaware that the truth body is no different from their essence. And so, heavenly Buddhas manifest, but these too are no different than one's essence. Eventually, after a harrowing encounter with terrific (as in terrifying) deities (who are also viewed as products of one's enlightened nature, manifested to peel away ego identifications), one then engages a life review, in order to attain an appropriate rebirth.

The key element in the postmortem phase concerns the disorientation that death produces and the concomitant feelings of attachment which remain strong, making it difficult to let go. In fact, the first counsel is to the entity still hovering around the dead body, dazed over what has just happened. "You are dead. You are no different than anyone else, for death happens to all. Do not be attached and prepare to let go." While many Catholics are quite familiar with the sacrament of Last Rites, we may be surprised to hear that a Buddhist monk performs "last rites," with substantive spiritual direction, on a corpse. But most religious traditions see some sort of spiritual element to the human person, even if, as in Buddhism, that element is not a permanent "driver of the bus," but instead is a changing consciousness conditioned by mental habits. In any case, while speaking to a dead body seems surprising, the counsel to the hovering consciousness is refreshingly blunt: you are dead, let go, prepare to move on.

And this is what we need to remember in the *bardos* of our lives, those uncomfortable transition spaces between the old and the new. These are the inevitable transitions of death and rebirth, in *this* life. And these become the training ground, the death experiments, where we become familiar with the requirement to let go, which in turn allows the great letting go at the end to be slightly easier. At times in our various crises, we are so disoriented, so afflicted by our pain, that we don't even know what is happening. And whatever it is we are experiencing, we nonetheless feel that "this can't be happening to me." And yet, some inexorable force seems powerfully to act, to pull away all previous assumptions and identifications, calling us to die this death. The avoidance of this brute, raw fact is denial. And, for a time, denial has its place, for we can handle only so much pain. In the dire crises of our lives, however, it is the mark of the honest kindness of good friends to remind us, as the Buddhist monk, that we have died. This brings awareness of the deep loss that we feel but do not have words to conceptualize. "The factory is closed." "The marriage is over." "You have cancer." The emotional death layered onto these realities highlights a difficult truth: the old is gone, the new is not yet. But there is considerable solace to the realization that we are not the only persons who have suffered so; others have gone through this too. Indeed, in the Tibetan tradition, this very counsel is offered to the anxious entity hovering around the corpse. "You have died; you are not the only one who has ever died, for death comes to all." And yet, death itself becomes the matrix for new life. And so the invitation is simply to die this death, to make the passage, to surrender to the sacred dark, the fertile womb in which we knit new life. T.S. Eliot, in *Four Quartets*, a poem suffused with deep wisdom and classic themes in mysticism, writes,

> O dark dark dark. They all go into the dark. . . .
> I said to my soul, be still, and let the dark come upon you
> Which shall be the darkness of God.[9]

This paradox of the sacred dark is found in many traditions, a paradox which suggests that darkness reveals its peculiar and profound illumination. While initially distressing, darkness, given its instrumentality for wisdom and compassion, becomes a mirror to our deepest flourishing. Although undeniably painful, it carries the potential for deeper wholeness. David Whyte addresses the mystery of the sacred dark in his powerful poem "Sweet Darkness." Following are several lines that resonate with the truth that entering the dark, rather than to be feared, is to be embraced, for it bears the new in a broader context of compassion:

Time to go into the dark
where the night has eyes
to recognize its own.

There you can be sure
you are not beyond love.

The dark will be your womb
tonight.

Addressing the call to deep inner freedom, he concludes his
poem with these lines,

Sometimes it takes darkness and the sweet
confinement of your aloneness
to learn

anything or anyone
that does not bring you alive

is too small for you.[10]

This is a hard truth, for it may require a leaving. We are called
to life; we are built for life, and we are invited to usher in life in
everything we do. The absence of this dynamic—in career or
relationships—may impel us redefine our priorities and focus.
To step out into the night requires honesty, courage, and faith,
but faith means, first of all, faithfulness to oneself, an authenticity grounded in love and acceptance.

We all suffer our deaths, beginning with the little deaths of
ego-sting. But the big ones—loss of a spouse, health crises, broken love, job loss—produce a devastating rupture and a roiling
mass of feeling and confusion. The wonder—and potential miracle—is whether and how to maximize the lesson, to transform
death to life. In this case when we surrender to the dark, when
we allow these crises to penetrate us, when we bravely drink the
bitter cup and consciously engage transformation, the Divine

hovers round us, and, in fact, *the Divine hovers round in any case*. The great Jesuit poet Gerard Manley Hopkins writes in "God's Grandeur,"

> Because the Holy Ghost over the bent
> World broods with warm breast and with ah!
> bright wings.[11]

We suffer the pain of change, yet the pain of change has the potential of becoming the miracle of change, with new layers of insight and love, new joys, unforeseen, unexpected, new ways of being, new mental habits that seed peace and deeper authenticity. To arrive at this place is not always smooth; sometimes our beneficent deity appears as a ferocious spirit, seeming bent to destroy us. Indeed, in a workshop on myth and poetry, Robert Bly focused on the Kali-like hag in old European fairy tales, evoking that spirit in his dramatic characterization. Bly made the sober comment that sometimes Kali, the bearer of chaos, visits us in order to provoke change, or perhaps cause grief, for "as Americans we have not suffered much." Kali shows up, gaunt and haggard, with, as I wrote in a poem, "ghastly teeth, sharpened on the bones of those she loves." Sharpened on the bones of *those she loves*. Kali's rage slays our illusions, our attachments, our tidy understanding. Kali ushers in newness, using the tools of chaos and suffering to slay ego, her rage offering opportunities to encode measures of wisdom born from loss. Sometimes, however, we feel overwhelmed with depression or despair, wondering if we are able to pass through the crisis or even if we *want* to pass through it. Hopkins himself struggled mightily with depression and anguish; this is clearly evident in his poem "Carrion Comfort":

> Not, I'll not, carrion comfort, Despair, not feast
>   on thee;
> Not untwist—slack they may be—these last strands
>   of man
> In me or, most weary, cry *I can no more*. I can;

> Can something, hope, wish day come, not choose not
> to be.[12]

In our deaths, we ask, how am I possibly going to get through this? And there is absolutely no way through it except through it, nor is there any guarantee that we *will* get through it. Some of us may be tempted to the extreme, to pull the plug on our pain and be done with it. Hopkins seemed tempted by suicide but seems to affirm, "I can; Can something, hope, wish day come, not choose not to be." The question before us may be, Can we let the pain be pain, suffer it, drink it deep, feel it through, and let it pass? Can we discover the truth of Rumi's words: "the cure for pain is in the pain." Can we sit in the acid of our aloneness and realize everything passes, including anguish? There is no way through it, but through it. The last lines of "Carrion Comfort": "That night, that year Of now done darkness I wretch lay wrestling with (my God!) my God." Many of us enter dark or difficult times when all the terrific deities emerge—devastating loneliness, bitterness, loss—and the challenge is to stay above the fray, not succumb to abject despair. And yet, we grope, stumble, "hope, wish day come, not choose not to be." And hope here must be held lightly, because anything other than feeling the fire burn through us teeters precariously on the brink of avoidance. Letting go is really letting go. Moreover, it may include letting go of our unnuanced conceptions of God. Jesus himself validates the truth of darkness at Golgotha and by the cross itself, asking for the cup to be taken away, weeping tears of blood, and crying out, "My God, my God why have you forsaken me?"—words that Hopkins evokes in his poem. And yet, Jesus surrenders. He drinks the cup. He says, "not my will, but yours." And, on the cross, he forgives.

Surrendering Hope, Surrendering Concepts

To surrender to death in one sense requires even letting go of hope. There is a strange dynamic to hope. It can surely provide energy to carry us through difficult times, but it also carries the tinge of attachment, the tinge of avoidance, the tinge to evaluate the now as inadequate or insufficient. The *Bhagavad Gita* clearly advises us to drop hope, because hope spells insufficiency of the now, the unacceptability of the present experience, and therefore generates the strain of striving. Striving is fine—we all need goals. But the corrosive logic of striving is that we are not enough as we are, here and now, and we will never be enough. Nikos Kazantzakis, the robust spirit who wrote *Zorba the Greek* and the *Last Temptation of Christ*, wrote this as his epitaph: "I am without hope, I am without fear, I am free." Or as the *Mahabharata* bluntly puts it, "hope is the greatest torture that exists, and despair the greatest happiness."[13] Hope, owing to attachment, inevitably breeds frustration and dissatisfaction; despair, albeit agonizing, creates the conditions for freedom: being here, surrendered. Hope indeed motivates—and we note that Christianity and Judaism are very much religions of hope—but hope also breeds the insufficiency of the now, a state laced with the fear of inadequacy, the fear of not being good enough. And fear, the most deadly toxin, *always* poisons love and life.

Is it possible to let it all go—our striving, our afflictions, our sins, our glories, our lives, even let go of God, that is, our limited understanding of God? This is perhaps the greatest death, the death of our conceptualizations of divinity. Is it possible to leap out of the plane without a parachute, free-falling into every death, including the death of our easy divinities? But this is terribly counterintuitive, counter to our usual patterns of conditioning. In the fire of our lives, in which things are consumed but formed anew, we might think of the training found in certain schools of Zen Buddhism. Here, the student is pushed to the limits of the rational mind, forced into a kind of conceptual wrestling match in order to provoke the great death—the death of categories, the death of presuppositions, the death of easy self-understanding, the death of self. To do this requires great courage. We must have heart (*coeur*) to do this, even if it requires the shattering of our hearts.

There is a dark night that each of us enters, and some of us, owing to temperament, conditioning, or neuro-chemical patterns, may enter these nights more often than others. These crises, occasioned by deaths of many kinds, propel us into vistas we never imagined—or even wanted. But they are there, and they invite us to new life. But getting there, walking through the *bardo*, is the hard part. Here's Eliot:

> Shall I say it again? In order to arrive there,
> To arrive where you are, to get from where you are not,
> > You must go by a way wherein there is not ecstasy.
> In order to arrive at what you do not know
> > You must go by a way which is the way of ignorance.
> In order to possess what you do not possess
> > You must go by the way of dispossession.
> In order to arrive at what you are not
> > You must go through the way in which you are not.
> And what you do not know is the only thing you know
> And what you own is what you do not own
> And where you are is where you are not.[14]

This is eminently challenging. We impute great cash value to our conceptualizations, our understanding, our standard way of seeing things; these become familiar and comfortable, even if this picture is incomplete owing to the distortions formed by our personal agenda and also because the depth dimension of life and humanity is in the end a mystery and, as such, is unfathomable. So to let go our views is not just a dry academic experiment but is fraught with emotional overtones. We usually have high investments on how we view things. "I'm right"/"you're wrong" provides a quick, easy, emotional payoff, but with little long-term benefit. To drop into the way of not-knowing and honestly admit it is terrifying; it feels like setting out on the ocean in a skiff. But the testimony of religious traditions suggests that in some sense the ocean is God itself, God here being the unconditioned supreme. We mightily struggle, yet even as we do, we are floating upon the sacred. Perhaps relaxing is required too. Perhaps trust, too, in the whole of it. Yet, suffering transformation in which our categories are shattered allows for the possibility of being here with new freedoms and capacities, especially in the internalization and expression of wisdom and compassion.

Zen traditions invite the shattering of categories in order to see reality free from our conceptual and emotional blinders. Zen aims to deconstruct our preconceptions, our assumptions, our habituated tendencies. So, monks might say, "Before Zen, tea was tea, and a cup a cup. During Zen, tea is no longer tea, a cup is no longer a cup. After Zen, tea is tea, a cup is a cup." In intense Zen training, all notions of separateness—including our fixed notions of the self—are dissolved, and instead we see reality as it is—flowing, movement, with everything and everyone connected in astonishing ways. Zen training aims to destabilize our easy categories and our mental constructs to trigger an awareness of reality in all its pristine beauty and freedom. This issues in the open heart, and it is in the open heart that we experience communion. The deaths, losses, betrayals of our lives might be construed as shattering epiphanies—our sense of self, purpose, relationship destabilized as the preconditions for new freedom. While this is unbearably painful, the radical shattering of assumptions allows for the reconstitution of everything—a new, freer sense of self, purpose, greater authenticity, the hallmark of holiness. One might say, in Zen fashion, "Before this crisis, I was I, and my life was my life. During the crisis, I was no longer I, and my life was no longer my life. After the crisis, I was I, my life was my life." The white heat of trauma forges new ways of being. And indeed, in traditional Zen practice, a crisis is exactly what training aims to precipitate, for it breaks down uncritical cognitive habits and prepares for new ways of perceiving, free from self-centered attachments.

In the Tibetan tradition following the *Bardo Thodol*, this disorientation is, understandably, profoundly disturbing. The entity feels the urge to incarnate as soon as possible, to throw off the discomfort of the in-between for the comfort of the embodied, the security of something familiar. But to do this would be a mistake, for we would lose the opportunity to maximize our learning, to grow in ways we need but never anticipated. Transitions—little and great deaths—are disturbing and destabilizing, but they are perhaps our most potent teachers, propelling us into the curriculum of transformation. They become "fierce grace," words that became the title of a extraordinary documentary on the life of Ram Dass.[15] This phrasing has special significance, for it bears witness to the lessons Ram Dass learned through a devastating stroke. Indeed, while a longtime practitioner of *bhakti yoga*, the discipline (yoga) of devotion, Ram Dass called his experience "stroke yoga," which implies the wisdom that he discovered in his profound health crisis. Many of us either have experienced or have friends who have experienced surprising growth attained through catastrophic medical crises. A friend once said about his heart attack, "It was the best thing that ever happened me." Other traumas sometimes eventuate in profound transformation, too, including marital crises, job loss, struggle with addictions, crises involving our children. Such transformations demonstrate that no trauma is beyond redemption, though clearly the miracle of change follows only after the pain of change. No one in the middle of a heart attack immediately celebrates it.

When death visits us *in this life*, however, we need to remember not to incarnate too soon, certainly not to revert to ways of being that have lost their authenticity—"the safety of straight-jacket habits and the supposed comfort of the old." We need to enter transitions with as much awareness as possible. This includes awareness of who we are at a given time—identity being relatively fluid—and what we really want in our heart of hearts. In the Tibetan tradition, one's next incarnation is predicated upon a review of life, an examination of karmic outcomes of endless thoughts, habits, and actions. To do this review really is an exercise of determining the curriculum for the next life. And this is why it is imperative not to incarnate too hastily, to get on with it as if merely to stabilize feelings of estrangement and confusion. The aim is to maximize the learning curve, not discharge the stress of unknowing by choosing a new life too soon.

When we die in *this* life—that is, when we suffer our losses and what-might-have-beens—we feel disembodied, disoriented, confused. There is a temptation to flee the pain and confusion and to embody too quickly, that is, to take up a new life (a new relationship, a new career) too soon. This could mean moving into a relationship on the rebound, or externalizing our anguish in self-destructive ways, or doing something rash or impulsive, such as leaping into an instant career shift, or moving away to escape pain. To do so may bring temporary relief from distress and even a measure of peace, but without internalizing the wisdom offered by death, we may only repeat the old patterns in different circumstances.

We cannot escape ourselves, our family histories, our biology, the momentum of our many choices. We carry all of this to every context of our lives. The external circumstances of our lives mean far less than the inner terrain, the plane where we finally befriend ourselves in all of our glories and traumas. The call is to die, to allow the pain to be pain, to drink the cup in all its bitterness, to feel our losses burn through us as if by acid—and somehow, impossibly, to do this without a clenched hold. A Zen dialogue:

> Where can we go to escape hot and cold?
> Why not go where there is neither hot nor cold?
> What kind of place is neither hot nor cold?
> When cold, let it freeze you to death. When hot, let it burn you to death. [16]

In this case, suffering comes from the mental labels "hot" and "cold" affixed to sensation. By letting the sensation be, without assigning value to it, we somehow touch a place free of suffering. Let pain be pain. Let suffering, as our mental overlays to our pain, go. If we return to the idiom of Islam, our obsessive focus on our suffering is *shirk*. The cure is to let go, do something unimaginable: trust. We can speak of selfishness, self-absorption, or self-addiction, and we can draw upon the resources of our religious traditions to help us to die our deaths, to learn to live in letting-go space, to be here. To do this, I think, involves something of a secret review of our lives, to see enfolded in all our becoming a certain soft spot, a certain disquiet or loneliness that cannot be met by anyone or anything. This is our secret tattoo, the site where we meet ourselves and the Holy One. To recognize this embraces our inner poverty, our authentic humanness, and this begins to weave new vibrancy in our unique paths of holiness. We live surrendered to the limitations of our humanness, and, in the quiet but decisive affirmation of that surrender, we begin to feel the kiss of God.

6

The Holiness of the Everyday

GAZING INTO THE EYES
OF THE BELOVED

Mother and Child

His steel blue eyes stare primitively into yours.
You wonder what he dreams at night.
Probably of your eyes, your round soulful browns.
He squirms, pouts, maneuvers for efficient sucking,
and you, for the hundredth time or five hundredth time,
smile, sing, swing him gently, coo to him.
He knows you too as he fixes his eyes,
speaks eloquently his simple silent stare, a long loving gaze.

Your days are different now.
That's clear.
You offer your body as in no other way
to this child who needily draws life and love,
storing for his days of stretching growth.

You are close to the holy one, too,
who took flesh, drew life from the beloved mother,
strength upon strength,
preparing in love great freedom and courage.

Sure there are many ways to serve.
But you have
the most common, hidden, and urgent
of them all
right now.

Thank you for what you do.

IF HOLINESS is to be understood as some supernormal power, then we are lost, for we are without supernormal power. Most of us stagger about doing the best we can, more than aware of our limitations and failings. Scriptures and legends of various religious traditions sometimes speak of extraordinary powers and miracles of saints, yet these ought to be viewed with a measure of skepticism, recognizing the agenda of the author and the need of an audience in the spinning of myths and legends. In Hinduism, the focus of my academic training, legends about saints are legion, and disciples even today speak of unusual experiences attributed to the power (*shakti*) of an adept or guru. And this seems reasonable, if we assume, as most seekers do, that the breakthrough of the sacred into the mundane happens in rich, diverse, and sometimes surprising ways, as if reality can be bent or angled by those who become prisms to the supreme.

I do not discount the unusual or uncanny stories of saints and seers and lamas and gurus and sheikhs who seem to bend reality in such a way as to allow us to witness a whole new range of existence and new worlds of possibility, new ways of being here. They, by being who they are, become a prism, as it were, angling everyday light to reveal the lavish color hidden within it. We may see things differently, as when a band of light from the evening sun is bent by the cut glass of a chandelier. Some teachers or saints are prisms who somehow angle light to reveal this truth. Perhaps they come to us in dreams, somehow welling up from our inner depths, coming to us as guides along the path of our becoming. The poet Coleman Barks writes of a powerful dream of the Sufi saint Muhaiyadeen which changed the direction of his life.[1] Christopher Chapple, professor of theology at Loyola Marymount, writes about having a dream, as an undergraduate, of Meher Baba, an Indian saint, who introduced Chapple to an Indian woman who later became his guru.[2] China Galland described having a dream of the Dalai Lama, which led to her study of the Black Madonna.[3] I also once had a dream of an unknown Tibetan lama, who came to me and touched my throat and released stopped-up sound and voice.

Whether welling from the depths of unconscious needs or from the depths of the mind, synchronicities, messages, visits, dreams, phone calls, little helps along the way assist us in our path of holy unfolding. But the word and example of the famous saints are mirrors of ourselves. It is not that we must become those saints. They are compelling precisely because they are who they are as they live their humanity. As we look upon them, we come to know ourselves in a manner far more lucid than endless rumination, which, if we're honest, may feel like cavernous self-absorption. It is difficult, if not impossible, to discover who we are in a vacuum, devoid of relationship with others, whether mentor, friend, companion, lover, teacher, or spiritual director. While Buddhism reserves a distinction for those buddhas who go it alone and attain nirvana by themselves, even this trajectory must admit many teachers in previous lifetimes. Indeed, the Buddha of this age, Siddhartha Gautama, is an "unexcelled completely perfect buddha" (*anuttara samyak sambuddha*) because he attained realization on his own (and then, out of compassion, taught others, the other criterion for a *sambuddha*). He himself, however, began the path to enlightenment many lifetimes ago by encountering Dipankara, the Buddha of ancient times. Seeing the holiness of Dipankara, something resonated in the buddha-to-be, something awakened in his heart, as if to say, "I want that, too." He then formed the resolve for enlightenment (*bodhicitta*). Resolve always becomes the arrow-like power, muscling choice upon choice, moving one toward one's goal. But I wish to underscore that even the Buddha of this age needed many teachers in the course of his long evolution. We cannot do the human thing alone.

The great novel *Siddhartha* intimates this truth as well. The young Brahmin, in his quest for self-discovery, realized, even in the presence of the Buddha, that there is no second-hand enlightenment; no longer aligning himself with any tradition or teacher, he affirms, in a freedom both liberating and haunting, "I will learn from myself the secret of Siddhartha."[4] And yet, while he rejected formal teaching and mentors, he in fact had many teachers, including Kamala, the courtesan, the villagers, Kamaswami, the businessman, and Vasudeva, who taught him to listen to the river, always flowing, always changing, always one: "it is good to strive downwards, to sink, to seek the depths."[5] Vasudeva taught him the value of listening well. Still, Siddhartha's greatest teacher may have been his son, who, in rejecting him, ushered him into his humanity. He felt the anguish of attachment, the suffering of loss, and the call to let go. This he finally did, and in doing so, he came home.

We need one another to help us become who we are. The mirror of the other allows us to see ourselves. The painful truth, when we go within to discover our true self, is that we often do not see ourselves in a clear mirror but instead find ourselves in a hall of mirrors and are lost because of it. We need friends, lovers, family, children, ministers, teachers, colleagues to mirror back what they see in us and hear from us, as we do the hard work of making sense of our life experience. Moreover, those we respect become mirrors of possibility too. And we need them, but not to put them on a pedestal, which distances them from us. Rather, we need them in order to discover that quality in them that strikes a chord in us. We see something in them that resonates with something deep in us, something that awakens in us a key stream of our being. This is the power of example, and it is hardly the domain of famous saints. It is found in the everyday holiness of our friends and acquaintances; in them we see something modeled well and lives lived with purpose and peace and we say, "I want that, too."

These persons awaken a quality that we ourselves have cultivated or are invited to cultivate. This resonance is particularly harmonic in the presence of someone who has cultivated these qualities in longstanding habits of the heart. What happens when we are in the presence of these persons might be likened to the harmonics of a tuning fork. When struck at staggered paces, the forks gradually become concordant, vibrating with the same resonance. Similarly, the chords of our soul automatically become attuned in the presence of a holy one. It is automatic because it resonates with our nature. This is not dissimilar to falling in love, but, following the observation of St. Ignatius, there may be a more lasting contentment, a more abiding joy, when these deeper chords are struck, for these are not dependent on external circumstances.

Pedro Arrupe, S.J. (1907-1991), the extraordinary superior general of the Society of Jesus, recognized the singular importance of sacred intimacy in one's holy unfolding:

> Nothing is more practical than finding God, that is, than falling in love in a quite absolute way, final way. What you are in love with, what seizes your imagination, will affect everything. It will decide what will get you out of bed in the morning, what you will do with your evenings, how you will spend your weekends, what your read, who you know, what breaks your heart, and what amazes you with joy and gratitude. Fall in love, stay in love, and it will decide everything.[6]

Striking these chords—falling in love—is possible in every time and in every place and in every moment. This is communion, and it is always available regardless of the emotional pitch of our lives. We have the capacity to access these chords, whether in community, alone, married, divorced, or in a nursing home. Living kindness, living generosity, living calm, living wisdom, this is who we are; and while we may be gifted with something extraordinary in our love relationships, this being-who-we-are is *our* domain, whether we are alone or not. Greg Corrigan, a priest, pastor, campus minister, and author, once offered this prism to me, angling the light in this potent inspiration: "Let the goodness you do be who you are." We have endless opportunities in our day-to-day lives to instantiate love and kindness in choice upon choice. Nothing is gratuitous or too little. As Mother Teresa herself counseled, every act, however simple, done in love, becomes infinite. "It's not how much we do, but how much love we put into the doing. It's not how much we give, but how much love we put into the giving." The cumulative effect of this way of being is a life lived well, authentic, generative, and satisfying.

The supernormal powers that are most meaningful and enduring are the endless gestures of kindness and self-sacrifice that add up to a life lived well, a life that emanates integrity and authenticity. This is shown in the following poignant example. Ronald Primrose, the father of a very good friend, lived his entire life in a small Illinois town. In ways that were quiet and unassuming, he made a profound impact on the lives of family and friends with everyday kindness and care. He was not a public figure nor did he serve on boards or construct ambitious programs for urban renewal. Moreover, being someone who enjoyed the quiet calm of home and family, he was not inclined to much entertaining. And yet, when he died, after a long illness, over six hundred people attended his wake—with many waiting outside in the rain—bearing witness to the undeniable impact he made in his community *in his own way*. And this is a key to our holiness, expressing our humanity in *our own way*, a way concordant with our soul.

Holiness begins with authenticity. We have considered the

lives of several contemporary holy ones and the wisdom that shaped their own authentic unfolding. In this chapter, I wish to affirm the holiness of those who are well known—and loved— by their families and friends but who are less well known by the broader public. They may not be recognized by the Nobel committee, but they are no less models of authentic living and loving, the hallmarks of holiness. All of us can think of persons in our lives who have shown us something of what it means to be here, to be alive, to be accepting of self and others, to live wisely and to love well. As this book really is a meditation on what it means to be human, this chapter will be my meditation on key people in my life, companions who show me something of what it means to be human.

The people whom I highlight in this chapter have shown me something of high quality, such that it registers in me, makes an imprint, and calls me to cultivate that quality too. These people are not perfect, but being here is not about idealized perfection. Indeed, a rather unflattering book about Mother Teresa, published several years ago, was all too eager to point up her flaws. And even a cursory viewing of the Petrie film reveals the fearless faith and indomitable will of Mother Teresa, impressive qualities but perhaps not easy to live with in community. And yet, in and through her flaws, real or imagined, Mother Teresa demonstrated an integrated life in which her being and doing were one. And thus her example becomes luminous.

We draw great power from the examples of the saints, gurus, and sages in the world's religious traditions, but the most vivid impressions we receive come from the very real, very human, very embodied people around us. In the ordinary yet exquisite examples of what it means to be human, most of us draw our greatest inspiration. Life is not an abstraction. Life is not an idea. We are built with bodies, and we need embodied, enfleshed examples of what it means to be human. And when something touches us, strikes a chord, our soul vibrates and we discover a little more who we are and what we need to do to be our best selves. We cannot know how to love without the embodied experience of being loved.

The Holiness of Motherhood

This chapter begins with a poem that tries to express the wonder and awe I have felt at the mystery and gift of exquisite embodied love: bearing children. Holiness is about creating, cultivating, and nourishing life, and there is no greater natural sign of this than childbirth. As a man, I will never know the emotional, psychological, and spiritual transformations that occur in bearing and birthing a child. But I have witnessed them. And these sometimes include a deep inward or collected composure. I recall Therese's pregnancies, and though it is risky to generalize from her experience, it seems that at certain times during pregnancy, a cloud descends on women. This particular liminal place is sacred, unknown by men, though men have their own liminal places of transformation, too. Liminal space, an inarticulate place of unknowing, is an essential, if uncomfortable, element in the organic process of becoming. The place of ambiguity or unknowing, however, has minimal cash value in a consumer society. There is little cultural permission to live in a grey zone of becoming. And yet mothers offer a model of inwardness and organic transformation: intimate communion of heart, body, and soul; life unfolding within the depths. In this case, mothers are consummate teachers for they model, *in their bodies*, a key truth: new life unfolds organically and in due course; it is wise to surrender to the process. Pregnancy, then, is a mirror too, or better, a sacrament, just as sexuality, in its truest expression, is a mirror and sacrament, too. Both intimate sacred oneness, real presence, life emerging out of love and surrender. Holy communion.

The change in gender roles that has occurred over the past forty years has provided enormous potential for creativity and spiritual growth for both sexes, but it has also produced great challenges and frustration when couples negotiate the territory of creating a home and creating careers. This certainly was the case in our marriage. Yet, despite our own unique permutation of an American pathology of busyness, there was, and is, something that I will always take as expressive of an exquisite and wholly natural holiness—the shared gaze of a mother and her nursing child. There is no shortage of social and psychological trauma associated with childbirth, which newspapers soberly report: babies born on crack, abandoned in alleys, traumatized by abusive parents. While these events sadly do occur, it is probably the case that—fear, anxieties, insecurities, and lack of sleep notwithstanding—most mothers know at least some moments of extraordinary communion in the holding and caring of infants. *And to be held by another in a loving gaze is the first step of holiness.* We know ourselves in the eyes of another. And there could be no more significant beginning in our path of becoming than being beheld by our mothers, who in peace and calm and quiet joy signal the first and most seminal message of all: you are beloved, you are enough; yes, we welcome you.

Growing up in Christian households, many of us have heard the phrase "charity begins at home." But this phrase could be modulated to "holiness begins at home," first and foremost in the holiness of motherhood. This is not at all to put pressure on women to be good mothers. The expectation to be a good anything—parent, professional, artist, or athlete—issues in the prison of outside approval. We are who we are, perfect imperfections. But mothers offer something unique in virtue of the physiology of immediacy. To be held in the loving gaze of a mother allows the child to be here, knowing, in a visceral, non-conceptual manner, that it is cherished and valued. The unspoken knowing of the child rings with the testimony of the disciples before Jesus, "it is good to be here." These indelible impressions naturally make it easier for the child to transmit the same to others many years later. We know the cost that accrues to individuals when the first transmission is absent or broken. But the suffering that such absence causes is not gratuitous or beyond repair. Muhammad, for example, lost both his father and mother by age six and was raised by his uncle, Abu Talib. Yet, the loss of his parents served to carve out a space in him—a capacity for reflection, inwardness, spiritual sensitivity—that allowed him to hear, many years later, the great revelation that became the Qu'ran. We all are endowed with pain—our loneliness, our shattered self-esteem and self-concepts, our heartache and losses—but our pain is not the end of the story. Pain is a teacher, too, leading us to the heartbeat of life, the pulse of compassion that issues from eternity.

The holiness of the everyday must begin with mothers, the mothers in all women, regardless of birthing history, and the "mothers" in men, too. For, while birth mothers are naturally graced with ineffable biological and emotional connection to their children, all of us access the same nurturing instincts when we behold another with compassion and kindness. Many of us are quite accustomed to the nurturing instincts of women, but it is a sign of social integration to see these nurturing instincts in men, too. For several months, for example, I shared an apartment with Richard Welch, a colleague who was preparing to move to Atlanta, where his wife had found a new teaching post. Being fairly quiet and reserved, I was a little unsure of what it would be like to share an apartment at this stage of my life. But I found myself moved by Richard's extraordinary everyday kindness and generosity, not to mention genuine nurturing instincts that are often found in women, owing perhaps to biology and social conditioning. I offer one example and its impact on me. Richard is an extraordinary cook, who generously prepared meals, with great care, for the two of us. I also enjoy cooking, especially as I prepare warm, hearty meals for my children—no doubt recalling the smells and warmth of my mother's kitchen as a child. Receiving Richard's kindness in cooking reawakened that impulse in me, and I very much desired to return the same care in breaking bread, which I happily did on occasion. Now, I am very aware of God's surprises, which often disarm us, and sharing an apartment with Richard was one of them. And yet, when I told my daughter about Richard's cooking and kindness, she said something that profoundly touched me—"He's like a dad." To me, she identified the nurturing qualities associated with cooking with a dad. And since I'm the only dad she has who cooks and tries to show love and kindness in cooking, I felt profoundly touched. Despite my flaws, she got it, the point of my cooking.

So, beginning with the gaze of a mother and child, I wish to recognize common holiness. It is common because it is close to home. Indeed, it is often in our homes, for most of us have family members—a parent or grandparent, an aunt or uncle, a sister or brother—who have shown extraordinary self-sacrifice, and these make deep impressions on our lives. Our own holiness—our unique paths woven with light and dark—begins in the home, by internalizing the positive examples and by reacting, for good or ill, to the negative examples. One distant, positive memory for me surfaced as I recently did a morning ritual for my six-year-old son. Before I left the house rather early to teach summer school, I knew Luke would be up before the other children. So I poured cereal into a bowl with a cup of milk beside it. As I did this, a memory dislodged from somewhere deep and surfaced. When I was a child, my father, a high school teacher, would leave a bowl of cereal, along with a tall glass of orange juice, for my brother Joe, who has cerebral palsy. As a young boy, I was very much struck by that simple act of kindness, very aware at that moment of a deep impression imprinting itself on my heart. And so it's not surprising that, almost forty years later, I found myself doing the same for my own son, and as I did, the example of my father bubbled forth from my memory.

We also find ourselves responding, consciously or unconsciously, to the negative examples of our homes too. No family is free of flaw, and most of us pray that the damage we cause is minimal. But all families—because they are human systems—are afflicted with doses of unwholesome patterns of behaviors—an absence of affection, untoward harshness, reactive anger, excessive criticism, or even more traumatic behaviors such as addictions or domestic violence. Each of these patterns, wherever or however it becomes manifest, constricts life; it does not nurture it. But these too are not insuperable obstacles, as the testimony of many families and lives bears witness. Moreover, as we are conscious of the negative outcomes of these choices, they become another model, a *via negativa*. They become examples of what not to do, examples that don't work for us because they do not provide abiding joy and calm. Instead, they generate death in the form of fear, anxiety, insecurity, or worse. As we respond to negative examples, consciously or unconsciously, we, in effect, are seeking our path; we are learning how to be here with awareness, freedom, and joy. We find our way through the labyrinth of our lives, seeking to come home, to come to the center, the place, in all our striving and doing, where we finally hear a message we may not have heard before: you are precious, you are beautiful, you are important, you have something to offer; the world is a little more fulfilled, now that you are here. This message, transmitted imperfectly in our families of origin, is nonetheless repeated by the gaze of the many "mothers" in our lives—our friends, lovers, spiritual directors, gurus, lamas, teachers, therapists—those who, by their sight, reveal to us ourselves, thereby generating the capacity to give such a gift to others.

I wish to consider the lives of several holy ones in my life, who have transmitted the same message of compassion and value. There are people that I will name, but there are many whose names I do not know also. The Hindu *sadhu* in Tiruvannamalai was one. The abbess of the French Poor Clare Colletines in Assisi was another. Once, on a flight from California, I sat next to an elderly grandmother who seemed to exude calm. Perhaps she was naturally given to be calm or perhaps life drew out this calmness, or both. In any case, she held her grandson's head in her lap with such exquisite peace and tenderness that, for me, her action became an instant, hidden example of communion. I wish to speak about those I know fairly well, but also one whom I know only through his professional capacity as physician. That person is Mark Bellinger, M.D., to whom I now turn.

Mark Bellinger

Mark Bellinger is a pediatric urologist at the University of Pittsburgh Children's Memorial Hospital. A tall, handsome man in his fifties, he guided our family through a medical crisis, the discovery of a congenital urological anomaly in my oldest son, Andrew, which required two surgeries. During this crisis, we learned that Andrew was born with one kidney, and that a large cyst had grown where the other kidney should have been and required surgery. This news was traumatic and disturbing— what did it mean? What did it imply about Andrew's health in the future? How would it impact his ability to play sports, and so on? But Dr. Bellinger was an ocean of calm, mixed with a sly and wry sense of humor that relieved our tension and put us at ease. Most of all, I was struck by his exquisite professionalism, deeply humane and suffused with calm.

After the second surgery, which lasted five hours, he made his rounds late at night, then returned in the morning by 6:00 A.M. I, who was staying at the Ronald McDonald House, came later, at 7:00 A.M. The doctor was there before the father! I commented to the nurses about Bellinger's commitment, and they were unanimous in their respect and admiration for him. While nurses might complain, understandably, about self-important and overbearing doctors, the nurses on the floor expressed nothing but high esteem for Bellinger. And despite a major medical practice in one of the country's top children's hospitals, he still managed to coach his children's soccer teams and crew teams. This is a person who lives well, who loves well, who knows what he values in key areas of his life and cultivates it with focus, energy, and creativity. This is a compelling example of how to do the human thing. After two years, I took Andrew—and Caitlin and Luke—for a check-up. His sense of humor was in full force, as I reminded him that he might do a scan for the other children. "For brains?" he asked, bringing a laugh from the children. When he did the ultrasound on Andrew, he said, "Yep, you still have one kidney. You've got the super-large economy size. You must have picked it up at Sam's Club." When he next performed an ultrasound on Luke, he wryly noted, "Yep, you've got two here, Luke. You win the Kidney Lottery."

Dr. Bellinger is a consummate professional, and he is a healer in the truest sense. His healing goes far beyond the technical cutting and stitching of surgery. It includes the "stitching" of calm in worried patients—and parents—by his confidence and compassion. Something far greater than his technical expertise showed through in his character. That something extra had more to do with Bellinger's humanity than with his career. It had more to do with the way in which he was *human* rather than the way in which he was a doctor. The truth of this is found in the impact such a presence makes on another. When we are in the presence of persons who lucidly model ways of being, we sometimes are left with the feeling, "I want that, too." It is not at all the case that I want to be a doctor; that would be disastrous, for others as well as for me. But Bellinger, even in our very brief contact, demonstrated something of high moral and spiritual value—calm, patience, care, compassion, and humor. And this he did in an exquisite way.

Doing so strikes chords in us; we know these chords, we sound them in our own way, and they resonate when we express them. We are reminded of that vibration when we see them expressed in other lives. And that's the point: we see kindness; we want to be kind. We see calmness; we want to be calm. We see courage; we want to be courageous. But this dynamic ought not to issue in standards of perfection; these inevitably cause frustration, because we are profoundly limited on this side of the fence. Holiness is not about perfection. It's about cultivating ways of being that resonate with our deepest chords, our deepest me. While we need to dispatch notions of perfection as an impossible ideal, we nonetheless have choices in each moment to grow more skillful in our living and loving. Bellinger strikes me as an extraordinary person, but he is not perfect, since no one is perfect. But he is skillful, not just in his medical expertise, but in his human being, in his particular way of being here. And it strikes a chord in us, resonant and concordant. When we meet the Bellingers of our lives, we walk away feeling better about the goodness in the world, the goodness of others, and even the goodness of ourselves. And if we are sensitive and alert, we learn a little more of how to be here in our own way, drawing on the resonant example of others. We are become more ourselves as we learn from others, and becoming our truest selves is our path of holiness, our path home.

Dinesh Khera

The next person whose ordinary holiness I wish to highlight is also a doctor, a good friend, Dinesh Khera. Dinesh is Hindu, and we became friends first by a shared commitment to raise awareness of South Asian religion and culture in Erie, a city that tends toward parochialism, despite the presence of extraordinary communities such as the Sisters of Mercy, who established Mercyhurst College, the Benedictine Sisters, known for so many diverse ministries and justice programs, Pax Christi, L'Arche, and the Gertrude Barber Center, an Erie institution long dedicated to meeting the needs of developmentally disabled persons and their families. Dr. Khera comes from a family of physicians in India. His father maintained a humble practice, and his father's own life of integrity and service had this effect: people saw something in him and turned to him, not just as a physician but as a good, honorable person whose life said something meaningful and helpful. His father, Ram Prakash, instilled the value of education in his five children, convinced that education, not material gain, was the one gift that a person could carry to any place and time. Indeed, of his five children, three became physicians, and one became a professor of dentistry. Dinesh's wife, Ritu, also is a physician and together the two of them have also instilled the values of education and service in their children. One, Puja, is in medical school; another, Amit, is in premed at Duke; and a third, Divya, is flourishing in her studies at Collegiate Academy, a charter high school here in Erie.

While there is much to note about Dinesh, what is particularly striking is his soft-spoken humility. Indeed, when we worked together on projects to bring well-known speakers to campus, Dinesh was the primary benefactor. He was convinced, as I, of the value and importance of sharing the wisdom of

India's religious traditions, and he provided generous support to do this. Yet, he insisted that I never thank him publicly at these events, eschewing any attention directed to him. As a prominent and respected physician in Erie, his hospital has asked him from time to time to do commercials or television shows, and he has always declined, preferring the humble day-to-day caring for his patients to fanfare and limelight. He has practiced what he has preached to his children. In our lives, he explained, as we prepare to set sail, each of us is required to build our own ship with the tools at our disposal—our training, education, and values. And that is the moral lesson: "You have to build it. But when you set sail, sail quietly. Don't try to seek attention. Do it well. That is enough."

The lesson of disinterested action comes straight from the *Bhagavad Gita,* which underscores the importance of action done without attachment to the fruits of action. This lesson was the cardinal impulse in Gandhi, too, who lived by the maxim, "take care of the means and let God take care of the end." Living this way is eminently freeing, a key touchstone on our path home, because the feverish need to achieve inevitably issues in the roller coaster of success and failure, praise and blame, gain and loss. These external determinants of identity and value are meaningless. This is why success and failure are imposters. They have nothing to do with our intrinsic worth. We are not required to achieve anything. Internalizing this, our actions become freer, truer, with less baggage attached to them, less emotional investment. As Mother Teresa once noted, "If we were humble, nothing would change us—neither praise nor discouragement."[7]

Dinesh models this humility, quietly demonstrating a way of being in the world of action that is self-possessed, sure, unruffled by reactivity. Dinesh is calm, unrushed, and comfortable with silence, even in conversation. When I asked him what made him tick, he was quite clear. "We all are endowed with a very powerful teacher, our inner voice. That is the basis of good conduct, listening to that voice. We know what to do. And when we suppress that voice and do something wrong, we automatically know it. We don't need others to tell us. Listen to the inner voice. Let it guide you." This conviction of the inner knowing is clearly conveyed in the Hebrew and Christian scriptures:

> For this Law that I enjoin on you today is not beyond your strength or beyond your reach. It is not in heaven, so that you need to wonder, "Who will go up to heaven for us and bring it down to us, so that we may hear it and keep it?" Nor is it beyond the seas, so that you need to wonder, "Who will cross the seas for us and bring it back to us, so that we may hear it and keep it?" No, the word is very near to you, it is in your mouth and in your heart for your observance. (Deuteronomy 30:11-14)

Dinesh's trust in the inner knowing accords with principles found in Indian religions for nearly three thousand years. And, while Dinesh draws from rich spiritual sources in all religions, another Hindu principle has been particularly formative, *satsang*, which can be translated as "association with the good" or "association with the real." It usually applies to a particular methodology in Hindu spiritual practice, namely, sitting in the presence of a guru and listening to spiritual teaching. In Hinduism, the holiness of the guru washes over disciples—like the fragrance of sandalwood—perfuming or purifying their souls. Grace is transmitted in the presence of a saint; perhaps an agitation is calmed or a capacity to live more wisely is enhanced. The *Dhammapada*, the Buddhist text on practical wisdom, suggests the high value of holy example:

> The wise one, the insightful, and the learned,
> Having the virtue of enduring, dutiful, noble,
> A person true, intelligent,
> With such a one as this, one would associate,
> As the moon the path of stars.[8]

Satsang addresses a key assumption in this book—that we need others to model key qualities and ways of being that resonate in us; it invites us to express those qualities too. We are required to build our own boats and set sail, but to do this we need all the available resources, and one sublime resource is the example of those who love well and live wisely. We see something in the example; we like it; and, in the context of our lives, we in turn embody it. This principle, of course, is well known by parents, because a key concern of parents is the company of their children. Attitudes, habits, examples tend to rub off, either negatively or positively. This is why most parents feel a sense of peace and even joy when our children are with other children who demonstrate kindness and consideration. This chapter and, in many ways, this book, is really about the association with the good in my life—sharing what I have learned from others and in my own experience. In the course of a person's life, there are occasions when others—perhaps colleagues or family—bear witness to one's grace and kindness. This sometimes occurs belatedly at funerals. In this book, I bear witness to those persons whom I have been fortunate to meet, to study, to listen to, or to befriend who have demonstrated great capacities for soulful living. This naturally stimulates two responses in me: gratitude for the opportunity to behold the Holy One in and through the holiness of others and the desire to internalize something of their example. Dinesh is a great man and a great friend, certainly as much a soul companion as anyone I've ever had the privilege of knowing. And for this, I am deeply grateful. He teaches me something of "how to be here" simply by his being.

To further unpack *satsang* in my life—all the while inviting you to consider the *satsang* in yours—I would like to turn now to two dear friends here at Mercyhurst, Mary Hembrow Snyder and Gerry Tobin. Let me address Mary's example first.

Mary Hembrow Snyder

Mary is a colleague in the religious studies department. She is a consummate teacher and scholar, earning a full professorship during her career at the college as well as recognition for her outstanding scholarship, teaching, and service. Mary is a dynamic teacher, challenging students to think critically as they engage questions of faith, justice, and the countercultural vision of the gospel. Her area of expertise is systematic theology, especially liberation theology and feminist theology. The first words that come to mind when I think of Mary, however, are generous and generative. She models astounding generosity of heart, mind, and means, often at great personal cost. Mary has demonstrated repeatedly, to me and to others, skillful listening, understanding, compassion, acceptance, and generosity. When I shared with her the trauma of my separation, she offered profound words of support and care, and immediately wrote a generous check to help me through my immediate financial needs. It was only later that I learned that she also wrote a check for the same amount to Therese, to help her as well. She has repeatedly shown a spontaneous, selfless generosity that continually impresses and inspires. It *resonates*, both in principle and in my own history, for at times I have shown similar generosity, even as a college student. As I prepared to go to India, for example, I saved a large sum of money over and beyond my travel expenses to donate to the mission of Father Schlooz. It is interesting to note that the amount was the same as that of Mary's two checks. Mary's generosity reminded me of my own and rekindled that same impulse in me. Her generosity stimulates the desire, indeed need, to express the same way of being, for in doing so, I feel more me. By activating that stream in me, I am more who I am. To see the holiness of others awakens our own holiness, quickens key streams in our being that need becoming, that need their proper expression for our full human flourishing.

Mary not only demonstrates material generosity but also generosity of service. She is a consummate leader at school, serving on many committees and governance structures, and serving as department chair for many years, division chair, associate dean and then dean of the School of Arts and Humanities. Her example, both in the classroom and in the college community, is a model of service. She is generous, unflagging, devoted, present.

Gifted and charismatic, Mary is eloquent and strong, quite capable of speaking the truth in professional and personal situations, even if this is sometimes eminently difficult. Being authentic requires being true, and this in turn requires the courage to stand in the heat of criticism, judgment, or misperception, if necessary. In addition to this, authenticity also implies the courage of self-restraint, the active choice, made out of genuine wisdom, not to correct the judgments of others. These key streams I have seen in Mary, and, seeing them realized in a dear friend, I know I can cultivate them, too.

But there is something that goes beyond the public expression of Mary's gifts and virtues. While I have always felt a deep kinship with her—feeling like a brother or a genuine soul friend—new depths to our friendship have developed over time in the shared experience of struggle. Most of us have, at some point or another, our dark and difficult times in which all bets are off, and from the deepest places of our soul, we wonder if we will survive. But we do survive, in no small part because of the companionship of friends who mirror back to us our intrinsic value, our worthiness of compassion, regardless of our flaws and errors. The message of God is this: you are beloved in my sight. I do not abandon you. I am here, with you, love you. And yet, in the maelstrom of our lives, life presents us with inevitable hurt and rejection, perhaps triggering primordial fears of abandonment and survival. In everyday life, even more so in our crises, it does little good to know *only* intellectually that we are beloved by God—*we need to see and touch and feel the Beloved in the eyes and embrace of another.* This is God made flesh for us. There are the persons in our lives, given by God to be God for us, revealing a consummate truth in a tender word: I am with you, for you, you are not alone, you are beloved. Mary is precisely such a person who has mirrored this important truth to me, the experience of which has been an extraordinary gift, one that has its natural outcome: the desire to offer the same to another. This is the impact of the holy ones in our lives.

Mary has shared meals, listened, offered insight, and we have shared our respective heartaches and struggles. Once, after Christmas, I returned after the long drive from eastern Pennsylvania where my children live with Therese. Although the college was closed, I went to my office, disconsolate, perhaps wanting to bury my heartache in work. I felt profoundly alone. On my desk was a small Christmas tree with tiny bulbs and a note from Mary wishing me peace in a season of pain. I burst into tears. The message was clear: you are not alone, you are valued, you are loved. Mary knew what I might be feeling and offered a simple, but powerful, gesture of thoughtfulness, one, incidentally that is quite typical of her. Even as tears rolled down my cheeks, I immediately recalled the bodhisattva in Buddhism, the archetypal saint who embodies wisdom and compassion and knows, skillfully, exactly which gesture is needed in a specific instance, not to remove edges and difficulties of one's struggle, but to offer an efficacious gesture in the middle of it. Mary has done this repeatedly for me and for many others. She is thoughtful. It is her nature. *And* it is instructive. It activates the desire in me to exercise similar thoughtfulness. Kindness begets kindness. For example, when my friend's father passed away, I went to her house to drop off a simple card to let her know I was thinking of her and her family (they were driving back from Illinois). As I did this, I consciously recalled Mary's kindness to me months earlier. I drove up to my friend's house to put the card in the front door, and on the porch were flowers and a card from none other than Mary herself. Thoughtfulness is her nature. Being who she is models a way of being that is not only luminous but informative. We see something of how to do the human thing; we gain strength for our way.

Mary has modeled a life marked by compassion, wisdom, generosity, passion, and the capacity to bear heartache. What I take from her example of being human is integrity. This includes the virtues often associated with integrity—honesty, truthfulness, and courage, for example—and these all apply to the capacity to bear pain. At different times in our lives we are invited to accept it, drink the bitter cup—whether loneliness, loss, broken love, or other trauma—bravely draining it, allowing it to sink into every cell of our lives. This returns us to the holiness of suffering, for suffering with integrity somehow creates the positive "reverb" that ripples to the banks of the pond. Moreover, while few of us choose suffering, suffering paradoxically can lead to deeper wholeness, generating new capacities for compassion and kindness. In the end, shared suffering can be healing. Mary and I once had a long, rich, soulful conversation over a meal, and afterward she said, "I feel like we just shared Eucharist." And we did. In the breaking of the bread, in listening to each other's story, we shared real presence, meeting the Holy One in the communion of hearts.

Gerard Tobin

Another keen listener is Gerry Tobin, the director of counseling at Mercyhurst. Gerry and I have a special bond owing to our training as Jesuit seminarians long ago, he as a member of the New England province, I as a member of the Chicago province. We knew each other as novices and scholastics, both of us leaving the order at different times during our training in philosophy in Chicago. Back then, Gerry looked like the poster boy of Boston Irish Catholicism, and even now he is still handsome, witty, and charming. Twenty years later—and a tad grayer—Gerry still "looks" like a Jesuit to me. In any case, Gerry is still living out his commitment to the *mages*, the more, but in the context of an intimate relationship with his wife, Michelle, who is also a very dear friend of mine. When I left the Jesuits many years ago, I brought the four boxes of my life to Gerry and Michelle's flat; I stayed with them for eight weeks as I transitioned back to lay life. After many years of friendship in Chicago, our paths diverged. We had both finally completed our Ph.D.s and were looking for college positions. I was offered a job at Mercyhurst; then, coincidentally, the position of director of counseling opened up one year later, and Gerry was hired. So our friendship continues and, in fact, is longer than our relationships with our wives. Ironically, during the initial phase of my separation, I again stayed at Gerry and Michelle's home with not much more than four boxes. I was received once again with kindness and generosity, and I could not help but recall the counsel of Jesus to care for the needy and least among us.

Gerry and Michelle have not been without their struggle, as no intimate relationship is spared that. But they've used everything to grow, as individuals and as partners. And Gerry, like most parents, sometimes struggles with his adolescent children as they begin their appropriate process of differentiation. But what I wish to highlight is the impact Gerry has made on me, and in doing so address the holiness of friendship, particularly longstanding friendship. Despite the edges and struggles of our lives, when we give ourselves to another, something lucid and magical happens that creates a distinct and unambiguous positive "reverb." In Gerry's example, I am struck by the quality of presence he graciously offered me during a difficult and dark year. While Gerry and I have always enjoyed each other's company, it was in that year that the depth of Gerry's friendship became clear. Gerry was generous with his time and his attentiveness, showing an extraordinary capacity to listen. One of the greatest gifts one can give another is to listen well, nondefensively and nonreactively. Soulful unfolding cannot happen without the space to tell one's story. True friendship requires the space of listening, holding another's story and way of being—indeed, one's authenticity—honoring its differences. To be met in that vast spaciousness is communion, the shared heart. Defense, control, power all objectify and enervate the soul of another. The place of compassionate listening is yet another sacred site where we meet God. We need a place where we can tell our story, and that is the nonjudgmental presence of a friend.

When we suffer traumas, the usual course of things seems to be that most friends eventually stop calling, expecting, rightly or wrongly, that the statute of limitations for support has passed. They have adjusted to the trauma; and their support, in part, facilitated their process of adjusting to your trauma. After a while, most people prefer not to hear about one's pain and confusion, perhaps frustrated by the hesitation to move on. It is the rare friend who is faithful, who listens well, who holds one's story empathetically, offering the sacred space for another to speak. Gerry, like Mary, has been such a friend.

During the course of the year, Gerry took it upon himself to call regularly, and, since we work at the same college, we took many walks together. Our conversation usually began with small talk but invariably segued into my sharing my heart. And while Gerry is exquisitely trained to listen—he is a psychologist after all—this commitment goes far beyond his professional capacity, for he and I have a shared history, a shared culture (Irish American Catholicism) and subculture (Jesuits), shared struggles, and, in some cases, shared neuroses, too. And so our soulful conversations, not bound by the limits of his profession, really were, despite the pain, an experience of communion—the sharing of heart and soul in the felt anguish of suffering. To share in such a way—to receive and be received—is to come home, to know the place of communion, or what Christians call the reign of God, or what Muslims call surrender, or what Buddhists call *karuna*, compassion. God, the Holy, is not an abstraction, and while we may know God in many ways, perhaps the most powerful is in the compassion of others. Mercifully, we are not without those who reveal to us the face of God in our poverty; in compassion, free of judgment, we see and hear the message we need: you are loved as you are.

What do I take from Gerry's example? An exquisite quality of presence and an astonishing capacity to listen. While I can think of many times where I have listened to another's story with compassion and understanding, the powerful experience of being listened to by good friends, especially Mary and Gerry, has revealed an important psychological truth: the experience of being heard is a profound human need and its absence comes at great cost.

Gerry's spacious capacity to listen reminded me of the character Vasudeva in *Siddhartha*, who, following Hesse's own Jungian sensibilities, clearly is the therapist who listens with nonjudgmental awareness. Vasudeva offered a model to Siddhartha, and seeing its fruit, Siddhartha naturally desired to learn to listen, too. Vasudeva *listened* to Siddhartha, and, furthermore, he encouraged Siddhartha to listen to the flowing stream of change and unity, "it is good to strive downwards, to sink, to seek the depths." Everything changes, yet change is comprehended in a unity, a matrix in which being and becoming are one. By listening well, Gerry helped me to listen to myself, to seek the depths, and thereby come to embrace my own matrix of being and becoming. The labyrinthine paths to holiness are always comprehended in wholeness.

One final thing that strikes me about Gerry is that he still very much seems like a Jesuit to me. Although he is without formal ministerial powers—he left the Jesuits, as I did, during philosophy—he nonetheless transmits, in a skillful manner, the truth of the priesthood of all believers. By his gracious, compassionate presence, marked with real wisdom and insight, he has been an *alter Christus*, another Christ. As I in turn listened to him, I could not help but remember the various important Jesuits in my life—including my great uncles, Ambrose and Paulinas—and the significant Jesuit spiritual directors, mentors, and companions along the way, beginning with my undergraduate years at Georgetown. As I reflect on my life, Jesuits and Jesuit spirituality have been deeply formative, deeply instrumental in my path of self-knowledge and self-acceptance. This realization dawned on me as Gerry and I walked one day. I felt Gerry's companionship, and, given our shared backgrounds, I resonated with his spirituality. Indeed, he occasionally drew on Ignatius's principles in helping me to sort things out. I felt as if I was sharing my soul with a Jesuit spiritual director. And, in some ways we're still Jesuits, for the values of spirituality, faith, justice, and scholarship are still very much alive for us, regardless of the context of our lives and despite our limitations and flaws.

All of us are graced with persons in our lives who show us something, reveal certain qualities that resonate within us. This resonance or vibration is a signal from the sacred, a hint of our essence that needs expression. It is not required, nor is it advisable, to take on whole cloth the life or example of another. Doing so means only living someone else's life and destiny. But as the disciples knew Jesus in the breaking of the bread—holy communion—so do we know ourselves in the breaking of bread, communion with another. We see hints, glances, notes in our soulsong, and these emerge in the holiness of friendship.

The persons in this chapter offer models of everyday holiness. In being who they are, they mirror back to me some stream in my own being. In my life, there are others who do this as well, even at a distance where I actually have little contact with them now. Greg Corrigan, a priest in the diocese of Wilmington is one. Generous of means and presence, wise and articulate, deeply in love with God, he models an exquisite life of service and presence. Brad Comann and I share deep appreciation for Buddhist spirituality, both of us seeking to make incremental growth in skillful living, despite the frequent stumbles in our inner landscapes. Chris Prucnal, in Chicago, home-schooled his two daughters while maintaining several flats. Chris has a superior can-do quality, with consummate skills in carpentry, plumbing, electrical wiring, and auto repair, all self-taught. More importantly, he is one of the calmest, most unpretentious, unflappable persons I've ever known. Grounded is the word that comes to mind when I think of Chris. My colleague Dave Livingston has demonstrated integrity in leadership, voicing truth, vision, and value in a context of compassionate awareness. Doug Villella is an optometrist in Erie who has established a clinic in Guatemala, one that has improved or saved the sight of thousands of Indians in the foothills. Jaap and Annalies Schiere-Brinkmann are Dutch friends who have worked many years for the Mennonite Central Committee in various places in South and Central America, showing extraordinary resolve and beauty in their work with indigenous people.

Each of these friends shows something lucid and potent; they angle the prism to reveal life's hues. They show something about how to be, and it resonates, and it leaves one with the feeling, "I want that" or "I want to be like that" or "I need that." Perhaps the deepest truth is "I am that too." This is not to say that I will ever be handy or resourceful in the way that Chris is but that I have certain qualities of calm, resourcefulness, and sacrifice, and these need to be expressed for me to be who I am. I may never do a Buddhist *sesshin*, as Brad, but I do feel called to practice meditation, however much my quiet time segues into daydreaming. I do not feel called to be a priest, as Greg, nor start a project in another country, as Doug or Jaap and Annalies, but the lucid quality of otherness is triggered in me by these friends, and I am reminded that a key stream of my being is giving of myself to others. And while the trajectory of my life currently emphasizes service in the form of teaching and writing, the example of my friends reminds me to actualize that particular stream in me. I need to do this to be more me. And so, for example, I take students to soup kitchens.

These are some of the persons in my *satsang*, the association with the good in my life. They "angle" something from God and become "angels" unawares. They show something of sacred embodiment, holiness in the flesh, and in doing so offer insight on how to be here. To see our examples and to internalize their lessons in our own unique way is essential to our path of holiness. These are just a few persons who have angled the prism of holiness to me. I recognize and name the gifts they have demonstrated, but above all they offer the gift of being who they are, speaking the cogent word of their lives by their habits and choices. The invitation I would leave with you here is to consider the *satsang* of your life. Who are the persons in your life who have shown exquisite compassion, calm, patience, simplicity, kindness, generosity? These persons are a profound gift, for they not only show something beautiful about being human, they show something beautiful about you, some key stream of your being, too, the evidence of which is the resonance you feel in the presence of your friend. To honor them is also honoring you. To cultivate the qualities that resonate from our friends cultivates our humanity and fulfills our vocation, for the only vocation we really have is the vocation of being human.

7

The Holiness of Brokenness

PERFECT IMPERFECTION

Broken Teacup

The monk in meditation delivers a mallet to a cup, shattering it.
He gazes at the broken pieces, and smiles,
then begins to knit them together
with liquid gold.

THIS CHAPTER IS ABOUT BROKENNESS, healing, and coming to terms with our conflicted inner world, an often chaotic array of distress and contest that mirrors the conflicted social world in which we live. The discord of our social universe is a reflection of our inner discord. And yet, in its widest scope, the external universe mirrors the deepest truth of our inner universe. If we take the grand view of things—say, the perspective from Andromeda—we no longer see ourselves at all; instead, we see a dazzling dark space illuminated by galaxies and stars. Here the brightness of the stars is meaningful only in the backdrop of darkness. The darkness holds the light. The light makes sense because of the darkness. The light *needs* the dark. The dark—the holy dark—gives relief to light.

Likewise, the inner dark is the backdrop for our light, our gifts and glories that we share with others; the dark contains the light, is the condition for the arising of our light. The dark is not evil, but a depth dimension of our being which colors our lives in unfathomably unique ways. Perhaps more so than our shining public displays, the dark provides intimations of key streams in our being. The holy dark—what Jungians call the shadow—is expressed in our urges, tendencies, untapped energies, fantasies, our neuroses and fears, even our bleak depression. Rather than flee these messages, better to listen to them, hear what they are saying, for according them space allows *their gifts* to be revealed even if these gifts are at first off-putting or disturbing. They can be demanding teachers, because they may require behaviors that are risky and threaten our comfort zone. They may demand new habits, a new career, new relationships, new ways of loving, new ways of being. While most of us, as children, have experienced primordial fears of the dark, we ought never to deny or underestimate the gift of darkness in our lives. Indeed, mystical traditions affirm that God is found in the dark. To enter the dark requires a different way of being for most of us—feeling our way by touch, not sight, processing information differently, proceeding slowly, exercising patience. This is not easy, but hanging in the dark, with great self-compassion, gives birth to new capacities and new freedoms, an authenticity born in the liminal space of unknowing.

The path of holiness begins with authenticity, our unique way of being in the world. And *our* way of being in the world—because it is human—*requires* our idiosyncrasies, flaws, and imperfections; these are not ancillary to our paths, they are essential to it. They reveal our honest complexity and give us the texture of our lives. If our lives may be likened to bread, the dark is the raw, unrefined, the whole grain, substantive and weighty. Denying husk and kernel in the batch produces airy fluff—insubstantial white bread. Embracing the whole grain of our lives produces a nourishing, substantive, weighty life. It includes everything, the whole of it, and that is precisely the call in the path of holiness: wholeness. And as we become aware of the tender, real, grainy places of our soul, we need the nourishment of companionship—and "companions," not incidentally, are those who share bread (*com-pana*). But as we move along our unique paths to wholeness, we *ourselves* become bread—we become nourishment for others. In the telling of our stories, the sharing of our struggles, and by extending our natural empathy strengthened by these struggles, we offer something substantial to others, something genuine and real borne of pain and heartache. Thus our presence becomes a gift to others and our words real soul food, free of pious sanctimony. Our examples, our efforts, and even our abject failures—and what we do with them—all these become bread for others.

Becoming bread is no more exquisitely expressed than in the Christian ritual of Eucharist, the ritual representation of the central event in Christian narrative and therefore a paradigm for our own becoming. As bread that is broken, we become food for others. But this becoming food is vivid in other traditions too. Shunryu Suzuki, a master of the Soto school of Zen, encourages faithfulness in the practice of meditation, relatively free of expectations—"I'm going to be a good meditator now"—though not without purpose and focus. Suzuki writes, "In some sense, we should be idealistic; at least we should be interested in making bread that looks and tastes good! Actual practice is repeating over and over again until you find out how to become bread."[1] For him, to "put ourselves in the oven" is the path. Meditation brings awareness of the whole of us, befriends it, and, having befriended ourselves, we are able to befriend others. In the Mahayana tradition, the natural outcome of wisdom is compassion. Every event contains the seed of wisdom and compassion. This compassion, first of all, must be directed to ourselves—showing ourselves the same kind of care we would naturally show to anyone suffering. Passing through our own struggles and thereby being baptized by pain grows the seeds of compassion others need in the trauma of their lives.

To become food for others is an ideal found in various religious traditions. The historian of religion Robert Ellwood speaks of the bodhisattva, the one who sees reality as it is, free of the limiting construct of self. The bodhisattva doesn't hesitate to throw his body before starving tiger cubs, knowing that to hesitate operates from a misguided premise in life.[2] And Shantideva, the great eighth-century Indian monk, captures the truest orientation—and outcome—of Mahayana philosophy in words that hearken back to the Sermon on the Mount:

> May I be medicine for the sick; may I also be their physician and attend to them until their disease no longer recurs.
>
> With showers of food and water, may I eliminate the pain of hunger and thirst, and during the intermediate periods of great famine between eons, may I be food and drink.
>
> And may I be an inexhaustible storehouse for the poor, and may I always be first in being ready to serve them in various ways. . . .
>
> I therefore dedicate this self of mine to the happiness of all beings. Let them smite me, constantly mock me, or throw dirt on me. . . .
>
> Those who accuse me falsely, others who do me wrong, and still others who deride me—may they attain enlightenment![3]

The poem concludes with the following aspiration, the daily prayer of the Dalai Lama;

> As long as space remains
> as long as sentient beings remain,

until then, may I too remain,
and dispel the miseries of the world.[4]

To become nourishment for others begins in the middle of our pain. There may be no better starting point in the path of holiness than acting on the awareness—in the terrible suffering and confusion we sometimes feel—that someone else not terribly far from us is going through a similar version of our own heartache and struggle. With the awareness that we are not the only ones who are suffering this particular trauma, we might pause, and even amid our terrible chaos, direct thoughts of well-being and kindness to that person or to those many persons, too. We might discover that our own pain is thereby relativized and feels less consuming. And that is the point; we feel related to others *by virtue of* suffering. No one wants needless suffering, but with an intention aligned for the good—"good" here not as some absolute standard but choices that bring life and freedom and calm—we may permit our suffering to carve out a space of compassion. This arguably is the most constructive outcome of suffering. And indeed it was the aspiration of Martin Luther King, Jr.

As my sufferings mounted I soon realized that there were two ways that I could respond to my situation: either to react with bitterness or seek to transform the suffering into a creative force. I decided to follow the latter course. Recognizing the necessity for suffering, I have tried to make of it a virtue.[5]

All of us suffer. No one escapes. All of us need compassion and healing streaming from the core place of being—the heart. In and through our traumas, we will understand with profound empathy the agonizing traumas of others. Having passed through the fire of our suffering, we are baked, we become bread for others. Our empathetic listening, the insight born of listening and deepened by our experience, becomes soul food for the other. Our self-awareness bears fruit as wisdom born of experience. After we pass through our crises, we are in a better position to serve, our humanity deepened by searing initiations. While the process of becoming is sometimes agonizing, a central dynamic for positive outcomes is befriending the process, trusting the organic growth of our paths, learning to live in letting-go space. In the end, it really means befriending ourselves. The first fruit of befriending ourselves is being here a bit more freely, a bit more at home in the universe. But quick to follow from this is the capacity to befriend others in a deeper, truer, freer way.

And so all of us stumble about doing our best, often laboring under external standards of good, evil, right, wrong. But the spiritual life seems to have profound acceptance at its core: acceptance of reality, acceptance of some embracing compassionate presence, and above all acceptance of oneself. The light and the dark dance with each other, need each other, come to completion only through the other, and this spells integration and wholeness. And being whole, being a true human person, is exactly what holiness is about. And if holiness is about our authentic way of being human, this must include the courage and *love* to be imperfect, knowing that we do the best we can under an endless host of conditions. This means that we do make mistakes, and we do hurt others. But from the perspective of Andromeda, everything has its place, everything works together in a great cosmic dance, nothing is gratuitous, not even our mistakes or failures. These are our teachers too, and probably our best ones; our failures become a peculiar nourishment for the growth of our soul. Moreover, our mistakes also become, oddly enough, a potentially fertile ground in the growth of the souls of those whom we've hurt, for the filmy boundary of love is extended by the choice to forgive, not punish, to offer unconditional love, not demand unconditional surrender.

Probably very few people consciously choose failure or personal disasters, but we sometimes do make unskillful choices that contribute to our chaos. Nevertheless, the seeds of renewal are latent in the chaos just as the seeds of trouble are latent in the calm. We all know the massive surprises in our lives—the meteor out there barreling past galaxies that crashes into our home—our inner home, our outer home, the home of our culture or religion. It happens, and the only question afterward is, "what are we going to do about it?" *How shall we be in our being here?* Authentically responding, in deep acceptance, we say yes; we allow ourselves to be open to the baking process, open to insight, self-awareness, and finally service, and thereby we arrive here more freely, we come home. Our mental or behavioral issues—cognitive and emotional habits, impurities, sins—become grist for the mill for our transformation. And whatever our particular constellation of light and dark—it is *ours.* It is our mix of weakness and flaw and charisma and compassion and wisdom and selfishness. It is who we are in our unfathomable uniqueness: there is, quite literally, no one in the universe quite like us. That, in the end, is our gift—to ourselves, to others, to the universe itself—and steeping deep this truth allows us to gather our soulsong back to God.

We all struggle in various ways on the path to wholeness. Suzuki Roshi speaks of the importance of mind weeds. These are our impurities or afflictions—our distractions, compulsions, fantasies—but there is no need to uproot them violently. They are us too, and to deny them in a dualistic pattern really is a micro-moment of self-loathing. But if we befriend them, watch them, smile at them, we allow their energies to nourish the garden. In an often-quoted poem, the great Spanish poet Antonio Machado writes,

> Last night as I was sleeping,
> I dreamt—marvelous error!—
> that I had a beehive
> here inside my heart.
> And the golden bees
> were making white combs
> and sweet honey
> from my old failures.[6]

Everything, including our failures, becomes opportunity for the sweet honey of redemption. Everything becomes opportunity in the alchemy of becoming. Everything becomes an opportunity to meet the Beloved. Indeed, as Machado's poem concludes,

> Last night, as I slept,
> I dreamt—marvelous error!—
> that it was God I had
> here inside my heart.[7]

Wisdom, while never denying the pain of hurtful choices, nevertheless often subverts our usual judgments of loss and failure, good and evil. When Thich Nhat Hanh writes that "We are imprisoned by our ideas of good and evil,"[8] he is not issuing a clarion call for antinomianism. Nor is he the standard bearer for the superficiality of New Age spirituality. Good and evil make sense only in relationship—as do most linguistic pairs (tall-short, north-south, father-son, teacher-student, writer-audience). We understand the one term because of its *relationship* to the other. Light makes sense only in relationship to the dark. And the darkness gives relief to the light. For Thich Nhat Hanh, interconnectedness, or interbeing, is the deepest truth of reality. But to lock terms in a dualistic separation denies their relational connection as well as the truth of transformation. In his commentary on the Heart Sutra, he notes that we gaze at the rose and are charmed by its beauty. We enjoy the rose owing to its excellence. Garbage, on the other hand, is bad, impure, something to be put away, buried, hidden. But wisdom sees the garbage in the blooming rose, and, in the garbage, the blooming rose. They are one and the same. Can we see the blooming rose in the garbage of our lives—our compulsions, addictions, agitation, sins? Can we make space for all of it, befriend it all, and thereby befriend ourselves? Can we see the decay latent in the growth, the growth latent in the decay? Can we do the unthinkable and let go—of tired patterns that no longer work, of concepts that no longer capture truth, of sorrow or guilt or whatever it is we nurse like a beloved invalid?

Every event becomes an opportunity for wisdom and compassion. And sometimes to weave this lesson into the fibers of our soul requires a shattering—of our categories, our sense of self, our happiness, and much more. But the shattering, while agonizing, offers the possibility for a new way of seeing things, a restructuring of identity based on new information. A new sense of identity, with new authenticities, is born, owing to the emerging gifts of darkness. But this birth into the new requires the dying of the old. The adepts, the religious *virtuosi* trained in the practice of dying well in daily deaths, see the new enfolded in the old, see the life layered in every death. Surrendering to this allows one to be in harmony with the course of things, rather than holding the tension that builds by resisting the natural process of growth and decay. Living in letting-go space, living in surrender, living in "amen" in effect creates a wider sense of identity rather than one constricted narrowly to private needs and desires. And in the surrender is freedom, above all the freedom to be here, free of striving, which always reveals the insufficiency of the present moment. Somehow the now is not enough. But not far from this logic is the notion that we are not enough. The wisdom of religion holds that we are enough as we are, not as we'd like to be; this mere presence is affirmed variously in the world's religions—the spaciousness of calm in Buddhism, the embrace of the Beloved in Sufism, the surrender of Islam or Shri Vaishnava Hinduism, the unconditional love of God in Judaism and Christianity. In these traditions and others, there is a key moment—I am here, with you, love you. Coming to this place or state is coming home. We soften, releasing the strain of becoming. This typically is a difficult lesson, especially for those of us afflicted with a tendency to perfectionism. We are set free by accepting, not an ideal standard of perfection to which we strive and which inevitably causes frustration because we do not meet it, but a different standard, a perfect imperfection, our unfathomable uniqueness, itself given texture and depth by our passions, gifts, *and* flaws. Our authenticity catalyzes our unique holiness, as the crystal flares out its beauty under its emergent conditions.

One of the conditions in our crystalline display is change. Change is often painful, but produces miracles, too. Dogen, the founder of the Soto school of Zen, held that impermanence itself *is* nirvana. Imagine the "mind twist" this could produce in us. Even early Buddhism tended to head for the hills with the awareness of the instability and suffering of the world. What would it mean to look with new eyes at the truth of change? Owing to our cognitive and emotional habits, we often don't recognize the change that is naturally unfolding in our lives and relationships. We slow things down, render change invisible, and thus we are stunned when it smacks us in the face. Rapid change, however, often is the quantum leap catalyzed by slow, unseen, growth *and* decay. To see this process with open eyes is a step toward freedom. Impermanence *is* nirvana.

The monk in the poem at the beginning of this chapter reveals a secret. His training sees beauty among the shards, new wholeness and beauty in the shattering. In the inevitable losses of our lives, we are invited to see the new beauty amid our broken shards. As Rumi says, "There's a shredding that's really / a healing, that makes you more *alive*."[9] We can internalize the wisdom from our shattering and see things anew. This may be realized only after the initial waves of heartache and loss pass. Dogen writes this poem:

> All my life
> right and wrong
> false and real tangled up together.
> But
> playing with the moon,
> ridiculing wind,
> listening to birds . . .
> All these years wasted looking at the mountain
>   covered with snow:
> this winter I suddenly see
> it's the snow that makes the winter mountain!

While Dogen's poem emerges out of particular meditative and spiritual training that seems, at first, to have little do with brokenness, what is relevant is the shattering of rigid categories—right, wrong, false, real—as convenient, tidy, conceptual boxes in which to organize—or orchestrate—the universe. Instead, this poem seems to intimate a value in the shattering of conceptual boxes and preconceived notions, a catalytic event that allows for seeing things anew. This is "beginner's mind," a vast spaciousness that makes all things possible. In this awareness, there are no things out there as discreet, separate, independent, substantial entities, but movement and flow, connection and nonseparation, "is-ness" or "suchness" (*tathata*), a dynamic dance in which being and becoming become one. In another poem Dogen writes,

> Four and fifty years
> I've hung the sky with stars.
> Now I leap through.
> Everything shatters.

To hang the sky with stars suggests ordering things. And we know the benefits of order: stability, a sense of safety, the feeling of belonging, and the emotional comfort that follows from order. But words, labels, and categories often fail to capture the mystery of complex events, and that includes just about everything in life. While humans are uniquely equipped to make meaning, indeed congenitally disposed to do so, sometimes the imposition of meaning—the drive to make sense of something—minimizes or violates the mystery of events. We all have heard bad advice in difficult times. Perhaps we were deeply grieving over the death of a loved one, and a well-intentioned friend says, "she's in a better place, now." Or, in the case of divorce, "You're better off without him." Statements such as these are particularly distressing because they, in fact, reveal the inability of the friend to be with *your* pain or to recognize the love you feel, however folded within heartache and anger.

Psychology is very good at imposing meaning—in the form of theories—on human experience. And this is valuable because there are, after all, shared patterns to human experience. But theories can be reductive, steamrolling the uniqueness of a person's story. While heuristically beneficial, theories or constructs do not always—some would say never—contain the depth and complexity of our human experience. Imposing a conceptual overlay can sometimes be an act of impatience—needing to make sense in order to move on, or, worse, it can be act of arrogance, an untoward assertion of ego and power. "Naming" expresses the power of the namer. To define the terms or to frame the story in a particular construct in a sense creates the reality. Meeting the person or event free of preconceptions or frozen judgments, eminently difficult to do owing to our habituated patterns, means living in beginner's mind. Good therapists do this, and so do good friends. To do this allows for a creativity born of authenticity and an open heart. As Suzuki writes, "In the beginner's mind there are many possibilities, but in the expert's there are few."[10]

"Beginner's mind" offers the invitation to recognize the mystery of our lives and our experiences. In the end, we are mysteries to ourselves and to one another. It is dubious and wrongheaded to presume to be able to concretize and neatly arrange all the layers of our complex personalities, needs, personal histories, and patterns of relating into manageable structures of understanding. This is not to offer justification for making choices that have negative outcomes. But things are probably always more complex than what is apparent. We might appreciate the sense of mystery in our lives—mystery as our unfathomable depths, not as a puzzle to figure out—from the perspective of Mahayana Buddhism. Early philosophers of Mahayana, especially Nagarjuna and Vasubandhu, taught that words, constructs, categories, are gravely problematic. While necessary at the conventional level, the use of conceptual constructs, in this view, actually distorts reality in two ways. First, they are the outcome of a faulty—if socially necessary—mechanism of perception. We see things out there where there are no things, no objects that are permanent fixtures of the universe existing on their own terms, independent of a complex weave of causes and conditions. The first problem then is perceptual/cognitive. We chop up the universe—we hang the sky with stars—with things, categories, constructs, and judgments, imputing, moreover, permanence to these fundamentally impermanent, interdependent streams of events. The second problem is emotional; we become attached to these permanent things—our BMW, our career, our neatly argued and well-defended take on things, our views, and perhaps above all our sense of self and identity. We crave meaning, but the meaning we make is dependent on a host of antecedent conditions, above all the gathered momentum of our sense of self and the habituated patterns used to reinforce it. Sometimes it may be a sign of mental health to hang in the chaos of a shattered identity, hang in the grey between black and white, the space of unknowing.

This is particularly difficult when life circumstances destabilize the external markers of our identity—our roles, our jobs, our web of relationships—which go a long way to reinforce our sense of self. But when these are taken away, as is often the case during profound loss, we may feel lost ourselves. And yet an opportunity exists to reimagine ourselves based on the data of our experience, and through it, emerge freer, less dependent on external markers of identity, which typically issue in the roller coaster of success and failure, praise and blame. The *Tao Te Ching* is quite blunt about these markers: "Success is as dangerous as failure. / Hope is as hollow as fear."[11] Why? They all proceed from the misguided premise of ego. The prescription: be empty. This leads to a real world counsel that is sometimes not easy to internalize: "Care about people's approval/ and you will be their prisoner."[12] Standing alone or even being alone, for many, is unbearably difficult, for it is in the quiet that we most poignantly feel the reverb of our many choices, both internal and external. Do panic, depression, anxiety, fear course through us? Can we stand the fire, let it bake us, and then let it pass, too? The process of cultivating inward strength during chaotic times is brutal, but the outcome may be a more spacious understanding of ourselves and others. This is a fruit that comes from patiently suffering the chaos of dissolution. As people hardwired to create order, hanging in ambiguity is not easy. But there are long-term benefits of doing so. As the *Tao Te Ching* affirms, "Not-knowing is true knowledge. / Presuming to know is a disease."[13] Approaching this from the Zen tradition of poetics, Yuan Li writes,

> I say a good poet does away with meaning;
>   where is the poetry?
> To this I say, get rid of words, get rid of meaning,
>   . . . *there* is the poetry!

Mystics in the world's traditions point the way beyond words, beyond our conceptual overlays. Whether from Western or Eastern traditions, there is a stream of wisdom that says all is comprehended by the All. And this notion itself destabilizes our quick judgments, our easy understandings. Good and bad are conceptual overlays that simplify the depth dimension of any moral event, however much this is necessary for social interaction. For social order, we apply these categories quickly and easily—people go to jail every day for violating them. But from another perspective, things are more complex, more richly interwoven with intriguing histories. These histories ought never to be used to dodge personal responsibility and account-ability, but our moral story is more complex than rigid black-and-white categories or oversimplified notions of causality. In the first case, to say "I'm good, he's bad," may offer a quick self-righteous fix, but it is not the truth. The truth is "I'm good and bad, and he's good and bad." Or, even prescinding from substantive categories altogether, "I have capacities for love and hate, and he has capacities for love and hate." That is the truth, the acceptance of which is our calling card into humanity, our settling into being here. In the second case, some thinkers make a distinction between linear and circular causality; the latter, which has strong parallels to Buddhist notions of interdepen-dence, speaks to the complex set of conditions that emerge in relationship. There is usually a more complex story than meets the eye, though complexity never should deny personal respon-sibility for one's contribution to discord and distress.

Forgiveness

The great saints speak to complexity without denying personal responsibility. Martin Luther King, Jr., addresses this truth in his essay "Loving Your Enemies." Forgiveness, perhaps the greatest call on the spiritual path, is a process that is organic, with a dynamism and logic unique to each person. Forgiveness can never be forced, and some psychologists defend the need to withhold forgiveness for a host of reasons. Without judging this strategy—because, no doubt, some people do feel a need to withhold forgiveness—we might nonetheless make an affective calculus to take stock of the emotional outcomes of withholding forgiveness. How happy, really, is the one harboring the hurt? Famous words in the *Dhammapada* bear witness to the negative momentum of funding our hurt. "'He insulted me, he hurt me, he defeated me, he robbed me.' Those who think such thoughts will not be free from hate."[14] There are two other key verses in this opening chapter; the first is this: "hate is not conquered by hate, hate is conquered by love; this is the eternal law." Forgiveness above all is an act of self-compassion, for the decision to forgive begins the healing of the one who has been injured. To do this rewires our consciousness, and it must be noted that the first step in this process is choice, a formal act of will. In due course, our feelings may catch up to our decision. The key element is choice and the committed resolve that follows it.

The second key verse indicates the importance of constructive formation of habits, in this case, mental habits. The first lines of the *Dhammapada* address the significance of our mental habits: "what we are today comes from our thoughts of yesterday, and our present thoughts build our life of tomorrow: our life is the creation of our mind."[15] Joy or sorrow obtains from the habits of our mind. We might be honest and ask ourselves what's the payoff for our mental choices? Are we happier? More at peace? There's little chance that we can do a radical makeover of the soul—we are who we are after all—nor is this desirable, since it would deny our authentic way of being who we are. We can, however, become aware of the unadmitted shadow elements of our lives, to bring the dark to light, and thereby become more whole. And wholeness, again, is always intimately related to holiness. A person who is whole is grounded, authentic, free to be themselves and therefore free to be with others. While we do not need to be anyone other than who we are, we do not have permission to stumble about completely blind to our unconstructive behaviors: we do need to become aware of the manner in which we are insensitive or hurtful in little or big ways. No one needs to be perfect, but we can become more skillful in our loving. And love itself is a choice, a habit, and a practice. While the natural course of things may mean that we may no longer be in relationship with a particular person, we can love that person—extend compassion and forgiveness—wish that person freedom from suffering, wish that one the joy of gathering one's soulsong back to God.

A space for the capacity to forgive is created when we realize that the act of harm does not absolutely categorize the sinner any more than the goodness of the injured. The person who causes harm also has done good things too. Even Mara, the Buddhist tempter, marshaled all his minions to bear witness to the positive merit he accrued eon after eon, even if he was the Buddhist "Satan," so to speak. Furthermore, from the Buddhist perspective of endless rebirths, we quite literally are related to one another. In this view, for example, we each have at some time been one another's mothers, a notion that may issue in a measure of tenderness even for the most benighted of us. Moreover, while we may not have committed egregious crimes, none of us is free from the acts of selfishness that have caused harm. When we recognize this, a space is created that helps us to let go of the harm caused by others. The time is finally ripe to let go. I am speaking here of the big sins—betrayal, theft, abuse, rape. Working through such harm becomes a life process, but if forgiveness is its fruit, it has to be a ripe fruit. Otherwise, it is bitter.

I once had a conversation with Locke Rush, a psychologist who lives near Philadelphia and who drew much inspiration from Bawa Muhaiyadeen, a Muslim saint from South India. He told the story of a woman who had been terribly hurt by a friend. Muhaiyadeen asked the woman to reflect on the situation, and rather than wait for the man to come to her and say, "I'm sorry," she was directed to go to the man and say "I'm sorry." This seems to turn our sense of justice upside down. The hurtful choice in all likelihood emerged out of ignorance or pain or out of a set of conditions to which the injured bears partial responsibility too. Muhaiyadeen's advice recognized this complexity. When she was ready, the woman was able to do this, and when she did, the man expressed his deep remorse for causing hurt, too. Healing occurred. Mother Teresa spells out the complexity of another's unhealthy choices this way:

> Who are we to accuse anybody? It is possible that we see them do something we think is not right, but we do not know why they are doing it. Jesus encouraged us not to judge anyone. Maybe we are the ones responsible for others doing things we think are not right. . . . Before we judge the poor, we have a duty to look inside ourselves.[16]

Thich Nhat Hanh also addresses complexity in his work for peace and justice. While never suggesting that reconciliation means "signing an agreement with duplicity and cruelty," real reconciliation arises from compassion, in turn born through the meditation on interbeing, the relatedness of all events.[17] Nhat Hanh has long been sensitive to the needs of the oppressed in his work for peace, always seeing broader social connections. In one striking example, he recognizes the complex social conditions out of which arise the Thai pirate who rapes a young girl on a boat in the ocean.[18] He obviously does not condone what the pirate does, but he sees the complex weave of personal and social histories. Similarly, he notes that there are prostitutes in Manila more because of unjust social structures than because of moral turpitude.[19] These conditions create destitution out of which arises, in the absence of viable options, the choice to sell one's body. And we are implicated in the unjust global structures that create destitution. Thich Nhat Hanh draws from the Buddhist theory of dependent origination, which examines how things arise out of a host of causes and conditions. This applies to broader social and political relationships as much as it does to personal relationships. There is always a measure of freedom in our choices, but our choices also emerge out of the host of conditions that have to do with our life situations, our personal, social, and soul histories.

Recognizing this opens a space in which compassion emerges. This is not to deny the real experience of hurt and anger, although anger itself is complex. While often serving to clarify values—its most important virtue—anger typically segues into the service of ego. Righteous anger often becomes self-righteousness. And, as is so often the case, anger all too easily issues into aggressive, hurtful behavior, typically exacerbating conflict. This redounds to our harm. A famous saying of the Buddha clearly makes this point, "You are not punished for your anger. You are punished by your anger." Most of us can recognize that we do not feel very content when we are angry. And the wisdom of the spiritual traditions and the counsel of our saints suggest that—when we are ready—we drop our self-justifying litanies and make the active choice to forgive.

We can do a calculus. What are we getting for our negativity, anger, even hate? In his life and teaching, Martin Luther King, Jr., called us to recognize that hate scars the soul of the one who hates. We therefore have a vested interest in working toward forgiveness, in letting go of our grievances and injuries, for what is at stake is our peace of mind and heart, a greater capacity to be here. But we also must recognize—and grant ourselves compassion—that this is a process, with its own organic development. We will let go when we are able to let go, and not a moment sooner.

The Dalai Lama is very clear about the importance of being aware of the negative outcomes of our mental states, and because of that, of working to change those states. Arguing that it is we who suffer the ill consequences of our anger and hatred, he says that meditation becomes "the process whereby we gain control over the mind and guide it in a more virtuous direction."[20] This process can lead, ultimately, to compassion even for the enemy. The Dalai Lama knows the dynamic of this process quite personally, having suffered and witnessed suffering from Chinese imperialism. And yet, from a broader perspective, "our enemy is our guru, our teacher,"[21] because the enemy calls forth deeper capacities for wisdom and compassion. In an earlier chapter, I quoted several verses from a hymn by Geshe Lanng-ri Tang-pa; below is perhaps the pivotal line from that hymn:

> When the one whom I had benefited with great hope
> unreasonably hurts me very badly,
> I will learn to view that person
> as an excellent spiritual guide.

It is important to keep in mind that from the perspective of Andromeda there is no enemy. Moreover, from the perspective of our religions, love of the enemy is the greatest call. Below are a few words from teachers of compassion, powerful in their unanimous call to a radical ethic of love:

> Ibn Imad (Islam): The perfect one shall render good to his enemies, for they know not what they do. Thus he will be clothed with the qualities of God, for God always does good to his enemies, even though they do not know him.[22]

> Paul Levertov (Judaism): In humility, the pious believer shall not return evil for evil, but forgive those who hate and persecute him. He shall say to himself that in the eyes of God, the sinner counts as much as himself. How can one hate whom God loves?[23]

> Mahatma Gandhi (Hinduism): It is no non-violence if we merely love those that love us. It is non-violence only when we love those that hate us. I know how dif-

ficult it is to follow this grand law of love. But are not all great and good things difficult to do? Love of the hater is the most difficult of all. But by the grace of God, even this becomes easy to accomplish if we wish it.[24]

Martin Luther King, Jr. (Christianity): Why should we love our enemies? . . . Returning hate for hate multiplies hate, adding deeper darkness to a night already devoid of stars . . . hate cannot drive out hate; only love can do that.[25]

Dalai Lama (Buddhism): I think therefore the concept of violence is now unsuitable. Nonviolence is the appropriate method. . . . Nonviolence does not mean that we remain indifferent to a problem. On the contrary, it is important to be fully engaged. . . . Nonviolence therefore is not merely the absence of violence. It involves a sense of compassion and caring.[26]

Buddha: Hatred does not cease by hate, but by love: this is the eternal truth. Overcome anger by love, overcome evil by good.

Jesus: You have learned, You must love your neighbor and hate your enemy. But I say, love your enemies and pray for those who persecute you . . . for if you love those who love you, what right have you to claim credit. Even the tax collectors do the same.

Each of these quotes calls our attention to the broader truth of love, a love in which even the enemy is embraced. Each person is our brother and sister, and the complexity of our histories, while never denying the accountability for our personal choices, extends a broader compass of compassion. In our path to wholeness we need to embrace our complexity—especially our brokenness—to recognize that our imperfection and flaws, our excesses and sin, are not separate from the cosmic dance at all. In fact, it is a vital element of the dance itself, the slingshot into transformation, the work of piecing together the shattered shards of our lives into an alchemical treasure. The broken teacups of our lives, stitched with liquid threads of gold, become a thing of great treasure and beauty.

And so everything becomes part of the path of transformation, even—perhaps especially—our errors and failures. Everything becomes the curriculum of the open heart, the place of communion. The poem at the beginning of this chapter intimates that with mindfulness, wisdom, and compassion, an alchemical transformation occurs in the brokenness of our lives. Our lives are like the monk's teacup—fragile, easily damaged. But the monk sees something extravagant and amazing in the broken pieces: a perfect imperfection. He sees something beautiful woven in and through the shattered shards. And he smiles. Again, in the brokenness of our lives, can we see the beauty amid the shards, the perfection amid the imperfection? Can we admit a presence, some inner intelligence to our paths that bears compassionate witness to our damaged lives and sees the weave of gold and beauty in them? What emerges from the brokenness is a treasure beyond words—ourselves, freer in our skin, more here. Surrendering to the process of transformation allows for the gift—our soulsong—to emerge.

Life has a way, life bursts out, sometimes with great birthing pains of newness, but life follows, life happens. Everything becomes opportunity for greater awareness, greater compassion, greater integration. Sometimes the requisite for this initiation is great loss or battering conflict or even abject failure. But many persons have testified to the spiritual efficacy of failure. It is not uncommon to hear persons who have weathered trauma or failure say, "it was the best thing that ever happened to me." But this of course is usually noted long after the hailstorm of shock and change. And this observation underscores the virtue of patience, not to mention courage, in our transitions. If we are honest, however, we never really know the value of any event. We want to win the lottery—we think it's good. We want a partner—that's good. We want to get into the best graduate school—that's good. We don't want a divorce—that's bad. We don't want a heart attack, that's bad. But none of these events has any intrinsic meaning or value. Their meaning and value are determined by us, imputed by our projections and preconceived notions. Getting into the best graduate school could have all sorts of unintended negative consequences, while having a heart attack may serve as a wake-up call to a more vital and healthy lifestyle. We know that divorce, while typically distressing, often is a choice for life, issuing in new capacities and freedoms. Bad events thus contain the seeds for greater wholeness. From death comes life. Everything becomes teacher, helping us gather our soulsong back to God.

A colleague once told me about a very difficult period in his life, the threshold moment when he needed to make a choice about the direction he wanted to go in his life. Chaos ensued, but after many months and many setbacks, events finally stabilized and he began to see the positive outcomes of his choice. He insisted that we never really know if a decision is good or bad until five years after we make it. Actually, I might suggest that any outcome can be good, if we maximize the learning, gain self-awareness, embody our wisdom in love. No matter what happens, the question is the same, "How will I be in my being here?" And yet, maybe we spare ourselves future grief by prescinding altogether from labeling our decisions as right or wrong or good or bad. Perhaps we just move in the flow of things, weaving love and kindness in the capacity with which we are endowed. In the end, we do the best we can. Our best efforts often will not meet the expectations of others, including those we love. Our best efforts have to be good enough for ourselves. If that is the case, we free ourselves from the prison of others' approval or blame.

Embracing Our Radical Humanity

The *Tao Te Ching* is rather dubious about worldly predications of good, bad, success and failure, owing to their instability, but it also bluntly asserts, "Failure is an opportunity,"[27] a potent little dictum, but again perhaps best articulated when the trauma has long passed. Yet if we are able to tone down our emotional reactivity, especially our fear, we may feel a thread through loss, failure, and even humiliation: you have been given a chance to be reborn, to begin anew. Indeed, for persons afflicted with tendencies to perfectionism, perhaps failure at some point in life may be *required* in order to break out of external determinations of acceptability and to access the deepest thread home: you are enough, and the universe is a little more complete with your being here.

In some Muslim traditions of carpet weaving, artisans deliberately weave a flaw into the carpet, thus avoiding the pretense of perfection and affirm the mundane fabric of reality. Insofar as the quest for perfection denies the whole cloth of our lives, it becomes an obstacle. Rote conforming to any external ideal spells the end of authentic personhood, the territory of the real marked always by limitation and need. The gap between the ideal and the real is exacerbated when one's sense of self is governed more by the expectations and opinions of others than by the genuine movements of heart and soul. If holiness begins with being oneself, perfectionism becomes an obstacle precisely because it denies being oneself. Being oneself, in this case, is somehow unacceptable, not good enough. Ironically, those of us who suffer the dis-ease of perfectionism may even need failure to come to deeper self-acceptance, freedom, and authenticity. The striving implied in the quest for perfection in fact pushes away the goal. I recall a time as a child, visiting, with my parents, the lake house of a neighbor and his family. I was quite small, and, though I knew how to swim, I was not a strong swimmer. The day was windy and we enjoyed the water. After a while I noticed a large inner-tube drifting away from the dock. I told our host that I'd go after it, even though I had some doubt because of the distance it had already drifted. But I swam to it anyway. And yet, I discovered to my dismay that as I approached it, the waves I made by my strokes only pushed it farther away. And, being rather small and quite tired, even when I did get close to it, my arms really couldn't grab hold of it.

Striving for perfection is like that. As an external ideal, we can never grasp it or get a lock on it. There is no perfection. And the very striving for it paradoxically makes waves that push it away. While discipline and cultivation are a part of all spiritual traditions, letting go of the thought of attainment, some sense of perfection, also has to go. An anonymous ninth-century Buddhist monk scribbled a poem on the wall of his cell, which included this last verse, "Even should one zealously strive to learn the Way, that very striving will make one's error more." The straining and the striving indicate a subtle judgment on the present moment. It's not good enough. And not far from this logic is the notion, "I'm not good enough." The path of holiness paradoxically requires the holiness of flaw, where we eventually come to terms with the sacred weave of our lives, and discover, through an encompassing presence of compassion, a perfect imperfection, a treasure beyond words.

We have opportunities in our crises, even those self-caused. Indeed, as I recall from my study of Chinese culture, the character for "crisis" means "the opportunity within the danger." It is appropriate to underscore the term "danger." We don't exactly know how we will respond to the crises that come to us, the meteor barreling past galaxies with our name on it. When this happens we don't even know if we will survive or retain some semblance of sanity. And it would be naïve to presume that positive outcomes always eventuate in our times of distress and trouble. We know people who are damaged by internal or external trauma and who do not pass through it. To use the idiom of the gospel, the reign of God does indeed break forth; miracles of love manifest themselves in forgiveness, comfort, solace, and healing, and these miracles are every bit as powerful as any command to "take up your pallet and walk." The reign of God bursts forth in the healing of broken hearts as it does in the healing of the body.

We would be disingenuous if we did not recognize that traumas sometimes create deep scars that do not heal. And there are persons who choose, if not entirely freely, bitterness and isolation. When I speak of the holiness of brokenness, I do not wish in any way to justify selfishness that causes suffering, much less illegal acts or, worse, catastrophic acts of destruction such as the cycle of violence or pillage or Holocaust. The question is, what do we do in our personal and social and political catastrophes? I recall the comment of a rabbi who was asked, after the twin towers of the World Trade Center collapsed, "Where was God?" He replied that God was climbing those endless stairs carrying axes and oxygen tanks to rescue victims. God was found in the choice to love within the catastrophe. And those firefighters, as all great holy ones, loved to the end, paying the ultimate price.

Every one of us is faced with choices, no matter how much our choices are conditioned by a host of antecedent causes. The key qualifying term here is "conditioned." Recognizing the stream of cause and effect in our lives, and the rut that is produced by our habituated patterns, we are nonetheless endowed with a measure of freedom in and through all our choices. And again, I say "measure" of freedom because most of us are burdened with psychodynamic patterns that vitiate our freedom. Guilt and fear are appropriate emotional reactions in some circumstances, for example, when we hurt those we care about or recoil from aggressive behaviors. But these emotions can also distance us from life and love when they become our automatic defaults. While they serve a purpose in our lives, we can also learn to drop them when appropriate. We can forgive ourselves. We can accept ourselves as we are. We can allow all the events of our lives to be great teachers.

If holiness means health and integration, reflecting a luminous quality of being here with a quiet joy and freedom, then we must become aware of our inner burdens, own them, name them, and where possible, *allow* them to be transformed. The vivid image that comes to mind is a gripping scene in *The Mission*, the feature film about the Jesuit missions in Paraguay in the sixteenth century. In the film, Robert de Niro plays a worldly nobleman who enters a process of conversion, a *metanoia*, a radical turn from his habituated patterns of selfishness and greed. But even in conversion, he attempted to exercise his power and strength by punishing himself with ropes strapped around his body that were tied to a host of metal barrels. He then tried to ascend the mountain, literally punishing himself with the burden of the weight. Yet his ascent was nonetheless still marked with ego and control; even the word "Enough!" of his confessor could not penetrate his heart. But finally a breakthrough did occur, and he fell weeping uncontrollably, finally realizing his own incapacity to achieve salvation by the force of his power and strength. He fell. And in the fall, there was healing. There are times when we *need* to fall. We need to let the muscles relax, stop fighting, let go of our burdens, our hold on our attachments.

In the film, the confessor "cut the cord," the rope by which he was attached to his burdens. The cord of our attachments—including our attachments to our suffering—tie us to a particular self-understanding, a way of being, or a particular way of life. And, however burdened or conflictive, these attachments become a lifeline to a particular identity. Living in letting-go space, cutting the cords of our burdens, free-falling in vast space for most of us is rather frightening, despite the freedom it promises. One might think of the astonishing account of Aron Ralston, the young hiker whose arm was pinned by an eight-hundred-pound boulder in a Utah canyon in 2003. He realized, after several days of coming to terms with death, that his only hope for survival was severing his arm, and to do this, he first needed to break his arm. The idea that saved his life was not that his arm needed to be severed, which he knew he had to do, but that he had to break his arm first, so he could cut around the broken bone. This life-saving idea came only after he had "died," that is, came to terms with death. Severing the last "twine-like tendon," he said, was like "sticking his arm in a cauldron of magma."[28] And yet the lesson couldn't be clearer: sometimes, pinned down by a burden that weighs heavily on us, slowly draining our life away, we need to do the unimaginable: sever the last twine-like tendon of attachment, despite the pain. Sometimes, we need to cut the ties that keep us from soaring, indeed, keep us from life itself. While doing this is unbearably painful—we all have our cauldrons of magma—it is often the only door to new life, a life we could never envision. In fact, Ralston said that he would never trade what he has gained from his ordeal for the arm he lost. Our catastrophes bear the seeds of new life, new futures.

But, oddly, we are often more attached to our pain than to our pleasures. We allow our suffering to shape our identity. What happens when we let go of this, too? In *The Mission*, while the nobleman was told he was not required to suffer need-lessly, his suffering, his own inner battle, *was* necessary to the extent that it finally wore him out. Exhausted, he finally let go. Moreover, he underwent a shift in self-concept, from proud warrior to burdened penitent. Each of those identities came lay-ered with self-constructions, reinforced by habits of thought and action. The burdened penitent—"I am a sinner"—was rein-forced by his muscular self-assertion: I will humiliate myself to achieve salvation. But forgiveness is not earned. It is pure gift. Both Buddhist and Christian traditions warn of the degree of selfishness that shows up in ongoing guilt and remorse. Chris-tianity urges us to be open to the love of God and to recognize that neurotic guilt is a kind of inverted hubris. And Buddhism too warns of the psychological ill health that obtains in obsess-ing over our unwholesome choices. Recognize the hurtful choice, resolve to engage in right action—right action here meaning wholesome and life-giving choices—and be done with it. But many of us linger and dally with guilt and shame, secretly validating some ancient self-concept. But at some point we need to ask, Can we forgive *ourselves*? And if not, why not? Can we stand naked, and just be who we are, in our radical humanity, replete with shadow and light, glory and pain, perfect imper-fections?

We have endless opportunities for growth and constructive change. While I speak about transformation and alchemical change, there is also a call not to change at all, but simply to be who we are, to accept ourselves in our entirety—the light, the dark, the lamb, the lion. None of us should be required to undertake a radical makeover of the soul. This is neither possible nor desirable. We are who we are after all, and yet, we also are capable of maximizing our learning and growing more skillful in our loving. This is the promise of the religious path. And it includes bearing witness, with lavish compassion, to the whole of our lives, those great movements of love and inspiration and the very real moments of need, desire, urges, and urgencies. Then everything, even our mistakes and failures, become an occasions for our own holiness—opportunities to heal and to be healed, to love, forgive, create, renew, grow in our exquisite humanness. And the kiss of God is in all this. This admits, with kindness and compassion, that the path of self-discovery is sometimes pressing and difficult. But the promise is this: in finding ourselves, we discover the Beloved. We come home.

8

Holiness

THE ROAD HOME

Speak

Speak, my soul,
your deep longing,
your grief over lost love
and fleeting passion.

Speak, my soul,
your voice
with blue sky clarity and
calm confidence
stilling every chaos
and confusion.

Speak, my soul,
your deep freedom,
your deep gratitude
for all of it:
bliss, loss,

the angel-voiced innocence of a beautiful boy,
the heartbreak of breaking hearts,
the pain of change,
the miracle of change.

Speak, my soul,
your deepest love,
your truest love,
the love that penetrates all loves and every infidelity.
The love that leads to life.

───────────────────────────

WE ARRIVE AT THE END of this book, but, to recall the words of T. S. Eliot, the end is always a beginning, or as I have written elsewhere, every true leaving is a footfall home. In the forward spiral of our lives we move forward, fall back, search new territories of wisdom and compassion, often bewildered by a lack of maps, but we move forward nonetheless, one foot following the next. In this book, I have tried to make forays into holiness, sometimes tending more to the poetic than the didactic. Poetry, emerging from the heart and soul of the poet, can trigger memory, feeling, and insight in the listener. And poetry, like meditation and self-awareness, is about listening. And so, too, is holiness. We listen to the questions emerging from our being and answer them in the cogent word of our lives. What does it mean to be human? What does it mean to be here? How shall I be in my being here? Holiness is a lucid response to these questions. It is both path and goal, because it embodies the goal in the path. It is the road home and home itself.

Holiness—far from the icons of halos and heavenly gazes—is nothing more than quality human presence or exquisite humanness. Perhaps as with other elusive terms—such as "religion" or "pornography"—we know it when we see it. We see the fruit of lives lived well—calm, kindness, gentleness, strength, compassion, care, freedom, spaciousness. No rush, no hurry. The saints, the holy ones, are here. We see in these lives a captivating luminosity. Something shines in lives lived well. And we, too, through practice, cultivation, and grace, sometimes *do* access strengths we never imagined; we *do* say potent things with compassion and calm; we *are* less preoccupied with our own needs and therefore more free in the presence of another. And, then, we shine, too.

There is a magnetism and beauty to holiness, and it is attractive. It is attractive in and of itself but because in some sense we see also ourselves and our own beauty. In witnessing the holiness of another, we behold mirrors of our becoming. We access deep streams of our being, capacities that we ourselves have or are invited to tap. Something resonates in the example of the holy one, and we say, "I want that, too." It is not surprising that such attraction sometimes segues into romantic attraction, the attraction itself merely revealing the deep human need for intimacy and communion. And that is what holiness is about in the end: communion—with self, others, and God. And God, for me, implies the unconditioned real, the compassionate intelligence of the universe somehow woven into every phenomenon and event of our lives. This depth dimension or presence in our lives lovingly and relentlessly calls us home, indeed *is* our home.

The Really Real

This depth dimension of being might also be called the really real. It is really real because it is saturated with being and meaning. Getting the promotion, the publication, the latest SUV—this all is real, just not really real; these things are passing, they arise out of conditions, they do not last. They are external markers of success and come with a dangerous price. When they pass, as they inevitably will, so will the contentment we derive from them. We may nod to them, we may smile at them, but our true home is free of success and failure, praise and blame, gain and loss, the roller coaster pattern of our lives. The goal is to arrive at genuine communion *now*, not when we've finally reached success in the marketplace or in the monastery. In one sense, we don't need to rack up endless hours of meditation, endure steamy sweat lodges, or land that bungalow by the sea to know that we've arrived. We do not need to justify our being here to others or even to ourselves. We are enough, as we are, now. This is not to say we are perfect. The saints *themselves* are not perfect. The saints are *themselves*, their authenticity shaped by experience, wisdom, value, and resolve. They answer the question of being with the cogent word of their lives.

Holiness requires authenticity. Authenticity implies self-acceptance and genuine humility, free of external determinants of value. From this place our creativity becomes more natural and spontaneous, less tainted by ego and the need for achievement. In the Oscar-winning film *Chariots of Fire*, we see a study of motivation in the racing careers of two British sprinters. Harold Abrahams, a Jew, was driven by a competitive spirit that extended to his legal training; he was prepared, as his character says, to battle each member of the British political establishment if need be. His sprinting was an expression of his competitive fire. Eric Liddel, the Scottish minister who also was a consummate sprinter, ran because he could "feel His pleasure." He recognized his gift as a gift from God. Not to run, in his view, would be an act of contempt before God. So he ran, his doing flowing from his being. As one accesses the soul, folded in the embrace of the Beloved, one cannot but express oneself in and through one's creativities. And these in turn become gift for others, the substance of one's soulsong back to God.

The really real concerns that which endures. Coming to understand this in the uniqueness of our lives requires intimacy with *ourselves*, the key to our holy unfolding. But this intimacy itself, given the wisdom of the world's religions, is enfolded within sacred intimacy. And while there is a rich diversity of words describing the sacred, offered by sages, saints, prophets, shamans, and scholars of the world's religions, one thing seems to be clear in the testimony of the holy ones: you are here, with us, love us, you being the Beloved, the Holy One, God. Intimate communion with the ultimate real will be endlessly diverse, owing to the endless diversity of humans; but the fruit is strikingly similar in the lives of the holy ones: calm, peace, courage, nonviolence, compassion.

While there is often considerable disagreement concerning the nature of the real, what is relevant here is the universal testimony of saints and sages that there *is* an ultimate real, intimacy with which provides a key to our authentic humanity and our destiny. This really real is here and uses every event and encounter and success and failure to track us down, call us to surrender, to open our hearts to be the person we have always been and have always been called to be: ourselves. Elizabeth Kubler-Ross eloquently captures the organic wisdom of our unfolding destiny.

> To see the truth is to know that no matter what may be happening, the universe is moving in the direction it is supposed to. That is why we can be in the discourse, but our destiny is never off course. Whether the events in our lives are the best or the worst, the world is set up to work, it is coded in a way that brings us to our lessons. It is designed to move us to joy, not away from it, even when we think things are going in the wrong direction. There is no problem or situation that God cannot deal with. The same is true for us.[1]

Becoming a True Human Being

When we live life as ourselves, we find the sacred thread home. And when we live this truly we become gift to ourselves, to others, to God. We speak, with our lives, the cogent word of our being; our lives then become soulsong, the song for which the universe has long waited. This is our holiness, our gift to ourselves and to others, the fruit of our authentic becoming.

This process may include looking at and even adopting elements of the example of others, and this is reasonable given the universal search for wholeness. But adopting the example of others will eventually become constricting and oppressive if it is not qualified as one's own. While mentors and guides provide important models of ways of being, any contrived conforming to an external pattern will eventually result in frustration and alienation. The reason for this is simple: it is someone else's path, not yours.

For our paths home, we are first required to be ourselves; only then are we able to gather our soulsong back to God. This does not presume that our song may be a sweet little ditty, always upbeat and joyous. There are dark tones in the greatest songs and poetry of the world. The dirge, the lament, the wailing cry—all this is soulsong, too, because it is real. To give voice to our lives, to sing our song, means above all to be ourselves, that is, to live and to speak authentically, even if this means—as it does for most of us at one time or another—suffering through anguish, heartache, and darkness. Nor does it mean always suffering well, as if we have halos fixed above our head. While it is always best to maximize self-compassion and compassion for others, we are not perfect. Depression, anxiety, or externalizing our pain will sometimes be part of the path to wholeness, too. And wholeness is the end of holiness.

To stand in our authentic selves is not easy, especially when it goes against the tide of public opinion, whether in a relationship, at work, or in the broader culture. This presumes that authenticity sometimes requires a leave-taking—so needing to be true to who you are may require a leave-taking, whether it be from a relationship, or a career, or a habituated way of being. This I take to be Mary Oliver's message in her great poem "The Journey," in which, in the poignant night of leaving, the voices of nay-sayers begin to die down and one slowly begins to hear another voice, one's own. Authenticity is the first, best, and most important step in our labyrinthine path home. And it is by no means easy to attain. Moreover, there are times when we may not even know what our authentic self is, given longstanding, habituated patterns conditioned by a host of stimuli found in family, society, and religion. We are also often quite good at fooling ourselves.

In another Oscar-winning film, *Dances with Wolves*, a Sioux holy man, played by Graham Greene, addresses John Dunbar (played by Kevin Costner), the U.S. Army officer alienated by the carnage of the Civil War who gradually adopts Sioux values and culture as his own. The character played by Greene says, "You are on the path of becoming a true human being. And this is encouraging." Becoming a true human being, authentic and real, is at the core of holiness. And this occurs over time, slowly, in the back and forth process of growing, learning, stitching cells of love in our chrysalis of becoming. Witnessing this process in others is encouraging, because it generates strength and inspiration in our own path of becoming.

Rumi writes the following quatrain underscoring the single most important requirement for full human living—authenticity. When we are truly ourselves, we begin to express the holiness of our lives.

> For years, copying other people, I tried to know myself.
> From within, I couldn't decide what to do.
> Unable to see, I heard my name being called.
> Then I walked outside.[2]

An important dynamic is clear here. We are often overwhelmed and bewildered by the array of thoughts and feelings and concepts that stream through our minds. In our exhaustion, we may finally befriend ourselves, say yes to who we are in our rich complexity. But Rumi's poem also suggests the importance of listening. When we listen well, we hear the call to step out, to be who we are, to live our lives in the way that is appropriate and true for us. This being who we are is facilitated by the love of the Beloved. We hear our name; we are called forth. We know ourselves in the call. Both Jesus and Buddha offered one simple word to disciples, "Come." We may hear the call in any number of ways—the felt ardor of a love relationship, the suffering of transition, the urge to give voice to new self-expression, the resonance we feel in the presence of a holy one—all this is call. Indeed, the word "vocation" intimates the response to call, to give voice to the invitation to come. But it is often difficult to know ourselves, much more so when we merely imitate what we have seen or heard or merely identify with roles.

The process of coming home is often painful, for it can destabilize our accustomed patterns of being in the world. We may even recognize that our habituated patterns are not particularly conducive to our best selves, but they at least offer the comfort, however dubious, of the familiar. The familiar, no matter how unhelpful or unwholesome, at least provides an organizing schema by which our expectations are met. The payoff is a sense of order, no matter how disordered the ways of being may be. But the unfamiliar is frightening, demanding responses that appear far beyond our capacities. Some of us may be tempted to return to former ways of being, for, despite pain, it nonetheless offers a certain comfort. It's far more vulnerable to stand in the new, far more frightening to be free.

And so many of us choose struggle over freedom. We resist change, above all death—not only physical death, but also the death of our self-concepts, our relationships, our accustomed ways of being in the world. Every change implies death. And it seems the better part of wisdom to become practiced at befriending death rather than fleeing it or fighting it, perhaps meeting it with kindness and compassion. As we become practiced at living our dying we may notice a certain calculus to our suffering: the degree of our pain is proportional to our clenched hold. As those who love to ride horses teach us, it is always better to ride loose in the saddle. Holding on too tightly will cause us to fall.

Surrendering in Love, Surrendering to Love

Holding the reins loosely, that is, holding our attachments lightly, living free of undue efforts to control—this is living in letting-go space. Living in letting-go allows for breath and life to flow. It creates the space required for movement and life. There is actually considerable space in the interstices of our body's cells which allow life forces to flow; there is comparatively vast space between electrons and neutrons, and the vast space in the cosmos upholds endless planets and galaxies. Space is the condition for life, for whether on the cellular or cosmic scale, it allows for growth, movement, change, and flow. On an interpersonal level, we know that space is the condition for freedom and growth, too, allowing our unique solitudes to unfold in creative expression. But to create space means to let go, to live a life of surrender.

> There's a necessary dying, and then Jesus is breathing
>   again.
> Very little grows on jagged
>
> rock. Be ground. Be crumbled, so wildflowers will
>   come up
> where you are. You've been
>
> stony for too many years. Try something different.
>   Surrender.[3]

Living in surrender is the key to holiness, for surrender here implies trust; it surrenders control of that which we cannot control—and that's often quite a lot indeed. It seems that the saints are those who radically trust the organic process of life's unfolding, woven as it is with a broader vision of grace and gift. And grace here is not only the comforting moments of good counsel, but, in the words of Ram Dass, fierce grace, the hurricane gales of loss and change that demand a dying to permit a rising, releasing greater capacities for authenticity and freedom. But there is no resurrection without death, no release of the heart without the release of ego, no nirvana without the end of a limited sense of self. A resolute faith in our holy unfolding, held in the embrace of the Beloved, seeds integration and releases fear, the worst toxin to life. Earlier, I wrote of the holy dark of our dark nights. Bede Griffiths, the great exponent of interfaith dialogue, once spoke of a profound conversion as a young adult in which he passed through great darkness. Afterward, the words of John of the Cross, evoking the Holy One, came alive for him: "I will lead you by a way you do not know to the secret chamber of love." Sometimes darkness itself is the unanticipated path to deeper love, the love that penetrates all loves and every infidelity, the love that leads to life.

Love is the clearest mirror by which we see and know ourselves. Love bears all things, weaving becoming with the thread of being. That is to say, love accesses some depth dimension of our being even as we undergo growth and change. The saints are skilled in loving well and living wisely; they unselfconsciously cultivate a way of being in the world that is especially magnetic. Their innate luminosity is perhaps less clouded by certain habits of mind and will that do not conduce to communion. This is not to say that they are perfect. Their limitations are real, probably most of all to themselves. But such awareness and self-acceptance actually contribute to their magnetism.

But this magnetism is enhanced, at least in part, because we project it upon them. This idealizes the holy one, renders a disservice both to the saint as well as to us. By idealizing the other, we subtly denigrate our own gift and beauty, and this gift is our exquisitely unique mystery of passion and pain, sin and saintliness. The saints know this about themselves. And our call includes coming to terms with ourselves, accepting ourselves in our *wholeness*, not just the good part. Embracing *our* realness, accepting ourselves as we are, is the first and most important step in being here. Doing so allows us to be who we are, the first and most important step in our unique paths of holiness.

Each of us is unfathomably unique, and this uniqueness enriches the great cosmic symphony, to refer again to the metaphor once used by Desmond Tutu. Tutu called us to recognize that the music of God is utterly incomplete without the crystal ting of the triangle. Every instrument plays a part in the symphony, and some may be more pronounced than others. But the symphony is incomplete without the discreet notes of every single instrument. Our own path to holiness begins when we recognize that *we* are a particular instrument built to sing a soulsong back to God.

When I was studying Sanskrit in India, my mentor, Dr. Mudumby Narasimhachary, gave me a small sandalwood statue of Krishna playing a flute, a classic image in Hindu iconography. And he wrote at the base of the statue these Sanskrit words: *nimittam matram bhava savyasachin*, "Be only an instrument, O Arjuna."

Krishna counsels Arjuna to be a tool in the service of the divine, much in the same way that St. Francis sang "make me an instrument of your peace." But the graphic image is God playing a flute. Be an instrument. You are a musical instrument of the Divine. Let the Divine *play you*. And, of course, the only way that the flute can be played is if it is empty. And so *we* need to be empty, too, in order to release stopped-up sound and voice. Our lives then become not only soulsong *back* to God but soulsong *of* God, too. This way of being is intimated in the poetry of the Sufis, none more so than Rumi.

> Who is the luckiest in this whole orchestra? The reed.
> Its mouth touches your lips to learn music.
> All reeds, sugarcane especially, think only
> of this chance. They sway in the canebrakes,
> free in the many ways they dance.
>
> Without you the instruments would die.
> One sits close beside you. Another takes a long kiss.
> The tambourine begs, *Touch my skin so I can be myself.*
> Let me feel you enter each limb bone by bone,
> that what died last night can be whole today.[4]

Our authentic personhood is intimately related to the Holy, the really real, the most enduring reality. Taking this in, seeing the sacrality of the external universe and our own inner universe is the encounter where we finally meet the Holy One. This is a place of great freedom. The beloved meets the Beloved, and we come alive. *"Touch my skin so I can be myself."* There we know the kiss of God. While the bliss of sacred intimacy—the kiss—brings us home, we know that life sometimes *suffers* us into receiving the kiss of God. But this too issues in deeper freedom, humility, and new capacities for being here.

We are on the way home, and everything is angled to bring us there. *Not* to live this will cause suffering, because we are stifled, bottling up beauty that must be expressed. Who we are *as we are* is unfathomably unique, and the way we live our being here, free from the constrictive expectations of others, free of unconscious identifications with roles, free of the suffering of perfection, releases our creativity and authenticity, the song of God in our soul, a song that creation itself needs for its own completion. For, if the flap of a butterfly's wings somewhere in the Amazon forever changes the structure of the universe, how much more our soulsong of love and kindness and creativity? The universe *needs* us and says, you are valuable, you are dear, you have something to offer. Come. Live your life. Enjoy the sweet freedom of being here.

Sacred Mirror

Sometimes, given human tendencies, this is not easy to believe, especially if we are prone to harsh self-judgments and the poison of comparison. These we may drop, for they speak the lie of inadequacy and insufficiency. Who we are *as we are* is more than sufficient; we, in our unique constellation of gift and glory and absurdity and sin, become like the pearl, formed by soft, subtle pain. Like the pearl, we too are perfect in our peculiar imperfections, a treasure beyond words. This does not mean abdicating our inner work, nor does it mean that we are acceptable despite our imperfections. We are acceptable *in* and *through* them. Moreover, our exquisite humanness is impossible without the whole of us. And this requires profound self-acceptance and self-love. For those drawing from the resources of religion, this healing acceptance can be tangibly felt in prayer and meditation. Being received as we are, not so much in our glory (this is easy to accept) but in our limitations and flaws, releases capacities for self-acceptance. We need to give this to ourselves as well; doing so breeds a confidence and joy in being here. But it is also an unfathomable grace to feel such acceptance from another. Most of us are more than aware of our imperfections and our occasional—or even habitual—unwholesome choices of mind and heart, and some of us, owing to neurosis or neurons or both, are never far from guilt or shame. Cultivating self-acceptance releases the song, and this is sometimes mercifully catalyzed by the healing love of another.

We've all encountered the comforting presence of persons who are really here—content in themselves, swimming in a sea of peace. These people are found in toll-booths, garages, classrooms, in offices and airplanes. The unknown grandmother on the plane, the kind stranger on the street, the Mary Snyders and Dinesh Kheras of our lives—these people are not famous, but they are luminous, exquisite examples of what it means to be human. While the persons in this book all had plenty of projects, what marks these people above all is the care and attention they have given to their greatest project, allowing their humanity to unfold in a context of love and faith. They are *themselves*, authentic and true; when we witness this, we meet the Holy One. And when we are *ourselves*, authentic and true, we meet the Holy One within. The lives of the saints, enfolded in the Holy One, are beautiful. But we cannot let ourselves be seduced by such beauty, because our project is to know and to express *our* beauty, our exquisite humanness. Our call is to know and to hear our own magical ting of the triangle. Loving ourselves as we are, lavishing ourselves with the compassion we naturally give others, this is the first step in being here.

The saints, those skilled in the human way, offer the greatest gift—being a mirror. We sometimes look into real mirrors and do not like what we see. This is often painful and humbling. Certainly, we may be less than impressed with our physical features and the toll age takes on them, but we also may have awareness of our inner features that causes us embarrassment or shame. In this case, seeing ourselves in our poverty and brokenness could be unbearable unless held in a broader context of love. But standing in the holiness of God, and especially the holiness of God embodied in another, allows us the courage to see ourselves in our completeness, the light and the dark, the saintliness and sin, the selfishness and selflessness. The gift in this particular fire is hardly the burning away of all our sins and negative predilections, but actually embracing them, even honoring them, because in doing so we honor ourselves, our unfathomable uniqueness, incomplete without the play of light and dark. Embracing the whole of us begins the weave of our holiness, begins stitching the sinews of someone really here. This becomes a great gift, and not for ourselves alone, for in really being here we can finally be here for others.

When we look into the mirror of another we have endless opportunity for discovery. What do we see in the mirrors of saints and saintliness? We see ourselves—our truest selves, our deepest freedom to be who we are fully alive, free. Saints are those who are clear, those with "little dust in their eyes," as the Buddhist texts hold. The mirror of the beloved reflects deep streams in our being. As windows to the soul, lovers see the other and also themselves, generating the blissful experience of feeling at home with the other and themselves. But the saints also offer clear mirrors of our being, our at-homeness with ourselves and the world. Through the holiness of the saints we see ourselves in our own belovedness and in that encounter are empowered to genuinely be who we are: beings of love for love, holy ones, too.

In *Fierce Grace*, Ram Dass and several of his companions describe their encounter with Neem Karoli Baba, a saint from Northern India. Ram Dass said that he felt *known* by the guru, but known in compassion and acceptance. The universal truth of his particular experience is that profound healing occurs through keen listening or even the mere being of others, the holy ones in our lives

Ram Dass felt held by his guru. He felt seen, *known,* and it was a knowing that was coextensive with love. Being *known-in-*

love, Ram Dass fell in love with God and God's people, creating service foundations, writing books, giving retreats, lecturing around the world. Being *known-in-love* releases our capacities for love. In rare moments we may have felt this, too, feeling a searing loyalty born by healing love. I recall a very powerful experience when I was a Jesuit novice many years ago; while I had long felt an intimacy with Christ, during the thirty-day retreat I again felt seen, held, loved *as I was* by Christ. The overwhelming feeling of loving acceptance has its own internal dynamic: it spontaneously leads to loyalty and commitment, "I will do anything because you have done this." In many ways, this happened again recently, as I made an eight-day retreat at the Jesuit Retreat Center in Wernersville, the former novitiate of the Maryland Province of the Society of Jesus. On that retreat, in that place, I had a peculiar feeling of coming home. Having been there as a student twenty-five years ago, I had plenty of material to review, some of it joyful, and some it painful, particularly the ending of my marriage. The pain, and my own complicity in it, was raw, but it was held in an ambient quiet, an extraordinary calm that contains all. In that calm, I could see again the Holy One and felt stunned again by the endless invitation of love.

For Ram Dass, being known-in-love catapulted him into a life of love and service. Profound acceptance by another stimulates profound self-acceptance, quite possibly the beginning and end of spiritual practice. For from self-acceptance and proper self-love comes right action. Our actions become true, less motivated to meet unmet needs. The signature of ego in our work begins to fade. One of Ram Dass's companions addressed the quality of presence of Karoli Baba. He said that it was not surprising in the least to see that the guru loved the world. That's the job description of a saint, as it were. What *was* surprising, said the disciple, was the intensity of the love which *he* felt for the world merely by being in the presence of the saint. In the presence of holiness, we come to know our truest selves and our capacity for connection with the world. But we need not lament that we never met Mother Teresa or the Dalai Lama. All we need to do is to register what happens in our hearts when we are with someone who loves well. And these people are not at all far away; they are our companions, parents, mentors, partners, and children. They are the grandmothers whom we meet on the plane.

Loving Ourselves, Loving Others

The principal dynamic in our holiness requires knowing and being ourselves, however much this is informed by the holy ones in our lives. Perhaps the first step in a life of holiness is to recognize our own unfathomable uniqueness. There is no one in the universe—and there never was and never will be—someone who quite sees the world precisely the way you do. No one with the same constellation of gifts and intriguing tendernesses, vulnerabilities, tendencies, all the issues that we work on yet visit us enough times in order that we might finally make peace with them, accept them, accept ourselves. As we are. Not as our persona. Not as we'd like to be. Not as others expect us to be. And not because we unconsciously buy into certain self-understandings conditioned by religion, society, family, or fear. Deep self-acceptance is the thread that wends our way home. And perhaps it is this home, the home of ourselves, that we come to know—and love—for the first time.

From this love, we find our capacity to love others more freely; we see others as the unique creatures that they are, singular constellations of love and longing, wending their way in intriguing paths of authenticity. Our holiness is the call to authenticity woven in the broader compass of love. And this real personhood includes, *requires,* our soft pain, our flaws and failures, our longing and need. But the message of the holy ones is that love is here. Love redeems. Love bears all things. Love is the master weaver, spinning the sacred threads of our lives, preparing us, like the chrysalis, for an unknown flight, or shaping us, like a pearl formed in the hidden silence of the deep, perfect in its peculiar imperfection, a treasure beyond words. We are all treasures beyond words, perfect imperfections.

Our imperfection is the tender spot calling us to truth, reality, and profound love. Religions insist that such self-unfolding is not merely a psychological path, that the whole of it—our glory and pain—is enveloped in a broader compass, a deeper intimacy with reality. God, Buddha-nature, Krishna, Allah, the goddess, Christ—some inner wisdom holds us up, whispers the eternal truth—*you are beloved to me.* Each of our paths, replete with our success and failure, is *ours,* and the way we live becomes gift to ourselves and to others. We walk our path, but we are never abandoned, we are never alone. The pearl, our beauty in and through the whole of it, often mercifully mirrored by others, emerges in due course, organically as if of its own accord. And we do well to remember that the pearl, in Zen poetry, is the inner plan, sacred wisdom and compassion folded into all.

The act of love, in service, relationship, even in our darkness shapes our authenticities, forms our holiness, which then becomes gift to others. Rumi writes,

> Let love lead your soul.
> Make it a place to retire to,
> a kind of cave, a retreat
> for the deep core of being.[5]

To live our path with as much awareness, courage, and love as possible—and in doing so discover our selves—is the path home, the path to our self, enveloped as it is in the arms of the Beloved. There are tools to develop this awareness, including the resources of religion, psychotherapy, indeed every event of our lives, for in the end, everything becomes a teacher, an occasion for wisdom and compassion. To do this with awareness is to be on our holy path, the road home.

To review the lives of holy ones is a celebration of spirit—the human spirit and the divine spirit weaving layers of beauty upon beauty. And this is an occasion for gratitude. That gratitude must also be offered for ourselves and for the many unseen acts of love and wisdom emerging from our own holy unfolding. We know that the words we speak sometimes become a cogent word, as if some gift or grace lifts them from us, and we touch another. In an exquisite moment, we leave tired banality and offer something rich, deep, a soulful word, above all, our very authenticity, and this in turn becomes the cogent word by which we speak our lives. Our authenticity, our real humanity, bravely lived, becomes our holiness.

To be ourselves, authentic and true, requires lavish self-acceptance and self-love. It also requires courage, for it will occasionally mean going against the tide of public opinion or developing new capacities and freedoms. To be who we are, our authenticities formed by experience and wisdom, undoubtedly means growing in heart, growing in courage. Indeed, it means doing something brave every day. And so, as I began this book with a poem in which I wished to speak to the giftedness of our lives, I will close this book with a final poem, "Every Day Do Something Brave." May it offer encouragement in the process of opening our hearts, knowing the holy kiss, speaking the cogent word of our lives. May it bring blessing and courage as we make the greatest journey of all, the journey home.

Everyday Do Something Brave

What is it today that will stretch your edge?
Pull you to places you never dreamed possible?

See them strapping on canisters in the subzero wind,
preparing to make the great ascent;

or hunting hidden orchids somewhere in the Amazon,
sweat splashing as machetes slash the path;

or rocketing fast on the Salt Flats, their jowls flapping comically,
the land speed record broken once again.

Where is the place beyond the possible for you?
Your Everests quietly await.

Try:

speaking the truth when terrified to;
dropping your ancient anguish,
so nursed and fed like a beloved invalid;
escaping the prison of others' approval;
standing alone;
being alone;
being yourself;
loving yourself;
being here in some sweet simplicity;
simply
being here.

Everyday do something brave.

Surrender your fear.
Surrender your shame.
Surrender.
Make that call.
Open your heart.
Touch.
Kiss.
Let yourself be kissed again.

Learn to dance, my friend.
And gather your soulsong back to God.

Acknowledgments

Grateful acknowledgment is made to the following persons or publishers for use of excerpts or selections from the following materials:

Coleman Barks, *Birdsong,* copyright © 1993 by Coleman Barks, used by permission of Coleman Barks.

Coleman Barks and John Moyne, *Open Secret: Versions of Rumi,* copyright © 1984, originally published by Threshold Books, used by permission of the publisher.

Coleman Barks, *The Soul of Rumi,* copyright © 2001 by Coleman Barks, reprinted with permission of Coleman Barks.

Robert Bly, *The Winged Energy of Delight: Poems from Europe, Asia, and the Americas,* copyright © 2004 by Robert Bly, used by permission of Robert Bly.

John Stratton Hawley and Mark Juergensmeyer, *Songs of the Saints of India,* copyright © 1988 by Oxford University Press, reprinted by permission of John Stratton Hawley and Mark Juergensmeyer.

"Now Is the Time" and "Get the Blame Straight" from *The Gift,* by Daniel Ladinsky, copyright © 1999 by Daniel Ladinsky, used by permission of the author.

"When Death Comes," from *New and Selected Poems* by Mary Oliver, copyright © 1992 by Mary Oliver, reprinted by permission of Beacon Press, Boston.

"In Blackwater Words," from *American Primitive* by Mary Oliver, copyright © 1978, 1979, 1980, 1981, 1982, 1983 by Mary Oliver, reprinted by permission of Little, Brown and Co., Inc.

"Sweet Darkeness" from *The House of Belonging* by David Whyte, copyright © 1997 by David Whyte, used by permission of the author and Many Rivers Press (www.davidwhyte.com).

Notes

1: Toward Holiness

1. *Mother Teresa*, produced and directed by Ann and Jeannette Petrie, 82 minutes, Petrie Productions, 1986, videocassette.
2. Herman Hesse, *Siddhartha*, trans. Hilda Rosner (New York: New Directions, 1951), 120.
3. Ibid., 122.
4. Ibid.
5. The Zen poetry in this book has been adapted and compiled from various traditional sources by Ronald Kidd, a Zen teacher in Chicago. I am grateful to Ron for sharing his insight with my students at Oakton Community College and for opening me to the world of Zen poetry.

2: The Holiness of Fire

1. Albert Schweitzer, *Reverence for Life* (Kansas City, Mo.: Hallmark, 1971), 28-29.
2. John S. Strong, *The Experience of Buddhism* (Belmont, Calif.: Wadsworth, 1995), 24.
3. The Dalai Lama, *An Open Heart* (Boston: Little Brown, 2001), 15.
4. From the Web page of Sivaraksa: www.sulak-sivaraksa.org.
5. Bobbye Middendorf, "Chicagoan Kathy Kelly: Agitating for Peace" *Conscious Choice* (June 2004), reproduced at www.conscious choice.com/cc1706/kathykelly1706.html.

3: The Holiness of Energy

1. T. S. Eliot, *Four Quartets* (New York and London: Harcourt Brace Jovanovich, 1971), 59.
2. *In Praise of Krishna: Songs from the Bengali,* trans. Edward Dimock, Jr., and Denise Levertov (Chicago and London: University of Chicago, 1967), 21.
3. The Dalai Lama, *An Open Heart* (Boston: Little Brown, 2001), 23.
4. The following anecdotes and quotes, unless otherwise noted, come from *Mother Teresa*, produced and directed by Ann and Jeannette Petrie, 82 minutes, Petrie Productions, 1986, videocassette.

4: The Holiness of Calm

1. *The Dhammapada,* trans. Juan Mascaro (London: Penguin, 1973), 40.

2. *The Bhagavad-Gita,* trans. Barbara Stoler Miller (New York and Toronto: Bantam, 1986), 67.

3. Cited in M. Darrol Bryant, "Dialogue at/with the Kumbha Mela," *Hindu Christian Studies Bulletin* 15 (2002): 33.

4. Rupert Gethin, *The Foundations of Buddhism* (Oxford: Oxford University Press, 1998), 29.

5. Douglas Villella, personal conversation.

6. John S. Strong, *The Experience of Buddhism* (Belmont, Calif.: Wadsworth, 1995), 50-51.

7. Klaus Klostermaier, *A Survey of Hinduism* (Albany: State University of New York), 395-96.

8. C. G. Jung, "Sri Ramana and His Message to Modern Man," foreword to *The Spiritual Teaching of Ramana Maharshi* (Boston and London: Shambala, 1988), ix.

9. John Moyne and Coleman Barks, *Open Secret: Versions of Rumi* (Putney, Vt.: Threshold), 5.

10. *The Gift: Poems of Hafiz, the Great Sufi Master,* trans. Daniel Ladinsky (New York: Penguin Compass, 1999), 160-61.

11. *Birdsong,* trans. Coleman Barks (Athens, Ga.: Maypop, 1993), 22.

12. Ladinsky, *The Gift,* 111-12.

13. Thich Nhat Hanh, *The Heart of Understanding* (Berkeley, Calif.: Parallax Press, 1988), 11.

5: The Holiness of Death

1. John Donne, *Selected Poems,* ed. John Hayward (New York: Penguin, 1950), 170.

2. Mary Oliver, *New and Selected Poems* (Boston: Beacon Press, 1992), 10-11.

3. Klaus Klostermaier, *A Survey of Hinduism* (Albany: State University of New York, 1989), 80-82.

4. *Songs of the Saints of India,* trans. John Stratton Hawley and Mark Juergensmeyer (New York and Oxford: Oxford University Press, 1988), 54.

5. Robert Bly, *The Winged Energy of Delight: Selected Translations* (New York: HarperCollins, 2004), 73.

6. Edward Conze, *Buddhist Meditation* (London: George Allen & Unwin, 1956), 88.

7. Mary Oliver, *New and Selected Poems*, 177-78. Originally published in *American Primitive* (New York: Little, Brown, 1983).

8. *The Soul of Rumi*, trans. Coleman Barks (San Francisco: Harper-Collins, 2001), 104.

9. T. S. Eliot, *Four Quartets* (New York and London: Harcourt Brace Jovanovich, 1971), 27.

10. David Whyte, *The House of Belonging* (Langley, Wash.: Many Rivers Press, 1999), 23.

11. *The Poems of Gerard Manley Hopkins*, ed. W. H. Gardner and N. H. MacKenzie (Oxford: Oxford University Press, 1967), 66.

12. Ibid., 99.

13. Cited in Mircea Eliade, *Yoga: Immortality and Freedom* (Princeton, N.J.: Princeton University Press, 1969), 29.

14. Eliot, *Four Quartets*, 29.

15. *Ram Dass: Fierce Grace*, produced and directed by Mickey Lemle, 93 minutes, Lemle Pictures, 2001, videocassette.

16. Richard H. Robinson and Willard L. Johnson, *The Buddhist Religion* (Belmont, Calif.: Wadsworth, 1997), 203.

6: The Holiness of the Everyday

1. *The Glance: Songs of Soul-Meeting*, trans. Coleman Barks (New York: Penguin Compass, 1999), xv.

2. Christopher Key Chapple, "Raja Yoga and the Guru," in *Gurus in America*, ed. Thomas A. Forsthoefel and Cynthia Ann Humes (Albany, N.Y.: State University of New York Press, 2005), 18.

3. China Galland, *Longing for Darkness: Tara and the Black Madonna* (New York: Penguin, 1991).

4. Herman Hesse, *Siddhartha*, trans. Hilda Rosner (New York: New Directions, 1951), 32.

5. Ibid., 86.

6. Kevin Burke, ed., *Pedro Arrupe: Essential Writings* (Maryknoll, N.Y.: Orbis Books, 2004), 8.

7. Mother Teresa, *In My Own Words*, compiled by Jose Luis Gonzalez-Balado (New York: Gramercy, 1996), jacket cover.

8. *The Dhammapada*, trans. John Ross Carter and Mahinda Palihawadana (New York and Oxford: Oxford University Press, 1986), 259.

7: The Holiness of Brokenness

1. Shunryu Suzuki, *Zen Mind, Beginner's Mind* (New York and Tokyo: Weatherhill, 1990), 57.

2. Robert S. Ellwood and Barbara A. McGraw, *Many People's Many Faiths* (Upper Saddle River, N.J.: Prentice Hall, 2002), 146.

3. John S. Strong, *The Experience of Buddhism*, (Belmont, Calif.: Wadsworth, 1995), 162-63.

4. The Dalai Lama, *An Open Heart* (Boston: Little Brown, 2001), 180, 7.

5. Martin Luther King, Jr., "Suffering and Faith," in *Peace and Non-Violence*, ed. Edward Guinan (New York: Paulist Press, 1973), 23.

6. Robert Bly, *The Winged Energy of Delight: Selected Translations* (New York: HarperCollins, 2004), 65.

7. Ibid., 66.

8. Thich Nhat Hanh, *The Heart of Understanding* (Berkeley, Calif.: Parallax Press, 1988), 34.

9. *The Soul of Rumi*, trans. Coleman Barks (San Francisco: Harper-Collins, 2001), 175.

10. Suzuki, *Zen Mind, Beginner's Mind*, 21.

11. *Tao Te Ching*, trans. Stephen Mitchell (New York: Harper & Row, 1988), 13.

12. Ibid., 9.

13. Ibid., 71.

14. *The Dhammapada*, trans. Juan Mascaro (London: Penguin, 1973), 35.

15. Ibid.

16. Mother Teresa, *In My Own Words*, compiled by Jose Luis Gonzalez Balado (New York: Gramercy, 1996), 55.

17. Thich Nhat Hanh, *The Sun My Heart* (Berkeley, Calif.: Parallax Press, 1988), 128, 74.

18. Thich Nhat Hanh, *Being Peace* (Berkeley: Parallax Press, 1987), 61-64.

19. Thich Nhat Hanh, *The Heart of Understanding*, 32-34.

20. Dalai Lama, *Open Heart*, 46.

21. Ibid., 21.

22. Cited in John F. Haught, *What Is Religion?* (Mahwah, N.J.: Paulist, 1990), 130. The quote originally appeared in Friedrich Heiler, "The History of Religions as a Preparation for the Co-operation of Religions," in *The History of Religions*, ed. Mircea Eliade and Joseph M. Kitagawa (Chicago: University of Chicago Press, 1959), 148f.

23. Ibid., 131 (149).

24. Mahatma Gandhi, *All Men Are Brothers* (New York: Continuum, 1980), 78.

25. Martin Luther King, Jr., *Strength to Love* (Philadelphia: Fortress Press, 1986), 51.

26. Dalai Lama, *Open Heart*, 11.

27. *Tao Te Ching*, trans. Mitchell, 79.

28. Marco R. della Cava, "One Hand Gone, but not His Spirit," *USA Today*, 7 September 2004, sec. A, p. 2.

8: Holiness

1. Elizabeth Kubler-Ross and David Kessler, *Life Lessons* (New York: Scribner, 200), 212.

2. John Moyne and Coleman Barks, *Open Secret: Versions of Rumi* (Putney, Vt.: Threshold, 1984), 7.

3. *The Soul of Rumi*, trans. Coleman Barks (San Francisco: Harper Collins, 2001), 21.

4. Moyne and Barks, *Open Secret*, 26.

5. *Soul of Rumi*, 15.

Index